ECOLOGY & WONDER

ECOLOGY & WONDER

in the Canadian
Rocky Mountain Parks
World Heritage Site

Robert William Sandford

AU PRESS

FRONTISPIECE: THE GRAND SENTINEL

The Grand Sentinel is a great stone tower located just below the summit of Sentinel Pass in Banff National Park. Were it located outside of the dense cluster of astounding natural features contained within Canada's mountain parks, it would be one of the wonders of the world. As it is, it is just one more landscape miracle that can be seen from the summit of the pass.

Photograph by R.W. Sandford.

© 2010 Robert W. Sandford

Published by AU Press, Athabasca University
1200, 10011 – 109 Street
Edmonton, AB T5J 3S8

LIBRARY AND ARCHIVES CANADA CATALOGUING IN PUBLICATION

Sandford, Robert W.
    Ecology & wonder in the Canadian Rocky Mountain Parks World Heritage Site / Robert William Sandford.

Includes bibliographical references and index.
Issued also in electronic format (978-1-897425-58-9).
ISBN 978-1-897425-57-2

    1. Canadian Rocky Mountain Parks World Heritage Site (Alta. and B.C.)--Environmental conditions. 2. National parks and reserves--Canadian Rocky Mountain Parks World Heritage Site (Alta. and B.C.)--Management. 3. Environmental protection--Canadian Rocky Mountain Parks World Heritage Site (Alta. and B.C.). I. Title. II. Title: Ecology and wonder.

QH106.2.R6S26 2010   333.7'209712332   C2010-900473-6

Cover and book design by Virginia Penny, Interpret Design, Inc.
Printed and bound in Canada by Marquis Book Printing.

This project was funded in part by the generous support of:

Parks   Parcs
Canada   Canada

For Vi Sandford, my partner on this amazing journey, and for our three children, Reid, Amery and Landon, who will inherit this West.

Contents

Foreword

What World Heritage Status Means
for the Canadian Rockies

SHORTLY AFTER HRH PRINCE PHILIP officiated at the unveiling of the plaque at Lake Louise to commemorate the inscription of the Canadian Rocky Mountain Parks on the World Heritage List, several reports appeared questioning the event. A *Calgary Herald* editorial asked, "Does this mean we are ceding control over our national parks?" (26 September 1985). Subsequent letters to the editor wondered if this meant that the parks were to be renamed and all development in the parks halted.

Confusion as to the meaning of inscription on the World Heritage List is found all over the world and clearly an educational shift is needed to explain it. What is the World Heritage Convention?

Some resources, both of nature and human culture, serve as bridges between the past and the future. Their importance to humankind transcends artificial and transitory boundaries devised for political reasons; they are relevant to all cultures and societies. Such resources do not "belong" only to the nations in which they are located or to the people who live in the twenty-first century. They are a part of the heritage of all of humanity and the legitimate inheritance of future generations, and as such their stewardship should be a matter of global concern.

These are the noble ideals enshrined in the World Heritage Convention, or as it is more properly known, the International Convention for Protection of the World Cultural and Natural Heritage. The adoption of this convention in 1972 united, for the first time, concern for international recognition and protection of the world's cultural and natural heritage. It placed this concern within a permanent framework that provides a legal, administrative and financial basis through which to implement the convention.

At the time of this writing 186 countries have become signatory to the convention and 878 properties have been placed on the select World Heritage List. Of these some 679 are cultural sites, 174 natural, and 25 of mixed designation. Canada at present has 15 sites on the World Heritage List, nine for reasons of exceptional natural qualities and six for extraordinary cultural heritage. These include L'Anse aux Meadows National Historic Site and Gros Morne National Park in Newfoundland; the old town of Lunenburg and Joggins Fossil Cliffs in Nova Scotia; Miguasha National Park on the coast of the Gaspé Peninsula and the Historic District of Old Québec in Quebec; Dinosaur Provincial Park, Head-Smashed-In Buffalo Jump, Waterton-Glacier International Peace Park, Wood Buffalo National Park and the Canadian Rocky Mountain Parks in Alberta; SGaang Gwaii in British Columbia; Nahanni National Park in the Northwest Territories; and Kluane/Wrangell-St. Elias/Glacier Bay/Tatshenshini-Alsek, which border Alaska and Yukon Territory; and the Rideau Canal in and around Ottawa.

Canada also has nine sites on the Tentative List for World Heritage Sites. These include Áísínai'pi (also known as Writing-On-Stone) in Alberta, which has the largest concentration of rock art on the Great Plains of North America; Atikaki/Woodland Caribou/Accord First Nations in Manitoba and Ontario, which is regarded as the quintessential Canadian Shield wilderness preserved in a landscape that speaks to the traditional lifeways of the Anishinabe; and Grande-Pré in Nova Scotia, the emotional and spiritual centre of the Acadian people. The list also includes Gwaii Haanas, the home of the Haida and old-growth coastal rainforests, diverse marine life and remarkable biodiversity, and Ivvavik/Vuntut/Herschel Island (also known as Qikiqtaruk) in the Yukon, which protects remarkable mountains, boreal forests, tundra and wetlands in the context of living Aboriginal adaptation to extreme environments. Also being considered is the Klondike in the Yukon and British Columbia, the most comprehensive and intact of all the cultural landscapes that illustrate life before, during and after the world's great nineteenth-century gold rushes; Mistaken Point in Newfoundland, which possesses the world's earliest record of multi-cellular life in ancient oceans; and Quttinirpaaq National Park in Nunavut, which testifies to the earliest evidence of human occupations of the northernmost tip of North America. The list ends with Red Bay National Historic Site in Labrador, which is the most complete and best-preserved example known of a sixteenth-century Basque whaling station in North America.

A growing number of the world's most outstanding natural areas have been granted World Heritage status. These include well-known places such as the Galapagos Island, Iguazu Falls, Great Barrier Reef, Serengeti and Sagamartha (Mount Everest) national parks. Other not-so-well-known World Heritage Sites include Srebarna Nature Reserve in Bulgaria, Kahuzi-Biega National Park in Zaire, the Willandra Lakes Region in Australia and Río Plátano Biosphere Reserve in Honduras.

There are also three properties on the List of World Heritage in Danger, all in Africa. There is also a second list of areas where the very reason they were designated as World Heritage Sites is under threat. It should also be noted that not all properties nominated are inscribed. Of thirteen sites proposed in 1984, just before the mountain national parks in Canada were designated, only seven natural site submissions were eventually approved.

The above, however, does not answer the question of what the Convention means. By ratifying the World Heritage Convention, Canada and the other 185 signatories accepted five basic principles of the Convention:

1. To hold in trust for the rest of humanity those parts of the World Heritage that are within its boundaries;
2. To support other nations in discharging this trust;
3. To exercise the same responsibility to works of nature as to the works of humankind;
4. To grant its co-signatories the right to observe the degree to which it is meeting its obligations under the Convention;
5. To adopt protection policies backed by legal, scientific, and financial measures to ensure that the integrity of World Heritage properties is maintained.

A state that is party to the Convention does not give up sovereignty over World Heritage Sites but it does recognize the special responsibilities it has to the international community toward the perpetuation of the values of the site.

Each state adhering to the Convention is required to make an annual contribution to the World Heritage Fund. The Fund is used primarily by developing nations to strengthen management of their World Heritage properties (e.g. for training, planning, equipment). In this sense the Convention is a mechanism for sharing global heritage responsibilities, which in turn provides developing countries with a material incentive to protect their outstanding natural sites.

Why were the Canadian Rocky Mountain Parks put on the list? The nomination document submitted by Parks Canada was processed by the United Nations Educational, Scientific and Cultural Organization (UNESCO), evaluated by International Union for Conservation of Nature (IUCN) and submitted to the Eighth World Heritage Committee meeting in Buenos Aires in November 1984. The Committee agreed that the site was of "outstanding universal value" and met three of the four criteria for World Heritage status (one is sufficient for approval). It was then formally inscribed on the List with the request that the adjacent provincial parks, Robson, Hamber, Assiniboine and Kananaskis, also be considered for inclusion as part of the site. British Columbia later pressed successfully for inclusion and Robson, Hamber and Assiniboine were added to the designation in 1990.

In making its recommendation on the national parks nomination, IUCN noted that the combination of natural features and superlative scenery in the four parks, Banff, Jasper, Kootenay and Yoho, were unsurpassed in the Rocky Mountain region. The integrity of the property was examined and also described in the statement: "Inside the boundary of the parks there are a number of localized sites that have been significantly modified to tourism or transportation purposes. These are contained within the defined intensive use development zones and are subject to elaborate environmental impact assessments. Over 90 percent of the site remains as undisturbed natural wildland." While new pressures exist today, that percentage was correct in 1990.

What are the implications for the Rocky Mountain Parks in terms of this designation? First, a World Heritage status confers prestige as one of the world's most outstanding natural areas. Increased publicity and tourism have been experienced in most sites, but this is unlikely to be significant for the Rockies. In many cases World Heritage status has led to increased budgetary appropriations and stimulated increased conservation measures.

Second, World Heritage status means increased protection in terms of Canada's obligations under the Convention. As a result, any threat to the integrity of the site is of international, not just national, interest. The best-documented case where World Heritage status has "saved" a site from inappropriate development is the Western Tasmania Wilderness National Parks. It has also served as leverage to convince the Yugoslavian government not to construct a dam in the Durmitor National Park World Heritage Site.

Third, World Heritage status does not mean restrictions on further development unless the integrity of the property itself is jeopardized. As noted, more than 90 percent of the property is largely undisturbed and it is unlikely that IUCN (who report on stewardship to the World Heritage Committee) would consider minor developments within the context of the zoning and management plans to be inconsistent with the reasons for which it was inscribed on the List.

Fourth, World Heritage status should provide a stimulus for a broader perspective on the Canadian Rockies whereby the national and provincial parks included within the designation are planned, managed and used as one natural unit.

Finally, World Heritage Status provides moral suasion and plays an important educational role in raising public awareness of Canada's international role and responsibilities in conservation. By making a public commitment before an international forum to give special status to the Canadian Rocky Mountain Parks, Canada has affirmed and reinforced the principles of this unique instrument of international cooperation for conservation. It is in the spirit of these principles that this groundbreaking book aims to celebrate the importance of the Canadian Rocky Mountain Parks World Heritage Site to Canada and to the world.

JAMES THORSELL
Executive Officer
IUCN Commission on National Parks and Protected Areas
Gland, Switzerland

Acknowledgements

ACKNOWLEDGING THOSE WHO contributed to a book that took 40 years to write is no simple matter. It is rather like determining who should be mentioned in one's last will and testament. You know there are so many to whom you owe acknowledgement but you know also that time and space will not permit you to include everyone who deserves to be recognized.

I would be remiss if I did not begin by acknowledging those who helped build the foundation of my great passion for that part of the mountain West that has been protected in the form of national and provincial parks that inspired this book. It is amusing to look back to when I was hired as a Park Naturalist in Banff National Park in 1970 and to recall the words of the personnel officer that offered me the job. "You were not our first choice," she said. I am indebted even to this day to Assistant Chief Park Naturalist Bruce Gordon for accepting a chemistry student into his service and for encouraging me immediately into the field to observe what was happening rather than trying to learn about landscape solely by reading scientific journals in the park library. From Bruce Gordon and from park wardens like Jim Rimmer and Larry Gilmar I quickly learned that direct experience is required to give meaning and value to science and vice versa. I am equally indebted to Bob Johnston, Doug Eastcott, Don Karasuik, Don Cockeron, Gail Harrison and so many others of that early era from whose example I learned that the only way to overcome your physical and intellectual awkwardness in any given mountain landscape was to spend every possible moment you could in it. Only by allowing yourself to be enlarged by the experience of the Canadian Rockies could you have any hope of comprehending such monumentality.

Early in my career I also spent two formative years in Jasper National Park where fortunately I came under the influence of great number of people of remarkable character. Among these I include Rory Flanagan, Dave Pick, Bob Pot, Bruce Rodger, Sue Wolfe, Jenny Clark, Bob and Pat Haney, Don Sears, Doug Wellock, Dale Portman, Bob Barker, Gordon McLean, Tony Klettl, Willi Pfisterer, Hans Schwarz and Gord Irwin. It was an expansive period in my own life and in the history of the parks service. For me it marked the beginning of a period of some seven years during which I spent months on end on trails and in the backcountry throughout what later became the Canadian Rocky Mountain Parks World Heritage Site. For Parks Canada, it marked a period of transition from early organizational structures and an explosion in visitation.

After Jasper I returned to Banff. I now had enough experience to realize that all of the contradictions that had been sewn into the purpose and function of our national parks system at its creation were manifest in our first national park which was in essential a Canadian version of Yellowstone. Banff was the place you went – and still go – if you want to work at the very leading edge of balancing landscape protection with broader human desires and ambitions. It is a microcosm of the larger reality in which human interests collide with planetary ecological life-support function. I met and worked with many highly competent and utterly committed people then and from that period on who were up for the challenge of balancing human use with ecological integrity. In addition to those named in the book, I must also acknowledge the influence, support and example of people like Andy Anderson, Tim Auger, Don Mickle, Peter Fuhrmann, Marc Ledwidge, Jim Davies and Lance Cooper.

This was followed by a brief but highly formative three years in Yoho where I was much influenced by the residents of Field, one of the most remarkable communities in the mountain West. Among those who influenced me most I include Gord and Bev Rutherford and their daughters, Karen and Lianna; Glen and Irene Brook and their sons Sid and

Alex; Men Camistral; Randall Robertson; Albert and Winnie Ashley; and a host of wonderful neighbours too many to name.

I would like to acknowledge the influence on my life and this book of a number of particularly influential mountain writers and artists. These include poets Charles Noble, Peter Christensen and especially writer Sid Marty. It also includes painters Illingworth Kerr, Ted Raftery, Terry McCue, Alice Saltiel Marshall, Marilyn Kinsella, Robert Sinclair and photographer Craig Richards. I owe a special and lifelong debt to Jon Whyte for the encouragement he offered that started me down the road ultimately to this book. I must also acknowledge the on-going artistic and aesthetic influence that Vi Korcsmaros, now Vi Sandford, has had on this book and indeed on all the books that led up to it.

This book also owes a debt to a number of other prominent scientists. I am much indebted to Dr. Stephen Herrero, Dr. Michael Gibeau and Colleen Campbell for all they taught me about grizzly bear biology and ecology. I owe a debt of gratitude to Ian Pengelly of Parks Canada for all he has taught me about fire ecology and to Dr. Cliff Whyte for all he has shared over time about how ecosystems in the mountain parks have functioned in the past and in the present. In terms of aquatic ecosystem science I am indebted to Shelley Humphries, Charlie Pacas and Jim Murphy. I am indebted also to Dr. Michael Demuth of the Glaciology Division of the Geological Survey of Canada and Dr. Shawn Marshall of the University of Calgary for all the encouragement and information regarding glaciation they have shared. I would also like to thank Dr. David Schindler of the University of Alberta, Dr. John Pomeroy of the University of Saskatchewan and Dr. Henry Vaux of the Rosenberg International Forum on Water Policy for their refreshingly candid perspectives on the importance of upland watersheds in all the Canadian West and for the valuable information they have shared on matters hydrologic.

I owe also a very substantial debt to senior people in Parks Canada who offered me the opportunity to experience all of the mountain parks and, indeed, most of the national parks in Western Canada. Without these opportunities I could not have written this book. Those I would especially like to acknowledge include Gaby Fortin, Don Sears, Jillian Roulet, Ron Hooper, Sandra Davis, Darro Stinson, Ian Church, Charlie Zinkan and more recently Bill Fisher. For the final chapter on the potential expansion of the Canadian Rocky Mountain Parks World Heritage Site I am particularly indebted to Mike Murtha of Parks Canada for allowing me to be involved at early stages of that planning process.

Invocation

The Magnificent Seven

OVERVIEW MAP
*Courtesy of Ali Buckingham,
Parks Canada.*

**REGIONAL IDENTITY AFFIRMED THROUGH THE RECOGNITION
AND RESTORATION OF PLACE**

THE PURPOSE OF THIS BOOK is to make three bold new claims related
to the history of Canada's mountain West. The first claim is that our
greatest cultural achievement in the mountain region of Western
Canada may not be what we have developed in terms of infrastructure,
industry, commerce or human population growth. While we mark their
development as central to history as we currently define it, railways,
highways, towns and cities only partly define our contemporary identity. The mountain West is different from the rest of the country – and
from most of the rest of the continent – in that it is not what we constructed out of the landscape that most deeply and enduringly defines
us as a people. It is not what we built that truly makes us unique as a
culture, but what we saved.

   We have saved something in this part of the country that has been
lost elsewhere in Canada and widely around the world. In the midst of
fragmenting and developing the mountain West, we recognized there

World Heritage Site and its surrounding buffers is that it essentially encompasses only one biogeographical and cultural region. And what a spectacular region it is. Few who have visited it, and none who have lived in it, would disagree that it is one of the world's most remarkable places.

The Canadian Rocky Mountain Parks World Heritage Site – or the Mountain Parks as they are called – encompasses four National Parks, three Provincial Parks, thirteen National Historic Sites and four Canadian Heritage Rivers. The Site encompasses 27 mountain ranges. Within it are at least 669 prominent peaks and hundreds of outliers and lesser peaks that remain unnamed. Within the World Heritage Site's boundaries are 12 major icefields, 384 glaciers and some 295 lakes. But it is the moving water that matters most. Within this combined reserve are a total of 44 rivers and 164 named tributaries. Only two of these rivers are dammed. If this were not enough, four of the greatest rivers on the continent are born here. These four rivers make the down-slope West habitable – for us and for the rest of the natural world. This book contends that, though the tourism potential of this expanded protected area is an important element of the Western Canadian economy, its role as a healthy watershed will be more important and more valuable to the future than we can even begin to imagine today.

Even the gaps that separate watersheds are important. This World Heritage Site encompasses 23 important mountain passes and at least 25 major airsheds. It encompasses three life zones and is home to more than 600 species of plants, 277 species of birds, and 69 species of mammals, including 13 different carnivores. One of these carnivores, the grizzly bear, is the symbol of the entire region. Its nature and habits embody what is truly unique about the mountain West and its culture. That such magnificent and wild creatures still exist within an hour's drive of Calgary, a city of a million people, demonstrates the iconic importance of the grizzly as a symbol of what is different about this region and the costs that locals are prepared to pay to sustain and celebrate that difference.

The relationship between the great bear and local culture has developed over more than 400 generations of human presence in the Rocky Mountains. Within the Mountain Parks are some 900 archaeological sites, dating from Early, Middle and Late Prehistoric times. In historic times the Mountain Parks were within the often-overlapping territories of at least 12 First Nations. Parts as well were the home of generations of Métis, the people of mixed European and Native blood who were the foundation of post-contact culture in the Canadian West.

At present there are four permanent communities within this World Heritage Site with a tightly controlled total resident population of fewer than 20,000 residents. These people live in the World Heritage Site for a reason: to operate and maintain these reserves and to serve and care for visitors. So famous are the Mountain Parks that they are the destination of more than 6 million visitors a year. But this number is deceiving. While a million people might walk down Banff Avenue in a year, there are valleys within this World Heritage Site that might be visited once a decade.

While most Canadians take the Mountain Parks for granted, this book argues that we should celebrate this accomplishment for what it means to us and to what it may mean to us and to the world as our populations grow and our climate changes. There is a great deal we can build on.

What we have created in the mountain region of the Canadian West is nothing less than one of the most expansive collective expressions of the will to protect national heritage the world has ever witnessed. In terms of upland watershed protection, it may also prove to be one of the best land-use decisions in Canadian history. We are quickly learning that ecology *is* economy. We are also learning that what we saved, might in the end save us.

The nature of our western mountain-protection achievement invites Canadians to think in different terms about how we might live in association with the remarkable landscape we have allowed nature to bring back into existence in our time. Realization of the dimensions of our accomplishment may also suggest that an opportunity exists now to work consciously toward creating a culture and an economy commensurate with the grand nature of the landscape we have preserved.

With each passing day we learn more about the value of ecological services nature provides to us free that would be beyond our means to provide for ourselves. It is now estimated that healthy ecosystems provide clean water and other natural benefits for less than one percent of what they would cost us to generate on our own. We may soon discover that our decision to preserve our upland watershed in the Rocky Mountains may ultimately allow nature to offer us the best deal it has offered humanity since agriculture: the gift of true sustainability.

This great reserve forms a baseline of understanding about the West that puts into relief what existed in the past so that we can appreciate the value of what we possess – and possesses us – now. In this region, it is still possible to use the past as an immediate foundation for planning for the future. Such latitude no longer exists in much of the rest of the world.

Recasting our history against the backdrop of such an extraordinary inter-generational public policy achievement allows our culture room to move in a time when natural systems everywhere are under great stress. We have not spent all of our natural capital. The fact that we have saved important functioning elements of our natural and cultural history allows us latitude others do not possess in choosing the future we want. What we have saved keeps the door open to the most important of all cultural options: the opportunity to create a new and inspired vision of what kind of West we would like to create for ourselves and for our children. But the West – and the world – is changing quickly. The door to the future we want is not likely to remain open long.

When we are unsure about what to do with our future, we should go to the mountains. By letting them speak to and through us, we affirm who we are and who we might become at our future and ultimate best. These mountains remind us that we don't have to accept diminishment and loss of landscapes and ecosystems as a condition of growth and prosperity as others have accepted elsewhere. These mountains remind us of what we can do for ourselves and for the world by honouring and protecting the places that mean the most to us. We should go soon and often to these mountains to be reminded of the wisdom of our great achievements, for change is heavily upon us and there is much we must do if we wish to create a sustainable society worthy of place in the mountain West.

Imagining and then creating the West we want may seem an impossible task. I hope, however, that this book will inspire a heightened realization of what is possible based on what we have already achieved. History tells us we can employ the power of mountain places in service of defining a unique Western Canadian identity. By caring about our mountains we have learned how to create the West we want.

ROBERT W. SANDFORD
Canmore, Alberta
January 2010

PART ONE

The West We Had:
Foundations of Place

1

A Walk into the Past

Setting a Context of Place

THE UNESCO CANADIAN ROCKY Mountain Parks World Heritage Site is so large that it is impossible to see in one lifetime. I am not as diligent and persistent as others have been in the quest to see it all, but I have worked at exploring as much of this great protected area as possible for the last forty years. I can honestly say that I know the map pretty well and can visualize the general geography of this entire vast domain. There are places, however, where mountains, valleys, glaciers and rivers are remembered only as end points in what could have been much more protracted explorations. There are valleys that, had I more time and energy, would have led me to missing places in my mental construct of this part of the mountain West. There are passes that, had I crossed them, would have taken me to fabled wild valleys only mentioned very generally in park reports. These places were only known in any depth by Park Wardens or Rangers who had spent their entire careers in the backcountry.

So it is that on the downslide from the summit of youth I still find myself with a long list of places I ache to visit, all of them remote. Most are in the Mountain Parks. And that is what our long-planned and much anticipated expedition to the backcountry was about: appreciation of the greatest cultural heritage achievement in the history of the Canadian West. It was also meant as an inquiry into how our mountains are changing and what, in the context of those changes, this protected place will mean to our future as a region and as a nation.

Our walking trip into the very southern part of Banff National Park was planned in association with a Parks Canada Warden who has worked extensively in all the mountain national parks. During the forty years he has spent with the National Parks Service, most of it in the specialty of mountain rescue, Gord Irwin has seen as much of the expanded UNESCO Mountain Parks as anyone I know. But even he has not seen it all.

We had been planning this trip for a long time, but for me there always seemed to be more urgent treks to make. Because there are so few who know enough about them or who can articulate good reasons for defending such unknown, almost secret, places from the fate that has already befallen so many other sanctuaries – many are lost without ever being known. The spring comes and the migrating birds arrive to find that another forest has disappeared, the vegetation gone right to bedrock or covered with houses. Travelling widely out of the cities as I do it is hard not to be overwhelmed by the magnitude of the change that is occurring. Everything of value on or beneath the surface of the West is being ripped out of the ground and shipped away to distant, often foreign places. Once one has witnessed the extent of transformation that has taken place in a single generation in and around the Mountain Parks, they begin to look and feel like an island amidst a West that is being flayed and then eaten alive.

There are many ways to enter the Mountain Parks. Most will know the highway portals: the Trans-Canada, which takes travellers through Banff and Yoho National Parks; the Yellowhead, which penetrates Jasper National Park and Mount Robson Provincial Park; and Highway 93, which slices vertically along the Great Divide through Jasper, Banff and Kootenay National Parks. There are also trails that can provide hiking, biking and horse access at dozens of points on all sides of the contiguous 400-kilometre-long and 150-kilometre-wide "wilderness."

As we wanted to access southern Banff National Park, we had a number of options. We chose, because we had only three days, to access the remotest part of the Spray River headwaters region from Burstall Pass in adjacent Peter Lougheed Provincial Park.

Irwin and I had company on our trip. He was accompanied by his partner, Marie-Pierre Rogeau, whom he met when she began research into the forest fire history of the mountain National Parks in 1991. Since

BURSTALL PASS

The trail to Burstall Pass in the Kananaskis is a popular day hike that takes in mountain scenery as spectacular as any found in the Rockies. Few, however, take the time to drop down the west side of the pass into the wild upper regions of the Spray River in Banff National Park. Left to right: M.P. Rogeau, Landon Sandford, Bob Sandford, and Gord Irwin.

Photograph by Vi Sandford.

that time, "M-P," as she is known, has become an acknowledged expert on fire succession in Canadian forests. I was accompanied by my wife Vi and our then-twelve-year-old son, Landon, who in the last year had taken an interest in where he lives and had asked if he might be included in this experience.

We did not get what locals would call an "alpine start." After dropping a vehicle off at Mount Shark trailhead we arrived at the beginning of the Burstall Pass trail at about 11:30 a.m. We were fortunate, however, that we were past the summer's peak heat. Even though it was only mid-August the light was already tending toward the oblique richness of autumn when every detail of the landscape is thrown into magnificent relief.

Less than an hour later, we stopped at the edge of an outwash plain where melt from the Robertson Glacier meanders through patches of willow to meet Burstall Creek. After lunch we started up the 2,380 metre pass. We stopped for a rest on the flats above the first big hill where we admired a great slab of perfectly smooth stone on the west face of Whistling Ridge that appeared to have been created by an enormous rock slide along a near-vertical fault line. Beyond the great slab we could see the massive walls of 3,400 metre Mount Sir Douglas, which dominates the head of the valley.

That I am not fit became clear as we climbed the last ridge of the pass. Landon danced all around me as I puffed and sweated my way to the summit. While pausing to catch my breath, we discovered a family of ptarmigan hiding stock-still among the rocks. Their adaptive colouration is so perfect you have to startle them to see them. It was as if the rocks miraculously produced a hen and four chicks only to have them disappear again when you stopped looking at them.

As we dropped a few metres down from the summit, the Matterhorn-like peak of Mount Assiniboine came into view. Just the sight of this great tower evokes myth. After a brief rest we began the steep descent into the utter wilderness that lay before us at the headwaters of the Spray. It was like crossing a border into a remote land I had dreamed for years of visiting. You could immediately feel the difference between the west side of the pass and the one we had climbed: like suddenly dropping back into time.

The trail on the west slopes of Burstall Pass has started to grow in from disuse. Moss on the path suggested to Irwin that more horses pass this way today than hikers. That did not mean, however, that we were alone. Within only a few kilometres we discovered signs of grizzlies, wolves, coyotes, martens, moose, elk and deer. There was something larger than us here and more ancient – a presence we didn't feel elsewhere. We descended step by step into the ineffable, into the sacred. As we followed the trail toward the valley, the tracks of a moose became the moose itself. We stared at it in silent awe, all five of us watching it watch us. What does it do to one, I wondered, to see such things and to see such places? Only good I suspect.

At a spring near the valley floor we stopped to drink water so good and so cold that every cell in my body thirsted for it. By the time we made the junction with the main Spray Valley trail, I was so tired I kept walking so I wouldn't fall down. Irwin, who as a fully accredited mountain guide is experienced in helping tired people reach their goal, made light of it. We jokingly formalized the Law of Relative Distance wherein three kilometres is always shorter leaving a backcountry cabin than it is when arriving, especially after a long day.

Vi, who had been carrying an enormous pack, unloaded enchiladas, wine and two cans of beer. There were appetizers and cold drinks. I drank glass after glass of water. No one was in a hurry to eat. There was nothing to hurry for, which allowed us time for simple conversation.

I said to Irwin that this part of the upper Spray River valley reminded me of the Rocky Forks area on the south boundary of Jasper National Park where I visited him just after he became a district warden in 1976. He replied that the similarity between Palliser and Rocky Forks was the main reason he was happy to come into this most southerly part of the Mountain Parks.

He went on to say, though it appeared completely wild on many maps, the block of parks comprising the World Heritage Site were in fact badly fragmented by national highways, roads, towns, railways, pipelines and heavily used trails. Fragmentation was being continually exacerbated by human use. There was a time, he explained, when protection goals were the highest priority in the management of the mountain park system. It was his view that Parks Canada had in recent years focussed on the quality of visitor experience as its central management priority, at the cost of core ecological values. He was concerned that the pendulum had swung too far in favour of visitor experience and too far away from protection.

Places like the upper reaches of the Spray, in his estimation, remained largely unaffected by front-country policy directions only because they had never been opened to mountain biking and other mechanical incursions. Though very accessible, they were seldom visited except by wardens on horse patrols and hikers committed to a multi-day backcountry adventure. Such adventurers, Irwin remarked, were becoming fewer. The recent popularity of backpacking, which began in the late 1960s and lasted into the early 1980s, has ended. Most hikers today want to spend the day on the trail and then return to civilization for a comfortable bed and a restaurant meal.

Another incursion the Palliser District had been spared, according to Irwin, was the intense focus of contemporary ecosystem management. In large areas of the Mountain Parks, landscape and environmental processes can no longer be described as self-willed. Put bluntly, these landscapes are no longer allowed to manage themselves. Instead, Parks Canada manages them according to its perceived needs and visitor expectations. In other words, having lost the self-willed capacity to change in directions defined by their own intrinsic qualities and dynamics, these landscapes are no longer wild. This is not a minor point but is the devil's bargain you make when a wilderness is designated a national or provincial park, at least in places where surrounding areas have been compromised by a variety of human uses. You are forced to manage at least as much for visitor needs as you are for ecosystem needs.

PALLISER MEADOWS
Due to its relatively low altitude, longer growing season, and abundant water resources, the upper reaches of the Spray River provide excellent year-round habitat for elk and moose, wolves and grizzlies whose tracks can be found everywhere in the valley.
Photograph by Vi Sandford.

We have reached the point where we have interfered so much with the greater natural ecosystem function of the Canadian West that the kinds of ecosystems we have created cannot continue to function without our constant intervention.

The foundation for contemporary management of protected areas in Canada's mountain West is a concept called ecological integrity. As cumulative effects of development and increased visitation in Banff National Park put into relief outdated wildlife management strategies such as predator control, exotic species introduction, wildlife population control and fire suppression, new concepts of ecological understanding have emerged. The most compelling of these is the idea of maintaining the integrity and connectivity of existing mountain ecosystems.

Ecological integrity, in the context of national parks, means the minimization of human impacts on natural processes of ecological change. This requires management of both people and the manipulation of natural processes. From an ecosystem point of view it means not letting your ecosystems become unnaturally fragmented or diminished in vitality. It means keeping all natural processes operative, including fire, predation, insects and even some forms of disease, which isn't as easy as it sounds.

When natural systems become islandized, they are subject to a whole range of influences we are only beginning to understand, all of which contribute to diminishment and ecological loss. We have learned, for example, that a newly islandized reserve will *temporarily* hold a full complement of its original species. What happens next, however, is that the big island is made into a series of smaller islands by roads, rails and trails. Wild landscapes are reduced to dysfunctional fragments. Species then begin to disappear. This is what is happening presently throughout the Rockies. Human population growth is tearing the wild out of the West.

Humans tend to overwhelm natural landscapes. Conservationists like Stephen Mayer in the United States have claimed the human presence is now so pervasive that we have effectively taken over processes of natural selection. Ecologists argue that our planet's remaining ecosystems are now divided into two types: intact systems and relic communities that have no hope of surviving over the long term without extensive human support. Relic communities are composed of ghost species – plants and animals that have no hope unless we help them. While the ecosystem that comprised much of the Mountain Parks was once considered intact, it is being increasingly islandized by outside land-use changes and uncomplimentary human activities. There is legitimate fear that some species like the mountain caribou, the grizzly and the wolf are already relic species and are expected to become ghost species by the end of the twenty-first century. For those who believe that the presence of these creatures is what defines the mountain West as unique, this is alarming news. Protecting endangered species is expensive. We don't know how many we have the knowledge to support. Some landscapes are changing so quickly, we don't know if some species can even survive in the circumstances that are emerging. Only one thing seems certain. The West is not as wild as it once was. It is not as wild as most Canadians think it is and it is nowhere as wild as we tell the rest of the world it is. Reality is coming up hard against some of our most cherished myths.

While Landon would have entertained us all night with his witty perspectives on our world, I pulled the thick wool blankets over me and by 10:30 p.m. had forgotten my aching bones in satisfying but strangely alert sleep. I felt I was returning to primal patterns of being that resided just below the surface of my civilized self. It was the sleep of the hunter – and the hunted.

The valley to which we awoke was filled with smoke. As is typical in late summer, there was a big forest fire burning to the south, perhaps as far away as the United States, and winds were pushing its smoke into the upper reaches of the Spray. Besides smoke, the valley was filled with history, mystery and names.

The names of the peaks and watercourses in this area derive from the patriotic obsessions of Arthur Oliver Wheeler, the commissioner representing British Columbia for the survey appointed to delimit the boundary between British Columbia and Alberta from 1913 through 1924. Wheeler made sure that British, Canadian and French generals were all remembered, major land and naval battles commemorated, and heroes elevated to permanent memory, by having peaks in the Canadian Rockies named after them. Burstall Pass, Lake and Mountain, for example, were named in 1918 for Lieutenant-General Sir E.H. Burstall, the commander of Canada's troops in Europe in World War I. In 1918, Wheeler named the highest mountain in the area, 3,400 metre Mount Sir Douglas, after Field Marshall Haig, the commander of British forces in France.

While Wheeler's commemoration of heroes of World War I is thought provoking, the real history of this valley is connected with the Palliser Expedition. John Palliser was born into an aristocratic Irish family of British descent in British-occupied Ireland in 1817. He grew up in Waterford County where he served in the military and eventually became county sheriff. At the age of thirty, Palliser made a trip to North America to hunt buffalo on the Great Plains. His book, *Solitary Rambles and Adventures of a Hunter in the Prairies,* published in 1853, was widely read in England and no doubt influential in his choice as leader of the government-funded British North American Exploring Expedition, which travelled over large areas of the unmapped West between 1857 and 1860. The instructions for the expedition were very clearly defined in a letter the Secretary of State of the British government sent to Palliser in late March of 1859:

> *From Fort Garry you will start, as soon as you have organized your party, in a westwardly direction, taking such course as you shall consider most advisable for acquiring additional knowledge of the country on either side of the Bow River or south branch of the Saskatchewan River and south of the southern branch, and thence proceeding westward to the headwaters of that river, you will endeavor from the best information you can collect to ascertain whether one or more practical passes exist over the Rocky Mountains through British territory, and south of that known to exist between Mount Brown and Mount Hooker.*[1]

While there were certainly plenty of political reasons for the British government to support such an expedition, the Palliser inquiry into the West also possessed a serious scientific focus:

> *It being the desire of Her Majesty's Government that the Expedition should, as far as practicable, be made available for extending general as well as specific scientific knowledge, I have to impress upon you the importance, in addition to maintaining a regular series of instrumental observations, of regularly recording the physical features of the country through which you pass, noting its principal elevations, the nature of its soil, its capacity for agriculture, the quality and quantity of timber, and any indications of coal or other minerals.[2]*

Palliser was also instructed to keep a journal of all the expedition's observations and to forward duplicate copies at every favourable opportunity to the Secretary of State for the Colonies, on Downing Street in London.

When the expedition reached the front ranges of the Rockies in the summer of 1858, Palliser split the duties of his men so as to ensure that they were able to explore as much of the region as possible. Palliser departed from Old Bow Fort on the Bow River on August 18, forded the Bow above the Kananaskis and then, with much difficulty owing to the amount of burnt and fallen timber, followed the Kananaskis to just below its origins at what is now called the Haig Glacier, and then crossed North Kananaskis Pass into what is now British Columbia. From the height of land at North Kananaskis Pass the Palliser party dropped into the valley of what is now known as the Palliser River, which they followed to its junction with the Kootenay River. After further exploration and a number of exciting adventures involving local Native peoples, they re-crossed the Rockies and made for Fort Edmonton, where they had arranged with the Hudson's Bay Company to spend the winter.

While Captain Palliser was exploring the Kananaskis, another member of his expedition was fighting for his survival in what is now Yoho National Park. James Hector was a geologist and medical doctor with a great interest in the Canadian West. While Palliser went south from Old Bow Fort, Hector went west. Following the Bow River to what he named Castle Mountain, he then crossed the Great Divide into British Columbia by what is now called Vermilion Pass. He then followed the Vermilion River to where it joins the Kootenay at what is now Kootenay Crossing Warden Station and then ascended the Kootenay to the height of land that divides it from the Wapta River, one of the principal tributaries of the Columbia. He soon found himself at the junction of the Wapta and a larger river that, after a dangerous incident involving a pack horse, he called the Kicking Horse. He then followed the river to its headwaters at Kicking Horse Pass where he crossed back into what is now Alberta. Hector next followed the Bow River to its source at Bow Lake, and then crossed Bow Pass into the Mistaya Valley in Banff National Park. He followed the North Saskatchewan to Rocky Mountain House and eventually to Fort Edmonton.

When we add up all these travels, we begin to appreciate why the Palliser Expedition is so important to this region and why the Palliser name carries such weight in the upper reaches of the Spray. While history focuses on the impacts of the Palliser Expedition on ending the Hudson's Bay Company's control over Rupert's Land, the definition of the Palliser triangle in agricultural history and the opening of the Canadian prairies to settlement, his influence was also very significant in the mountain West. Fur trader and map maker David Thompson may have travelled more in areas now encompassed in the Mountain Parks, but his detailed observations are eclipsed by the careful accumulation of scientific observations made in the region not just by Palliser himself, but by geologist James Hector, botanist Eugene Bourgeau and Astronomer Royal Thomas Blakiston.

My front-step meditations on names, naming and the history of this valley were interrupted by the sounds of an approaching helicopter, which surprised us by landing right in front of the cabin. The purpose of the flight was to drop off equipment to be used in an ongoing study of genetic diversity in existing grizzly bear populations, to better understand genetic dispersal along linked corridors in the Yellowstone-to-Yukon conservation study area. The goals of this study are a reminder that even the Mountain Parks are not an ideal wildlife reserve. The assemblage of reserves is not the right shape to optimize survival of islandized species. A round reserve will sustain more species than an elongated one and clusters of reserves have a better chance of keeping their original complement of species than one alone. The DNA study will assist in identification of critical bear habitat at any given time of the year, and avenues of connectivity between different bear habitats. While I recognized the value of such research, I could not help but hear the voice of Stephen Meyer whispering to me in the wind generated by the helicopter blades:

*Our most common tools for preserving biodiversity – prohibitory laws and regula-
tions, bioreserves, and sustainable-development programs – are themselves powerful
engines of human selection, tweaking (for our pleasure) but not fundamentally altering the outcome: massive species loss with the attendant disappearance
of the wild.*[3]

Here we were in the middle of one of the last truly wild places in
Banff National Park and the cavalry had just arrived to help advance
further human direction of natural selection. Critics of national park
wildlife management programs wonder why Parks Canada bothers
putting so much effort into saving the grizzly bear. The answer is
simple: without this species the West is not the West as we know it.
Though originally designated for their remarkable geological features,
the Mountain Parks would not be a wilderness if we lost the great bear.
Whatever it costs, we should do everything within our power to save
this species, for in saving it we save everything it symbolizes.

When the silence returns after the departure of the helicopter, I am
suddenly very interested in walking to Leman Lake where a number of
bear-rubbing trees have been identified and modified to unobtrusively
collect grizzly hair for DNA analysis. The very thought of grizzlies in this
valley makes me feel alive.

There was a bald eagle circling high above us as we left the cabin. As
we walked through the buckbrush we stirred up thousands of white
butterflies that circled us as we walked. The butterflies have one or two
dots on each quarter-sized wing. Likely they are *Pierus marginalis*, or a
related species of what are common known as the Veined White.

As we crested the old moraine that confines the waters of Leman
Lake, M-P pointed out one of the bear-rubbing trees. It was an alpine fir
right on the trail, perfectly located to allow grizzlies to scratch itches
on their backs. An "x" was constructed of barbed wire at the bottom of
the likely scratch zone to collect hair that would later be analyzed for
its DNA content. This would allow the identification of the individual
bear that left the hair and establish its relationship to other bears in the
area and larger region. Some 46 trees were apparently rigged in this way
to unobtrusively determine the health of the grizzly gene pool in and
around this area of the Mountain Parks.

As we reached the log jams on the shore of the lake, we noticed that the
fire smoke had become thicker. While bald eagles floated in circles above
us, we talked, skipped rocks into the water and ate a leisurely lunch. We
were two kilometres from Spray Pass. Irwin explained that the pass is

now accessible from British Columbia by high clearance two-wheel drive vehicles. An all-weather road can take motorists to within a 40-minute walk of the boundary of Banff National Park. This same distance can be covered in less than 15 minutes on one of today's high tech all-terrain vehicles and even more quickly in good conditions on a snowmobile.

This is how such places are irreversibly lost. First they become surrounded. Old trails into the great sanctuaries are upgraded to seismic or logging roads. Then they are gravelled and opened for year-round use. Today hunters are less of a problem than they used to be, not just in relative but also in absolute numbers. While hunting traditionally put some pressure on wildlife populations, its current impact is slight compared to the damage caused by snowmobiling, the unregulated use of all-terrain vehicles and the opening up of mountain biking trails. Together these activities have not only fragmented landscapes but also resulted in far greater stress on wildlife, especially at critical times in their life cycle.

As Yellowstone National Park managers learned to their deep regret that, once such activities are permitted on a large enough scale to support commercial enterprises, the lobby they create makes it impossible to end their use, no matter how much damage they may cause. While park managers very prudently eliminated snowmobile use in Canada's Rocky Mountain national parks in 1972, it is permitted up to the boundaries on all sides of the Mountain Park block.

As I was still tired from the walk in, Landon and I headed back toward Palliser Cabin while the others walked the two kilometres to Spray Pass. Bushwhacking from the lake shore back up to the trail, we found white geraniums among the cow parsnip and the hellebore. I had never seen white geraniums in Banff National Park. It isn't just the machines entering the park, but a northward shift of many species of plants and animals with the increase in average night-time and winter temperatures. There are already nearly 100 invasive plant species in the Mountain Parks. Most of these, however, were introduced from Europe or Asia and brought to the mountains on the wind, accidentally on trains, in the wheel wells and on the tires of cars, or in feed for horses. Climate warming will likely exacerbate the problem of invasive species by creating circumstances favourable to weeds that do well in disrupted places. The problem with invasives is that they take over ecosystems and use a disproportionate amount of their limited energy. Over time they choke out endemic species and reduce biodiversity.

As we have caused and continue to cause considerable landscape disruption in the Canadian West, we should expect a great many new

TOWARDS LEMAN LAKE
Its low elevation and proximity to Palliser Pass make Leman Lake an excellent place to study the grizzly bear movement into and out of the Canadian Rocky Mountain Parks World Heritage Site. Gord Irwin poses for a photograph, on the trail in the midst of ideal of grizzly habitat.
Photograph by Vi Sandford.

arrivals of species from the south and be ready for other problematic arrivals from Europe and Asia. We know that our mountain ecosystems have already begun to disassemble under the influence of changing climate and have begun to reassemble in ways we can't predict. Historically, these ecosystems were largely defined by cold. When cold becomes less of a factor, the ecosystems can change dramatically in as short a time as a single human generation.

Back at Palliser Cabin I drank three litres of cold, clear water drawn from Birdwood Creek. I found myself thinking about our increasingly water-scarce world. The Mountain Parks generate most of the water in the prairie West. We know, however, that climate change is already affecting the timing and extent of precipitation in these mountains. Most people in Alberta don't see these changes because they are buffered by the ecological composition, extent and character of the Mountain Parks. This vast area of relatively stable, long-established ecological relationships slows down the galloping influence of outside changes and invasions. By minimizing human impacts on this fragile landscape we slow the impacts of climate change on our ecosystems, allowing ourselves more time to mitigate undesirable causes and adapt to projected changes. In so doing we also protect the water resources crucial to the entire West and buy time to learn more about managing changing ecosystems toward stability and sustainability.

These unimpaired landscapes of the mountain West are the headwaters of our unique identity. Seen in this light, nature here is offering us the best deal it has offered our species since it provided us with the when a down-going slab of oceanic crust melted and sent hot rock upward in a process called subduction. The hot rock then melted the overlying continental crust to send huge volcanic mountains skyward. While still very much a product of continental drift, the Canadian Rockies were formed in yet another way.

THE CONTINENT SHUDDERS AND MOUNTAINS ARE FORMED FROM COAST TO COAST TO COAST

NORTH AMERICA HAS NOT always been where it is now. It moves slowly, jostling the other continents on its way across the spinning world. When the eastward-tending North American plate reversed direction about 200 million years ago, the oceanic crust off the west coast of the continent slid beneath it. Island arcs on the surface of the subducted oceanic plate rode up onto the advancing North American plate and were added to the continental land mass. This process is called accretion and the land masses added to a continent in this way are called terranes.

Over the past 200 million years, the North American continent acted as a wedge, peeling terranes from the underlying oceanic plate. As many as 50 different terranes have been added to the northwestern edge of North America through accretion, most from the southwest. Some terranes may have moved three to five thousand kilometres northward before being captured by our wandering continent.

The North American continent has grown wider over time. Much of British Columbia was not originally part of North America and arrived as an accumulation of terranes. This accumulation also caused horizontal compression of the sedimentary rock that already covered the surface of the North American plate. This horizontal compression created the mountains of Western Canada.

The first period of mountain building, known as the Columbian Orogeny, took place about 175 million years ago. Compression continued into the early Cretaceous, a period that began about 144 million years ago. The mountains of British Columbia kept piling upward and mountain-building advanced slowly eastward; 120 million years ago, the western ranges of the Rockies began to pile up too, and the main ranges began to rise. About 85 million years ago, North America "docked" with the massive Vancouver Island and Queen Charlotte terranes, causing the last major horizontal compression across Western Canada. It was this last great compression, the Laramide Orogeny, which created the

MOUNT KITCHENER, JASPER NATIONAL PARK
The Rockies have been carved by rivers and glaciers out of the thrust-up sediments of an ancient seafloor. Over time, a four hundred million year-old sea floor has been pushed three kilometres into the air. Now these mountains are being worn down and carried away into distant seas. The rocks of ages cycle like water but over much longer periods of time.
Photograph by R.W. Sandford.

foothills and front ranges of the Rockies. Thereafter, plates slid along the west coast of North America rather than ramming into it. Horizontal compression of this kind resulted in the deformed and thrust-faulted ocean sediments we now know as the Rocky Mountains.[1]

AS THEY GO UP, THEY COME DOWN

EVEN AS THE PRIMORDIAL mountain ranges of the West were being born, they came under the same multiple forces of erosion that created the sediments of which they were composed. The rising Rockies were worn away by the mechanical action of rain, running water, and the alternate freezing and thawing of frost and ice. Relatively soft sedimentary rock eroded, through the mechanical and chemical breakup of readily dissolvable minerals and through natural breakdown by plants. By the time the Rockies stopped rising, they were already hip-deep in their own debris.

If the geology of the Canadian Rockies could be summarized into a single brief statement it would be this: they have been carved by rivers and glaciers out of the thrust-up sediments of an ancient seafloor.

expansion in life forms is seen to be evidence of what is often referred to as the Cambrian Explosion. The Burgess Shale, the first World Heritage Site designated in the mountain West, is one of the best places on Earth to witness evidence of this explosion.

The first to understand the significance of the fossils in the Burgess Shale was Dr. Charles Doolittle Walcott, the Secretary of the Smithsonian Institution, who literally stumbled upon them during a visit to the Rockies in 1909. Between 1909 and 1911, Walcott collected and exported to Washington D.C. some 65,000 specimens from a quarry on the shoulder of Mount Field, representing some 170 species of plants and animals.

Over the next century, four generations of palaeontologists studied the nearly perfectly preserved creatures. One of the greatest of these was Desmond Collins, a palaeontologist from the Royal Ontario Museum. Dr. Collins and his colleagues and students mined the Burgess quarry for nearly 20 years. Based on his testimony on the value of this treasure trove to our understanding of Cambrian life, the Burgess Shale was nominated as a World Heritage Site.

For the first 20 years after the Burgess site was designated in 1981, everyone seemed satisfied that the rare creatures discovered there had been fully appreciated for what they told us about the evolution of life. Then in 2003, British palaeontologist Andrew Parker caused the Cambrian to explode all over again. Using an electron microscope to examine the fossil remains of particularly well-preserved Burgess fauna (*Wiwaxia*, *Canadia* and *Marrella*) Parker discovered the remnants of diffraction gradients. Their presence suggested to Parker that these animals were iridescent. If there was light and colour, Parker surmised, then animals could "see." The capacity to see meant the existence of an eye.

What Andrew Parker discovered was that the "Big Bang of Evolution" that took place between 544 and 543 million years ago apparently was the result of the new ability to see. The eye allowed the rise of a whole new kind of creature: the active rather than the passive predator. With the evolution of the predatory hunter, new defences were urgently required. "In the blink of an eye," armour was invented. The number of creatures with shells exploded and life filled all the seas in the Cambrian ocean.

The Burgess Shale is of inestimable value to us today because it is one of only a tiny number of places on our planet where fossils tell the tale of how nature turned the light switch on. These fossils represent a turning point in the history of life on Earth.

DR. DESMOND COLLINS
Since the discovery of this amazing fossil bed by the Secretary of the Smithsonian, Charles Doolittle Walcott in 1909, the Burgess Shale has attracted some of the world's leading paleontological researchers to the Rockies. Dr. Desmond Collins and his colleagues at the Royal Ontario Museum in Toronto affirmed to the world the importance of Yoho National Park through a series of important new discoveries in the 1970s and 1980s.
Photograph by R.W. Sandford.

With the rise of the eye, evolution got out of first gear. A new sense demanded adaptive strategies for prey seeking escape from animals with eyes. New musculature appeared. So did jaws, teeth and shells. The eye led to the rise of armament and ornament in nature. By way of evolution, adaptive colouration appeared in the world. In a world where animals could see, there was an explosion of new niches that life could fill. A broader food web came into existence, which led to creation of the first true ecosystems and to early animals with backbones: chordates like *Pikiai*. The chordates led to the first vertebrates, which led to us.

The eye caused a rapid advancement of evolution. In only a million years, the world was changed forever. Close your eyes. Keep them closed. Now open them. The world became ours the moment the first eye recognized light. That eye may have first opened above a seafloor that was since pushed three kilometres into the sky to form the Rocky Mountains.

THE NORTH
SASKATCHEWAN RIVER
Because of their elevation,
the Rocky Mountains play
an important role in the
hydrological cycle of the North
American continent. Fed by
rain and snow, rivers in the
Canadian Rocky Mountain
Parks World Heritage Site
have been flowing without
interruption for more than
10,000 years. As the glaciers in
the Rockies continue to melt,
however, that may change.
Photograph by R.W. Sandford.

THE BURGESS SHALE AND MASS EXTINCTIONS

DESMOND COLLINS, WHO worked on the mysteries of the Burgess Shale
fossils for much of his life, contended that one of the deeply disturbing
lessons offered in our time by the Burgess record relates to the pre-
cariousness of life: existence is a gamble. Chance plays a huge role in
determining what survives and what does not. "If you re-wound and
replayed the video tape of time," he was fond of saying, "you might not
get *Pikai* – and you might not get us."[2]

The Burgess Shale offers other sobering lessons on the history of
earthly life. Its layers were laid down during a long period of stability.
The geological time scale is founded upon the presence throughout
history of such long periods of stability, followed by massive extinctions
caused by horrific natural catastrophes. There are no guarantees against
disasters from within or without. In other words, contingency is a fact of
existence. During the past 570 million years, the span of time that hard-
bodied creatures have lived on Earth, there have been as many as fifteen
major periods of extinction. Five mass extinctions involved as many
as half of the species then alive on Earth. Two major catastrophes were
even more devastating.

The first extensive extinctions occurred about 245 million years ago at the close of the Paleozoic, or Age of Primitive Life. The end of the Permian Era is defined by something that caused more than 90 percent of species to vanish. Geologists examining the Permian-Triassic boundary have found an abundance of fossils that suddenly interface with a lifeless black mudstone, which upon analysis reveals a period during which there was little oxygen as billions of bodies decayed at the bottom of the sea.

Research has suggested that the catastrophe that caused the great Permian extinction was the explosion of a chain of Siberian volcanoes that introduced enough CO_2 into the atmosphere to heat the oceans sufficiently to force methane out of salt-water solution. The combined temporary impacts of increased atmospheric concentrations of these two gases may have caused a runaway greenhouse effect that eliminated much of life on Earth. Geologists are now able to model the extent of the temperature rise that brought about the loss of 95 percent of life on this planet. It is interesting to note that the sudden temperature rise that occurred in the Permian was on the order of about 6°C, which – interestingly enough – is about the upper limit at which the United Nations Intergovernmental Panel on Climate Change has projected for mean annual temperature rise if we do not curb greenhouse emissions in our time.[3]

Life on this planet underwent yet another cataclysm 180 million years later, at the end of the Cretaceous. In *The End of Evolution: On Mass Extinctions and the Preservation of Biodiversity*, geologist Peter Ward describes the scene.[4] An asteroid or the nucleus of a comet at least 10 kilometres across and travelling approximately 40,000 kilometres an hour approached the earth. Its huge velocity rammed a hole through the atmosphere. Moments later it slammed into the earth, causing an explosion more powerful than the detonation all of the modern world's nuclear weapons, creating a crater nearly 300 kilometres across. Rock in the impact zone, as well as the entire mass of the asteroid itself, blasted upward through the hole in the earth's atmosphere created by its entry. Some of this rocky debris was flung into orbit around the earth. The heavier material re-entered the atmosphere but fell back as blazing fireballs that set fire to many of the earth's forests. Over half of the vegetation on the planet burnt in the ensuing fires. Stratospheric winds carried the impact debris around the world. Debris and the smoke of the burning forests blocked out the sun for months. Shock heating of the atmosphere caused atmospheric oxygen and nitrogen to combine into nitrous oxide, which fell as poisonous acid rain. The acid concentration in the rain dissolved the calcareous shells of all the creatures in the upper 100 metres of the world's seas. After months of darkness, the "impact winter" gradually ended. But radical increases in the concentrations of carbon dioxide and water vapour in the atmosphere permanently altered the weather. No wonder the dinosaurs died.

We remain both fascinated and troubled by evidence of disasters of a planetary scale, with good reason. Scientists are concerned that a die-off could be occurring that might rival the impacts of the astronomical event that brought the Cretaceous to a close. Many experts believe that the period during which humans came to dominate the earth may mark a period of extinction in which more actual species disappear than during the two great die-offs of the Permian and Cretaceous periods combined. That dark view, however, supposes we don't do anything to slow or stop the massive extinctions we are causing.

What we have done as a society in the Rocky Mountains suggests other more positive possibilities. Hope for the future invites us to carefully examine the most recent periods in our planet's geological history and the earliest chapters of human presence on the North American continent, with the goal of determining what we might do in our time to slow this diminishment and loss and to allow current biodiversity to sustain us in the future.

The Creation

People and Place Before European Contact

OUR PART IN THE STORY of these mountains begins in the Pleistocene, which began about 1.8 million years ago. The Pleistocene is important to us because it was during this epoch that the assemblage of plants and animals we find in the Rockies today came into existence.

As we shall see, it is back to this period that Parks Canada's current ecosystem restoration goals have tended, as exemplified by the idea of bringing bison back into the Canadian Rocky Mountain Parks World Heritage Site. But re-wilding, as it is often called, doesn't just involve wildlife. A cultural component accompanies all re-wilding ideals.

The second thing that is important about the Pleistocene is that we see a theme emerge during that epoch that remains with us today. That theme is diminishment and loss of species and diversity.

If there was ever a place to contemplate early human presence on this continent it is the east slopes of the Rockies. Many archaeologists believe that the First Peoples travelled along the margins of the mountains on their way to permanent residence in North America. When continental glaciers reached their recent maximum, sea level was 90 metres below what it is today. Somewhere between fifty and twenty-five thousand years ago Siberia and Alaska were joined by a wind-swept plain now known as the central Beringian Land Bridge.

It has long been thought that at this time an ice-free corridor existed between what is now the Yukon and the U.S. along the front ranges of the Rockies. It would have been right along the edge of what is now the east boundary of Banff National Park. Unfortunately, no archaeological evidence of human occupation from that early date has been discovered, but there have been important discoveries from later periods.

Lake Minnewanka in Banff National Park has long been regarded as a significant prehistoric Native occupation site. Since 1974, five Clovis projectile points have been located in the area, indicating human occupation dating back ten to twelve thousand years ago. The presence of these large points suggests that the earliest people to camp on the shores of the lake used spears to hunt large animals such as bighorn sheep and bison.

Between nine and five thousand years ago, the mountain climate warmed. Evidence suggests that the treeline in the Rockies was higher than it is today and that the people who visited the Lake Minnewanka area at that time had advanced their hunting techniques with the atlatl, a device that helped them throw spears further. It was not until 2,000 years ago that the bow and arrow appear to have come into common use among the peoples of the western plains and mountains.

There is a great deal we do not know about early Native history in the Rockies. In the spring of 1993, a team from the University of Calgary found 115 lithic objects (stone tools) indicating prehistoric occupation of an important lakeshore site. They also discovered intact stratigraphy in the lake shore sediments to suggest that the site might yield some very early material. Unfortunately, the team had only three weeks to excavate before the water backing up behind the Minnewanka hydro-power dam inundated the site.

Archaeology is important for what it has to say about the relationship of early peoples to the landscape and the possible impact their hunting activities may have had on the current wildlife assemblages in North America. Some archaeologists believe that Native peoples may have had a huge influence in determining which large mammals survived a major Pleistocene extinction to populate this continent in our time. Fossil evidence tells us that a significant number of mammals of over 45 kilograms existed near the end of the Pleistocene in North America that do not exist today. They include a number of species which, had they survived, would have resulted in a very different assemblage of animals

KTUNAXA DANCERS

At least a dozen First Nations peoples lived in and around what is now the Canadian Rocky Mountain Parks World Heritage Site for generations before the area came under protected status. For many of these peoples, traditional ways of life can only be sustained through the perpetuation of place and landscape-based ceremonies. By protecting the landscapes that are at the heart of Aboriginal culture, we keep the hope alive that one day all of humanity may one day live sustainably within nature once again.

Photograph by R.W. Sandford.

today in both North and South America.[1] The North American bison is the largest mammal from the Pleistocene to have survived.

According to Paul Martin of the University of Arizona, six genera of large carnivores also disappeared considerably before we arrived on the scene. Five more became extinct during a period when their disappearance could have been witnessed by humans, and four others survived into the present. Among the species that disappeared are the dire wolf, *Canis dirus*, two bear species, a scimitar cat and the sabre-toothed cat. We also lost the North American lion and a cheetah.

While most of us would hardly consider such disappearances relevant in the context of our time, the ghosts of these missing predators are with us still today. Consider the pronghorn. At the end of the last Ice Age, this animal was the central prey species of the North American cheetah. While the pronghorn is still capable of the extraordinary bursts of speed that would have been necessary to escape such a fast predator as the cheetah, that predator no longer exists on the Great Plains. The cheetah is gone and the pronghorn finds itself rather in the incredulous position of the incorrigible speeder who has continually improved his vehicle so as to outrun the police, only to discover that the police no longer exist. If you live in the west you may have witnessed pronghorns trying to keep up with cars. One wonders if they miss the Pleistocene cheetah that once chased them hungrily across these same plains, or if they are simply being pursued by ghosts.[2]

It appears also that the two bears that disappeared in the Pleistocene were much larger than the related species of today. The short-faced bear, *Arctodus simus*, was probably nearly four metres tall when standing. This bear would have attracted considerable attention when it stood up suddenly in the willows by the river. When early North Americans confronted this bear – as surely they did – they found themselves in the presence of one of the great natural symbols of the Pleistocene; they beheld the spirit of the greatest of the great bears. Through knowledge of this animal they were able to define ceremonially just how much wild

Though they spent most of their time on the other side of the Continental Divide, the Salish and the Kootenay, who call themselves Ktunaxa, travelled east across a variety of mountain passes to hunt buffalo on the plains. Later they crossed the divide to exchange furs at early trading posts. The Shuswap also lived on the west side of the Great Divide. They spoke a dialect of the Salish language and travelled extensively in the Rockies as far north as Jasper. It was they who built pit houses on sites near the Vermilion Lakes in Banff National Park and on what is now the Banff Springs golf course.

The Stoney arrived in this region from the east, perhaps 300 years ago. In historical records they are also referred to as the Assiniboines. The Stoney are a Sioux-speaking people who separated from a larger group that lived in the area of the Great Lakes. They moved into the Kootenay Plains area along the North Saskatchewan River in the 1820s and settled in the Bow River Valley by 1840. They later travelled widely throughout the region now encompassed within the mountain national parks. During and following the fur trade there were Iroquois in Jasper, and since contact, Métis were everywhere.

Each tribe had their relationship to land and place, the implications of which still surface in Canada through Native land claims. But the fact remains that no one can claim the Rockies as their sole home.

The long presence of Aboriginal peoples in the Rockies belies the fact that contemporary historical interpretation of the mountain West remains Eurocentric. We often act as though nothing happened here until the train chugged into town. If we are to create a culture worthy of place we need to transcend unsupportable romantic notions and false stereotypes about Native presence in the mountain West. The first thing that must be put into proper perspective is the duration of Native presence and its relationship to notions of "European discovery." Europeans discovered little that was not already known about the West by locals.

Another myth that needs to be dispelled is that early peoples were a passive, almost benign presence on the landscapes of the West. The First Peoples have been influencing the nature and character of the western landscape since their arrival. The landscape that we experience today passed into our hands from theirs. But before we took it from them, it passed through the hands of the fur trade.

Exchanging What We Had for What We Want

The Fur Trade Era in the Canadian West

THE TRANSFORMATION OF the Canadian West from a wilderness to an outpost of European culture was as much commercially as politically motivated. It is no accident that corporate interest was sewn into the very fabric of the history of the Canadian West and into the process through which our national parks system came into existence.

The corporation as we know it today was a product of a new wave of thinking that swept Europe in the sixteenth century. Before the notion of limited liability – which is the foundation of the corporate ideal – debt was held to be trans-generational. Quite simply, the debts of one generation were passed on to direct descendants in the next, which severely restricted the amount of risk that merchants were prepared to take in development of their businesses.

The discovery of the New World radically altered the degree of risk required to take full advantage of the opportunity to profitably exploit fabulous new resources and markets. Fortunes rode on precious cargoes that were all too often lost in shipwrecks or to the enterprise of pirates and thieves. It soon became clear that the old debt system was not adequate to the opportunity that was emerging in an increasingly global marketplace. Early state-chartered corporations were created to underwrite the liability of shareholders in bold new trading endeavours in the New World.

On May 2, 1670, during the reign of Charles II, the Hudson's Bay Company (HBC) was incorporated by Royal Charter to trade in those regions of North America draining into Hudson Bay. Though it took more than a century, the Hudson's Bay Company and its rivals gradually advanced westward across the seemingly limitless continent toward the Rocky Mountains. The Bay's influence on the lands and peoples of the West would go far beyond the mere harvesting of furs. Aboriginal cultures would be utterly transformed by the desire to trade.

The corporate ideal proved enormously successful. Granted access by various governments to vast tracts of the freshly colonized America, the corporation set out to profit from the expanding geography of the New World. In so doing, corporations reshaped the history and culture of every place they touched.

At the time of European contact, the tools and implements North Americans possessed were principally made of flint, stone or bone. The people of this continent instantly recognized the advantages of European iron tools and woven goods. All they had in quantity to be traded for axes, pots, blankets, guns, powder and shot were the skins of the abundant animals around them. In exchange for the goods they so desired, Native peoples entered into a market economy that yanked them, often in a single generation, from the Stone Age into the Iron Age. The impact on their lives was profound. In the end the fur trade would leave many Native peoples without a means to earn a living and without a way to return to their pre-contact lifeways. In the opinion of many historians, it was not the land hunger, political greed, disease or rum that destroyed many of the Native peoples of the West. As Wallace Stegner pointed out, it was iron and steel, guns, needles, and woollen cloth that altered Native way of life, the things "that once possessed could not be done without."[1] Native culture was not all that was altered irrevocably by the fur trade. The impact on the ecosystems of the North American continent was catastrophic.

It is estimated that there were between 60 and 400 million beaver in North America at the time of European contact. (The figure of 60 million, calculated by naturalist Ernest Thompson Seton, seems more likely.)[2] Seventeenth-century fashion was not as fickle as it is today. The beaver hat was the rage for 200 years. While a continent was explored in search of it, hundreds of Native peoples came under the spell of the

ATHABASCA FALLS
Not far downstream from where the Sunwapta and Athabasca rivers meet, the entire flow of the Athabasca River tumbles over a wall into a canyon so narrow the river has to change shape to pass through it. When the river is in spring flood, the roar of the falls can be heard kilometres away.
Photograph by R.W. Sandford.

European trade system. The beaver ultimately became the symbol of our nation as well as our national park system.

It should not be forgotten, however, that the beaver is also a symbol of the power of self-generation of habitat, biodiversity and natural systems of water purification. Though they are hardly threatened, beaver populations are likely only a fraction of what they were in Canada two centuries ago. Much of the wetland they occupied has been drained and altered. No one in this country knows what kind of impact the virtual elimination of the beaver has had on the water resources and aquatic ecosystems of this country. All we know is that the West today bears little resemblance to what existed before the fur trade.

The fur trade had an obvious impact on wildlife populations and on natural ecosystems throughout the continent. While hardly anywhere in the West was not in some way affected by the fur trade, the area within what is now the Canadian Rocky Mountain Parks World Heritage Site most associated with it is Jasper National Park. If what happened at Jasper House is any indication, its impact on wildlife populations must have been stupendous.

In Jasper the Native prehistory is far more extensive than most residents suspect. The park alone has 474 historic sites, of which 221 are

PORTRAIT OF DAVID THOMPSON

Admirers see David Thompson exalted as a model of what a fur trader should be: understanding of his customers and partners, the First Nation's peoples; phenomenal in physical endurance, covering more than 90,000 km (55,000 mi.) in his travels; and pious, sober, and faithful. Detractors see a different man: a man who was disloyal to employers, bore grudges, and shaved the truth in his narrative of his adventures. Everyone, however, even detractors, agree that Thompson was the greatest North American land geographer of his time. There is no likeness of David Thompson in existence. This remarkable painting by Alice Saltiel Marshall of Canmore was pieced together from descriptions of Thompson offered in the journals and accounts of those who knew him.

Photograph courtesy of the artist.

prehistoric dwelling sites. We now know that the main ranges of the Rocky Mountains were of marginal ecological and cultural importance to the Native peoples of the regions. Native use of the area during the period of early European contact was seasonal. The great majority preferred to live and hunt in areas outside the mountains with more game and shorter winters. While in the Rockies, however, they hunted wood and plains bison, woodland caribou, moose, mule deer and the ever-popular bighorn sheep. They also fished and hunted waterfowl when available.

To Native peoples the mountains were not barriers as they were to early Europeans. The highest peaks of the Great Divide were permeated with passes used regularly by Native peoples for hundreds of years before the arrival of the first Europeans. Through pre-history the major route through the mountains of what is now Jasper National Park was Yellowhead Pass. With the advent of fur traders, however, far more travellers used Athabasca Pass, which connected to the Columbia. The man responsible for both the trade and the change of route was map-maker and surveyor David Thompson. To understand the impact of the fur trade on the West, it is important to understand the period in which David Thompson lived.

Thompson was born poor in Westminster, England on April 30, 1770. At 14, he became indentured to the Hudson's Bay Company and, in 1784, found himself aboard the *Prince Rupert* bound for Hudson Bay. Of a largely independent nature, Thompson disliked his job as post clerk and soon used his mathematical skills to begin work on behalf of the HBC in mapping and surveying. During this time, however, it became clear there would be limited opportunity in these fields, especially compared with what was being offered by the North West Company (NWC), the Hudson's Bay Company's only serious rival.

In 1797, armed with a promise from the NWC that he would be able to explore and map to his heart's content, David Thompson left the venerable HBC. While working with the Nor'Westers, Thompson was encouraged to explore new passes across the Rockies in a quest to secure the lucrative furs said to exist on the upper reaches of the Columbia River.

The first major pass across the Rockies that Thompson explored was near the headwaters of the North Saskatchewan River. By following the west fork of this river with a band of Kootenays in 1807, David Thompson was able to find his way over what is now called Howse Pass to the Columbia, and establish successful inter-montane trade with Native peoples in the interior of British Columbia. The fierce Peigan, or Pikani as they called themselves, were not excited about the establishment of trade and the selling of guns to their hereditary enemies, the Kootenays. They blockaded Howse Pass and threatened to take Thompson's life should he attempt further trade with their enemies.

In the winter of 1806-1807, the American Fur Company under John Jacob Astor conceived a plan to capture all the trade at the mouth of the Columbia and to deliver the entire unclaimed region to President Jefferson. When Astor invited the North West Company to join, they declined. They had their own ideas about the future of the West coast of British North America, which did not include the Americans.

In July of 1810, the NWC instructed Thompson to cross Howse Pass to the mouth of the Columbia before American Fur Company could establish a post there. When they presented him with a parcel of tiny British flags that he was instructed to give to every chief and to plant on the fork of every major river, Thompson recognized that his was more than just a trade mission.

When men sent to bolster Thompson's party reached the traditional route up the North Saskatchewan, they were confounded to find their way blocked by four tipis of hostile Peigans. After discovering that Thompson was waiting for them on the Brazeau River, they eluded the Peigan, joined their leader and began the difficult march north to the next pass they might cross to reach the Columbia. Due to delays in travelling through the mountainous terrain, Thompson and his twenty-four men did not reach the Athabasca River until December of 1810.

It is often claimed that David Thompson was the first European to visit the Athabasca Valley. But even Thompson noted that there were others in the valley when he visited in 1810, for he passed a hunter's cabin on an island in Brule Lake. It has also been said that the Athabasca River Valley was a desirable route for Thompson and the fur trade, but it was not. Even before departing for Athabasca Pass in the fall of 1810, Thompson noted that the use of a northern pass "would place us in great safety [from the Peigan], but would be attended by great inconvenience, fatigue, suffering and privation."[3] He was not wrong. As Thompson and his men approached the pass, the cold of the January peaks chilled their bones. One of the Native persons accompanying the expedition argued that the pass was the known haunt of the mammoth. Though they found no evidence of the creature, all were in great fear. At the summit of the pass, Thompson wondered what would happen next. A new world lay before them, unknown and unnamed. With his men ready to desert, Thompson wondered if he could get to the mouth of the Columbia in time to head off the Americans. They did indeed but the issue of the future of the Columbia quickly became a larger geopolitical issue between Britain and the United States.

After his exploration of Athabasca Pass in January of 1811, Thompson established it as part of Canada's first national highway to the west coast. Since Thompson was only passing through, he left William Henry behind to establish Henry House. Later, in 1813, the NWC built a post on the northwest shore of Brule Lake in the Athabasca Valley. It was one of the loneliest and most remote posts in the entire fur trade system. It appears that the first trader stationed there permanently was Francois Decoigne. Early travellers through the area noticed that Decoigne's primary role was not the trading of furs but the maintenance of the house as a provisioning depot serving the needs of brigades returning to and from the Columbia. It was only open in spring and fall. In summer and winter, the trader usually repaired to more comfortable and less remote Fort Edmonton.

When Ross Cox crossed Athabasca Pass in 1817, Decoigne's remote cabin was named Jasper House, after Jasper Hawes, the factor who now occupied the post. In 1824, three years after the amalgamation of the North West Company and the Hudson's Bay Company, governor George Simpson of the HBC concluded that there was enough work at the post to require the services of an additional clerk.

In 1830, Michael Klyne rebuilt the dilapidated Jasper House at a new site further up the Athabasca River, near the point where it becomes Jasper Lake. In 1846, the artist Paul Kane described Jasper House, which consisted of

> only of three miserable log huts. The dwelling-house is composed of two rooms, of about fourteen or fifteen feet square each. One of them is used by all comers and goers: Indians, voyageurs, and traders, men, women, and children being huddled together indiscriminately; the other room being devoted to the exclusive occupation of Colin Fraser and his family, consisting of a Cree squaw, and nine interesting half-breed children. One of the other huts is used for storing provisions in, when they can get any, and the other I should have thought a dog-kennel had I seen many of the canine species about. This post is kept up only for the purposes of supplying horses to parties crossing the mountains.[4]

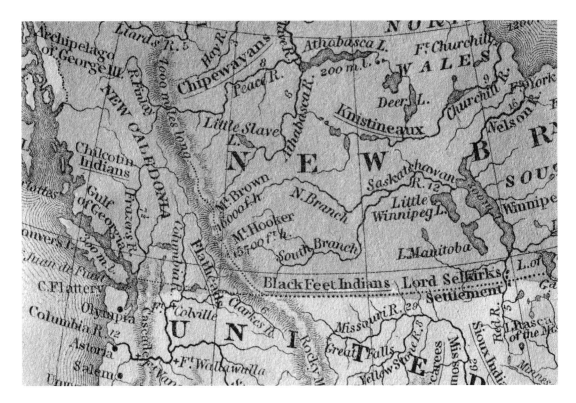

MOUNT HOOKER AND MOUNT BROWN

Botanist David Douglas returned to England in 1827 to report Himalayan-sized mountains in the Canadian West. Soon, Mount Hooker and Mount Brown began to be represented on maps as being among the ten highest peaks on the continent. The mystery of the height of these mountains was not solved until Toronto geologist Professor Arthur Philemon Coleman visited Athabasca Pass in 1893. This story is well told in a novel written by Jerry Auld called *Hooker & Brown*, which was published by Brindle and Glass in 2009. This image is from a map from the late nineteenth century.

From the collection of R.W. Sandford.

Jasper House in its various incarnations had a profound impact on wildlife in the Athabasca Valley. Prolonged hunting pressure associated with the need to supply food for Jasper House traders, their families, and passing brigades had reduced bighorn sheep and moose populations. Father De Smet's account of his visit to Jasper House, also in 1846, gives us an idea of the nature of the problem. He observed that during twenty-six days, Jasper House hunters killed twelve moose, two caribou, thirty bighorn sheep, two porcupines, 210 hares, a beaver, two muskrats, twenty-four geese, 115 ducks, twenty-one pheasants, a snipe, an eagle, an owl, thirty to fifty whitefish a day, and twenty trout. It is not surprising that a few years later the game was gone and the Hudson's Bay Company had to prohibit freemen from hunting within 50 kilometres of Jasper House. But the reduction of wildlife populations by hunting was insignificant compared to the impact of the fur trade itself.

In a good year, North America exported to Europe the pelts of 300,000 beavers; 50,000 wolves; 30,000 bears; 22,000 otters; 750,000 raccoons; 40,000 lynx; 50,000 to 100,000 pine martens; and 250,000 foxes. For decades this was a normal annual take, during the heyday of the trade. By 1700, the beaver was gone from the east coast of the United

States. While efforts to sustain beaver populations in Canada kept numbers at harvestable levels, at least for a time, the thirst for more and more furs drove traders farther and farther west, with predictable results.

EARLY RECOGNITION OF CONTEMPORARY IMPACTS

ONE OF THE FIRST to recognize contemporary human impacts on extinction rates was William T. Hornaday, who voiced concerns about the future of the grizzly bear early in the twentieth century. As the Director of the New York Zoological Park, Hornaday travelled extensively in North America and abroad. In 1913, he was home long enough to publish *Our Vanishing Wildlife*, a book in which he reported that, except within nature reserves, there was no place on Earth where wildlife was disappearing faster than in North America. Hornaday was appalled at the evidence in both Canada and the United States that, in every state and province, proved that "the existing legal system for the preservation of wild life is fatally defective." He went on to claim that the carnage taking place early in the twentieth century was greater than what had occurred during the 1870s when, he maintains, nearly sixty million buffalo and hundreds of thousands of antelope, deer, elk, bears and wolves were slaughtered on the Great Plains.[5] But the diminishment of wildlife populations was just one of many changes taking place in the mountain West. Ecosystems were in visible decline, but even more hard hit were the cultures depending upon them for subsistence.

The Coming of Death

Diminishment and Loss among the First Peoples of the West

BY THE TIME ANTHONY HENDAY arrived at the foot of the Rockies in 1754, Native culture had already been dramatically influenced by European contact. The Plains peoples had horses by 1732. They had acquired mounts though trade, theft, and war from tribes further south who had in turn obtained them from Spanish conquistadores.

The Spanish Barbs – small tough horses that originated around North Africa's Barbary Coast – were the ancestors of modern North American mustangs. Native peoples cultivated the natural toughness of these horses and bred them for speed. The horse allowed them to hunt over greater areas. It allowed Native peoples to be more mobile and expand their material culture. As European settlement pushed Native peoples ever westward, the horse helped them to advance into new terrain. The horse was also a weapon of war. With the horse, the Blackfoot were able to dominate the western plains.

The horse was not the only early benefit to Native peoples in what later became a rather one-sided cultural exchange. They acquired the gun from Europeans, which further revolutionized the way they hunted and waged war. With the gun and the horse, the Blackfoot were able to drive the Ktunaxa over the Divide and keep them there.

While the horse was the first great biological innovation to be introduced to North America from Europe, it was not the last. In his remarkable book *Ecological Imperialism: The Biological Expansion of Europe, 900–1900*, Alfred Crosby dramatically reveals the extent to which Europeans making their new homes in Canada made the West resemble biologically the places they came from in Europe.

Crosby substantiates his point with a reference to the old American folk song "Sweet Betsy from Pike." As Crosby explains, Betsy is from Pike Country, Missouri. She crosses the mountains "with her lover Ike, two yoke of oxen, a large yellow dog, a tall shanghai rooster, and one spotted hog." Crosby then makes the point that Betsy and her menagerie were part of an invasion of North America that went far beyond the settlers. What occurred in the nineteenth century was nothing short of "a clucking, crowing, grunting, lowing, neighing, bleating, barking, buzzing, meowing, self-replicating and world-altering invasion of North America by Europeans and their livestock and weeds." Much of southern Canada, as a consequence, has become a neo-Europe.[1]

In the wake of the horse came hundreds of introduced plant and animal species. Some such as cows, pigs, goats, sheep, dogs, cats and bees were introduced intentionally, but others were not. The European invasion of North America also occurred at the viral and bacterial levels. Here the ecological history of the West overlaps with historical epidemiology. The period from the fifteenth to seventeenth centuries was a perilous time for the human species. Growing concentrations of humans in crowded, dirty cities created circumstances ripe for epidemics. Bubonic plaque struck on a cyclical basis during this period and diseases like smallpox became so commonplace that Europeans developed immunity to them. That, however, does not mean that the rest of the world did.

Native peoples in North America had little or no resistance to the diseases Europeans brought to the New World. The resulting loss of life among Native peoples was so substantial it led many Europeans to believe that the mountain West was un-peopled and therefore suitable for resource exploitation and European settlement. This is evidenced by John Palliser's account of the area that is now the southern part of the Canadian Rocky Mountain Parks World Heritage Site. Palliser reported finding only 225 Stoneys between the North Saskatchewan River and Canada's present border with the United States. Why Native peoples were few in the Canadian West at this time is one of the saddest stories in our history and one we don't like to tell.

By far the most devastating of the diseases introduced from Europe was smallpox. Caused by a pathogenic virus, it was normally spread by "droplet infection," usually in a sneeze or by direct physical contact with a person in the infectious stage. It could also be contracted from corpses for up to three weeks after death and from items that had been in close contact with a diseased person, for a period of up to a year after death. Once a person contracted the disease there was little that could be done.

It is important to compare the mortality rates of various epidemic diseases and smallpox as they affected Native peoples. The average mortality in a typical bubonic plague or smallpox epidemic in Europe was about 30 to 40 percent. The ebola outbreak that terrified the world in 1989 infected 315 people. Of those infected with this horrible hemorrhagic fever, 244 died, a mere 77 percent mortality. I say "mere" to highlight the fact that smallpox mortality among the Native peoples of North America was much higher: in many tribes, the death rate reached 90 percent.

Why was the mortality so high among Native peoples? The first reason, obviously, was that they lacked any kind of immunity. Epidemiologists call the four major smallpox outbreaks that happened in the West "virgin soil" epidemics. These are disease outbreaks in populations that generally lack acquired or inherited immunity to new diseases and do not have the cultural experience to deal with them.

Another reason why the mortality was so high was the terrible nature of the disease itself. The following account was written by William Bradford who witnessed an outbreak of smallpox among Native peoples on the Connecticut River in 1634:

> [F]or want of bedding and linen and other things they fall into a lamentable condition as they lie on their hard matts, the poxe breaking and mattering and runing one into another, their skin cleaving (by reason thereof) to the matts they lie on. When they turn them, a whole side will flay of[f] at once as it were, and they will be all of a gore blood most fearful to behold.[2]

Both Native people and Europeans made fatal mistakes in managing these epidemics. The latter failed to recognize the need to contain each epidemic. Given the inter-connected nature of Native family structures, it was impossible to prevent a wavelike spread of the disease outward from its epicentres. Despite the close-knit and caring nature of their culture, Native peoples did not have the means with which to deal with this class of disease. Two traditional approaches to healing the sick were particularly dangerous in highly contagious viral infections

*Giving Meaning to Mountains and
Making Them Ours*

Mountaineering and the Aesthetics of Place

WE DO NOT KNOW WHEN MOUNTAINS were first invested with super-natural powers. Perhaps the first sacred summits were volcanoes, their thunderous anger reaching with hell-fingers into villages of innocents unsure of how they had offended their gods.

Perhaps the first notions of hell were belched up from these burning summits, the very breath of brimstone carried on the wind with the smoke and glowing ash. Certainly, weather came from the peaks. When clouds boiled over the mountains, it made them look like displeased stone gods punishing evil with fire and flood.

Faith, too, seems to have been born on the summits, those sacred places where the earth reached up to the sky out of which all things seemed to come. With so much riding on the wind and the rain, where else could the peaks be pointing but to heaven, that vague seat from which an absolute power pronounced on the likelihood of crops and the fortunes of men. To such summits the first prophets climbed, seeking peace, wisdom and pronouncements from their gods. Time has swallowed Zarathustra, who wandered in search of truth until on "the mountain of the Holy Communing Ones" he heard "the soul of the earth" lamenting to heaven the devastation of the land below.[1] Was it

■ 47

he who first made the whole planet sacred, the entire spinning sphere a god? Ours might be an era in which revisiting early ideals could be worthwhile.

In the Bible, God tells Abraham to offer his son up as a sacrifice "upon one of the mountains which I shall tell you." To the mountain they went but just as he was about to slay his son, God blessed him and his people and they went forth with their faith to rule a sizeable portion of the known world. Abraham, being on the inside of such things, knew the almighty as El Shaddai. Many translate this name to mean "one of the mountain." From this we can imagine a deity watching over his peaks, rather in the manner of a retired mountaineer fondly recalling earlier climbs.

It was clear that Abraham's mountain had a lot of power. It was upon this mount that Solomon placed his temple.[2] Later a mosque was built on the site for from this summit Mohammed, the founder of Islam, went to heaven. Mohammed was wise about mountains. He was the first to unequivocally state that the climber had to go to the mountain as it was unlikely to come to him, a comment with a great deal of philosophical merit. In this regard, it could be said that Mohammed was the founder of the expedition, for his philosophies would later send a great number of people into the mountains to ponder the profound wisdom of his seemingly self-evident truths.

All of this summiteering was good for the image of mountains. It was becoming increasingly obvious that gods did dwell at least on some peaks and those who went to visit them shared their power. The prophet Ezekiel really got this idea going. Though it was not clear he had this vision on a mountain, what he described is a phenomenon seen in mountains. Ezekiel saw an enthroned man surrounded by a rainbow and a wheel burning within a wheel. He described what he saw as the Glory of the Lord. In *Earth Wisdom,* Dolores LaChapelle notes that this kind of vision only seemed to appear when the subject was veiled by cloud. She indicates that, though it may be hard to prove, the phenomenon may have been a sun halo. A sun halo, or what is also called a "glory," is a visual effect produced by unusual conditions of mist and sunlight.[3] This phenomenon is referred to in mountaineering as the Spectre of the Brocken. It was first described by an Englishman who witnessed it on the Brocken, the highest peak in the Harz Mountains, in central Germany.[4] The glory is produced by a backscattering of light similar to how a car's headlights can be reflected from an animal's eyes at night. It is a rare natural phenomenon because conditions, such as the angle

MOUNT COLUMBIA AND ITS GLACIER

A spectacular glacier flows down the shoulders of Mount Columbia. The Columbia Glacier is the headwaters of the Athabasca River, a major tributary of the great Mackenzie River system. *Photograph by R.W. Sandford.*

of the sun and the quality and concentration of water vapour in the air, must be just right to produce a vivid rainbow halo around a figure moving in the mist. The extent of the glory can be much enhanced when oblique sunlight projects the haloed shadow outward into surrounding clouds. In such conditions, the rainbow figure can appear several kilometres tall as the illusion is projected outward from its source. To witness this is an unnerving experience. Imagine a rainbow taking your shape, radiating outward and projecting your movements hugely into the mist over the surrounding valley. If you didn't know that it was an illusion created by light and water vapour, you might imagine yourself entering a mid-zone between heaven and earth.

Before the very eyes of his disciples, Jesus was said to have assumed the brightness of the sun and was ablaze in rainbows. It sounds much like the Spectre of the Brocken. To this day, icons of Jesus wear a halo, the glory of the mountain. Throughout his life, Jesus meditated and consulted God on a variety of peaks. He was on yet another mount when he died.

The Buddha was also bathed in the holy light of the mountain. He, too, saw his figure glowing with rainbow light. Buddha referred to four sacred mountains as the cornerstones of his faith. These mountains have mythical association with the four elements of the Buddhist cosmos: earth, air, fire and water. Temples and monasteries were built on the shoulders of these sacred places. Some became famous if only because on occasion even pilgrims could be lit by the rainbow of their belief. Sometimes acolytes would over-react to the presence of the sacred light. Glowing in rainbow mists, they would throw themselves from the peak into the arms of Enlightenment itself.

The first was support for eastern manufacturing; support for raising tariffs to bolster Canadian manufacturing had helped Macdonald get elected in 1878. The second element was a strong desire to settle the West so that its natural resources could support eastern manufacturing. The third was construction of a transcontinental, all-Canadian railway that would provide a physical link between East and West.[13] The railway created an agricultural economy on the prairies and a tourism economy in the Rockies and Selkirks. The basis of tourism was the hot springs on Sulphur Mountain in what is now Banff National Park. Spas in the late nineteenth century were very popular among the well-heeled in Europe and eastern North America.

The Canadian Pacific Railway's tourism business grew into a full-scale resort operation as its transcontinental passenger traffic increased. Although the federal government and the railway were partners in tourism in the mountain West, the federal government had little money to put into developing the park system and chose to spend what it did have on the hot springs reserve at Banff.[14] As the CPR had a vested interest in developing the parks created around Mount Stephen House, Glacier House, and later at Lake Louise, the company established a trail- and bridge-building program that would result in the creation of facilities appealing to a new breed of mountaineers and tourist-explorers.[15]

A good deal of this new interest in hiking and climbing in the mountains of the Canadian West had been stimulated by a remarkable new book published in England in 1890. *Among the Selkirk Glaciers*, by William Spotswood Green, documented the author's visit to Glacier House with his cousin, Henry Swanzy, in the summer of 1888. As no map existed of the area beyond the tracks, Green and Swanzy decided to create one. The intrepid pair hiked and climbed for six weeks, naming peaks and passes and mapping more than 500 square miles (1,295 square km) of rugged mountain terrain.[16] The widely read book inspired British and American climbers to take the train to Western Canada.

Partly as a result of Green's book, Glacier House became the earliest centre of Canadian mountaineering and tourist-exploration. Tucked neatly into the hemlocks, cedars and aromatic firs on the Illecillewaet River just below Rogers Pass, Glacier House was an ideal location for a mountain resort. The view of the Illecillewaet Glacier from near the hotel was staggering indeed, as were the views of peaks that rose from the surrounding ice stairways that led blue-white to the skyline. In 1891, the prominent American climber Walter Wilcox visited Glacier House

**THE CPR PROMOTES
LAKE LOUISE**
In 1888 two British
adventurers stopped in to
see William Cornelius Van
Horne at the Canadian Pacific
Railway headquarters in
Montreal, to recommend that
the railway build a chalet at
the most beautiful place they
had seen in Canada. That
place was Lake Louise. Within
a decade, the CPR made Lake
Louise the most famous
tourism attraction in the
Rocky Mountains.
*Photograph courtesy of Canadian
Pacific Hotels and Resorts.*

and found it filled with tourist-adventurers "who were accustomed to gather every evening around a blazing fire and read selections from Green's *Among the Selkirk Glaciers* just as our forefathers were wont to read a daily chapter from the Bible."[17]

AN ACCIDENT WAITING TO HAPPEN

FOREMOST AMONG THE EARLY tourist-explorers in Canada's mountain West was a group of eastern climbers who belonged to the Boston-based Appalachian Mountain Club. The club's energetic president, Charles Fay, pioneered an enthusiasm for mountaineering not just in the United States but in Canada as well. Fay and his wealthy associates saw in the Rockies a personal vision to be fulfilled. Great peaks could be climbed and history made in climbing them. It was a golden age. Ambitious urbanites simply got off the train and walked toward the summits of unclimbed, unnamed peaks and named them for their friends.

Without guides, however, and with so little training, early climbers in the Rockies were accidents waiting to happen. On August 3, 1896, Philip Stanley Abbot fell from the upper cliff bands on Mount Lefroy to the col below. He died before Fay and his companions could summon medical help.[18]

Like the accident on the Matterhorn three decades earlier, Abbot's death caused a stir. Many North Americans wanted to ban climbing to prevent further accidents. Undeterred by the bad press, the small mountaineering community decided it was time to bring professional

LAKE MCARTHUR
This stunning body of water
located near Lake O'Hara is
named for the great Canadian
surveyor James Joseph
McArthur, who mapped the
mountains on either side of
the main line of the Canadian
Pacific Railway inside what
is now the Canadian Rocky
Mountain Parks World
Heritage Site.
Photograph by R.W. Sandford.

mountaineering expertise to the challenging problem of climbing in the
Canadian Rockies. If they could avenge the death of Abbot by "conquering" Mount Lefroy, they reasoned, the image of mountaineering as an
uplifting and worthwhile enterprise would be redeemed.

Before the fatal accident on Mount Lefroy in 1896, Fay and Abbot had
climbed in Switzerland with Professor Harold Baily Dixon. Dixon was
an accomplished academic and a respected member of the Alpine Club
in Britain. It had been Abbot's vain hope that Dixon accompany the 1896
expedition to the Rockies and Selkirks.

At the insistence of Abbot's father, who was anxious to prove that
the mountain on which his son died could be climbed, Dixon agreed
to form part of an 1897 attempt on Mount Lefroy. Dixon also invited
some influential friends. Among them were George Percival Baker of
the Alpine Club, and John Norman Collie who had already made a name
for himself in the Alps and in pioneering climbing efforts in the Himalayas. Though competent in their own right, these Englishmen did not
come alone. They paid all the expenses of having a professional guide
accompany them to the Rockies. That guide was Peter Sarbach of St.
Niklaus, Switzerland, with whom both Dixon and Abbot had climbed in
the Alps. While his clients made it clear that Sarbach was invited on the
expedition to strengthen an already excellent climbing team, Sarbach
became the first professional mountain guide to climb in Canada when
he arrived at Lake Louise in 1897.[19]

A large international party guided by Sarbach made the first
ascent of Mount Lefroy on the anniversary of Philip Abbot's death on
August 3, 1897, and went on two days later to make the first ascent of
Mount Green, later known as Mount Victoria. On August 11, a large
party guided again by Sarbach arrived at the Bow Glacier, which they
crossed to access the Wapta Icefield. After making the first ascent of
Mount Gordon, the Americans departed for home. Collie, Baker and
Sarbach proceeded north in search of a large peak they had seen from
the summit of Mount Gordon. Crossing Bow Summit they entered
the valley of what Collie called Bear Creek, later known as the Mistaya
River. On August 25, Sarbach guided Collie and Baker to the summit
of a 3,155 metre peak near the confluence of the Mistaya and the main
branch of the North Saskatchewan River. Collie named it Mount
Sarbach in honour of their guide. Though persistently bad weather pre-
vented any further summit attempts that year, the value of professional
guides had already been established.[20] The Rockies made a deep impres-
sion on the climbers. In 1898, Collie returned with Hugh Stutfield and

Herman Woolley to search for the David Douglas giants, Mounts Hooker and Brown, though the myth of Himalayan sized peaks in the Rockies had already been dispelled; the trio discovered the Columbia Icefield.

THE ARRIVAL OF THE RAILWAY GUIDES

A CAMPAIGN TO ENCOURAGE the railway to consider full-time professional guides in Canada had been launched even before the arrival of Sarbach and the Collie party in 1897. Dr. Joshua Stallard was a close friend of the Vaux family of Philadelphia. George and William Vaux had spent several summers studying glaciers in Rogers Pass with their family starting in 1890. In 1896, Stallard had joined the Vauxes at Lake Louise and had met Charles Fay and Philip Abbot just before they departed on their fatal attempt on Mount Lefroy. In September of 1896, Stallard wrote a letter to the CPR passenger traffic manager responsible for the Rockies, extolling the virtues of Swiss mountain guides, based on climbing experiences in the Alps dating from 1852. Stallard went on to suggest that the fatal accident on Mount Lefroy might not have happened had the Fay-Abbot party been properly and professionally guided.[21]

Passenger Traffic Manager David McNicoll passed Stallard's correspondence on to T.G. Shaughnessy, then vice president of the railway, with a letter outlining his support for Stallard's idea. "As you and I know," McNicoll wrote, "I have all along been of the opinion that we must provide increased accommodations and facilities in the mountains if we expect people to visit them and stay among them, and I understand a little has been done at Louise, but I think a great deal more needs to be done. The same applies to the different points of interest in the neighbourhood of Glacier Station."[22]

In March of 1897, Shaughnessy wrote to Archer Baker, Canadian Pacific's European Traffic Agent in London, to find out how the railway might engage professional guides for service in the Canadian West.

Senior railway officials like McNicoll and Shaughnessy clearly saw the value of professional guides and were anxious to import them to Canada. The writings of William Spotswood Green plus the photography and glacial research of George and William Vaux had already done a great deal to advertise the natural attractions of the Glacier area to potential tourist-adventurers.[23] No one wanted any more climbing deaths. The great engine of the railway's administration was bent on bringing mountain guides west.

In the autumn of 1898, the Canadian Pacific Railway used the Thomas Cook Company to help locate Swiss guides interested in coming to Canada for a season. Contracts were signed with three perfect specimens from Interlaken. Christian Häsler and Edouard Feuz (the closest approximation in English is "Foits") would be sent to Glacier House and Charles Clarke would be sent briefly to Banff to promote mountaineering at the Banff Springs Hotel.[24]

The arrival of Swiss guides at Glacier House caused a sensation. First, there was their unusual appearance. Here were men in tweed jackets, waistcoats, and ties, wearing nailed boots and knickers with long wool socks. Climbing ropes hung from their shoulders and they held ice axes. Though most visitors didn't know what to make of them, climbers were impressed. "No pair of twin brothers," wrote Charles Fay, "were more nearly duplicates in raiment, no two guides ever more supplemented one the other in excellencies."[25] Fay got to know the two Swiss guides immediately. With Fay and Herschel Parker as clients Feuz and Häsler made their first ascent in Canada on August 13, 1899. Fay wrote a full account of this famous ascent for the hotel register at Glacier House, which concluded with his assessment of the value of professional mountain guides on new and dangerous terrain:

> The ascent of a peak so remote, should properly take three days; one to reach a suitable camping place at the base, one for the ascent, and a third for the return to the Hotel. Our party took but one and one half days, and made a correspondingly forced march.[26]

On August 20, 1899, George Vaux Jr. visited and commented just as positively on the benefit that professional guides would bring to the Glacier House experience. The presence of guides was making his research into the movement of the Illecillewaet Glacier safer and more productive:

> During the year which has intervened since I last wrote in this minute book, Glacier has lost none of its charms.
>
> The most valuable improvement has been the bringing here of the two Swiss guides. Thoroughly safe, and competent in every particular, there is thus afforded to the general visitor the opportunity to get a true insight into the attractions which mountaineering affords. The visit to the Illecillewaet Glacier may now be supplemented by a trip into the ice itself under the guidance of Feuz or Häsler, which cannot fail to delight with its beauty and novelty. Entire confidence may be reposed in the guides, the chief requirement being an implicit obedience of their directions.[27]

Guides were making the summits accessible to people who could not make it on their own. It did not take long for word to get out that the great peaks of the mountain West could be climbed *if* you went with a guide.

The decision to experiment with guides at Glacier House at Rogers Pass in 1899 completely changed the rules of membership in the climbing community. Until this time, climbing had been the almost exclusive domain of those who held membership in an alpine or mountaineering club. As there were only a few of these in North America, and none in Canada, it was difficult to acquire the skills and experience necessary to become a competent climber. With resident professional mountain guides available at reasonable cost, it became possible to learn to climb without terrifying or fatal results. With the opening of the 1899 season, anyone who was reasonably fit could step off the train at Glacier House and receive a safe and relatively inexpensive introduction to mountaineering in one of the most stunning alpine settings in the world. One needed no equipment, no membership – only a sense of adventure and determination.

FAMOUS CLIMBERS AND FAMOUS GUIDES

THE START OF THE TWENTIETH century brought more Swiss guides to the Canadian Alps. Karl Schluneggar, Friedrich Michel and Jacob Müller signed contracts with the railway and made their way to the western mountains in the summer of 1900.[28]

In 1900, Edward Whymper crossed Canada by train and had been much taken by the scenery and nature of the Canadian peaks. The following winter, Whymper proposed to the CPR that he would favour the landscape attractions of the railway and its hotels in newspaper articles and public presentations in England and in Europe, in exchange for an all-expense-paid visit to the Rockies in 1901. As Whymper was the most famous mountaineer in the world, the railway took quick notice of his offer and placed its considerable resources at his command for the entire climbing season of 1901.

To ensure a successful 1901 climbing season, Whymper brought four Swiss guides with him: Christian Klucker, James Pollinger, Joseph Bossonney and Hans Kaufmann (the only one with previous experience in the Rockies).[29]

The railway, having footed the bill for this expensive expedition, was anxious to see Whymper make the first ascent of Mount Assiniboine, the mountain widely known as the Matterhorn of the Rockies. Privately,

ARTHUR OLIVER WHEELER

A.O. Wheeler is a legend in the Rocky Mountains. He wrote the first book by a Canadian on the mountains of the West. He was the co-founder of the Alpine Club of Canada. He mapped the boundary between Alberta and British Columbia. And he was a tireless promoter of mountain adventure everywhere mountains could be found in Canada.

Photograph courtesy of the Wheeler family.

Whymper had no interest in the great stone spike rising out of the Great Divide south of Banff. At 62, he was the first to suggest that his really difficult climbs were already in the past and that a younger man would have to put a stone-man on the dangerous summit of a mountain like Assiniboine.[30]

Though he had with him some of the most competent guides in the world, Whymper confined most of his climbing to easy peaks in and around the Yoho Valley. Four major first ascents were recorded, up Mount Habel (now known as Mount Des Poilus), Mount Collie, Trolltinder Mountain and Isolated Peak. When Whymper was forced to return briefly to Field to find another horse wrangler, he met a British vicar named James Outram and invited him to join the party. When Whymper concluded his 1901 climbing season after the trip to the Yoho Valley, outfitter Bill Peyto informed Whymper that a bold American attempt on Mount Assiniboine guided by Edouard Feuz and Friedrich Michel had very nearly succeeded. Peyto suggested that he could get Whymper to the mountain in time to capture the peak before another American attempt could be mounted. Whymper wasn't interested, but James Outram was. Outram hired Christian Häsler and Christian Bohren as guides and headed for the peak. On August 3, 1901 they made the first ascent of Mount Assiniboine, one of the classic mountaineering peaks in the world.[31] It should also be noted that Christian Bohren's granddaughter, Loni von Rotz of Canmore, made a centennial ascent of Mount Assiniboine in 2001 to honour her connection to her family heritage.

SWEET ELIZABETH AND THE BIRTH OF THE ALPINE CLUB OF CANADA

ONE OF THE FIRST CANADIANS to be exposed to the burgeoning Canadian alpine aesthetic the Swiss guides inspired was a young surveyor named Arthur Oliver Wheeler, who established an early reputation for cartographic genius with a survey of the Rogers Pass area in British Columbia beginning in 1901. Wheeler was a tireless champion of a uniquely Canadian sense of the alpine.

Despite the fact that Canada was a world centre for mountaineering by the turn of the twentieth century, Wheeler found it very difficult to create interest in an alpine association in this country. Though many clubs all over the world had been formed in the tradition of the Alpine

Club created in England in 1857, Canadians didn't seem interested in forming an organization of their own.

After several attempts at creating a Canadian organization, Wheeler was ready to accept Charles Fay's offer to establish a wing of the American Alpine Club in Canada, but only as a last resort. He refused to give up until he had explored every avenue of possible Canadian interest. For three years after the AAC offer, he wrote letters to major Canadian newspapers trying to garner support for a wholly Canadian organization. Ultimately it was a letter from Wheeler to the *Winnipeg Free Press* that hit the nationalistic nerve and brought the notion of a Canadian Alpine Club to life. That letter prompted an article in the paper by a staff writer, who claimed that it would be downright un-Canadian to subject local mountaineers to the dictates of a foreign alpine institution. The article went on to give Wheeler a tongue-lashing for his lack of patriotism and imperialistic zeal. The author of that article was Elizabeth Parker.[32]

Parker lambasted Wheeler's idea of affiliation with an American club, which prompted the astute Wheeler to ask for press space and editorial support to promote a separate organization, which became the Alpine Club of Canada. Supported by the newspaper, Parker then set out on a tireless campaign of articles about the club and its objectives. She organized the club's founding meeting in Winnipeg in March of 1906, at which Wheeler was elected president and Parker the organization's first secretary. At last a Canadian mountaineering organization existed to incorporate an appreciation of mountains into the evolving culture of this huge new land.[33]

THE ACTION MOVES BACK TO THE ROCKIES

RIDING THE CREST OF GROWING interest in mountaineering in Europe and the United States, the railway advertised these spectacular parks as fifty Switzerlands in one, and promoted the role guides played in enjoyable and safe mountain travel.[34]

In 1911, the Canadian Pacific Railway built a "Swiss Village" at Golden, B.C. to house the guides and their families in a location central both to the Rockies and the Selkirks.[35] Soon a second generation of Swiss guides was working at Canadian Pacific's mountain resort hotels. These *bergführers* rightly became as famous as the men and women they led on hundreds of first ascents all over the Canadian West. Edward Feuz made more than one hundred first ascents of mountains taller than

3,050 metres, taking with him many of the most famous climbers of his time.[36] Clients would come from all over the world to climb with him.

The high profile and enormous success of the Canadian Pacific Hotel mountain guiding program did not go unnoticed by CPR's chief rival, the Canadian National Railway. In 1924, Canadian National began importing Swiss mountain guides to Jasper Park Lodge. Even though some climbers were arguing that they would have preferred to avoid the cost of professional guides on first-ascent expeditions, almost all of the early first-ascent parties on major peaks always included at least one guide.[37]

The central focus of the guiding tradition has always been safety. Though there was one particularly close call in the Death Trap at Lake Louise, over the more than fifty years during which CPR offered guiding services in the Canadian Alps, there wasn't a single mountaineering fatality in the thousands of climbs that Swiss guides led.

GRUMPY ARTHUR AND THE GREAT SURVEY

WHILE THE NORTH AMERICAN mountaineering community remained obsessed with the first ascents of unnamed peaks throughout the West, the Dominion Land Survey was already well into the planning stages of a much larger project. Its ambition was to map the entire Alberta-British Columbia boundary from the 49th parallel northward to the 60th degree of latitude at the southern boundary of the Northwest Territories. The Boundary Survey, as it was called, was the most ambitious program of mountain exploration ever undertaken in this country.

A.O. Wheeler was one of the principals involved in the Great Survey. As one of the founders of the Alpine Club of Canada, Wheeler knew as much about the mountains of Canada as anyone. Between 1913 and 1924, the survey mapped the spine of the Great Divide from Akamina Pass at the American border to the 120th meridian. During the survey, hundreds of mountains were climbed, and thousands more described and placed on maps. These maps remain the foundation of what we know about our mountains today. The next step after the creation of accurate and reliable maps would be the construction of refuges in popular places to ensure the safety of climbers and a growing number of hikers attracted to the glories of the western mountains.

It was around concerns for safety that the first alpine huts were constructed in what are now the Mountain Parks. Abbot Hut was the first. In 1921, Edward Feuz proposed that access to classic climbs on Mount Lefroy and Mount Victoria would be made a great deal easier and safer if a shelter were built on the narrow saddle named for Philip Abbot that separated the two peaks.

Feuz argued that if you could "just get some cement up to the pass and a good stone mason and a few building materials, you could build yourself a hut which would make the place almost as civilized as Switzerland."[38]

Feuz and fellow guide Rudolf Aemmer drew up the plans and showed them first to national parks officials and then to the railway. There were no takers. It looked like too much work and risk for too little benefit. Feuz, however, was not one for giving up. Finally, he found a supporter in Basil Gardom, Superintendent of Construction and Repairs for CPR's western hotels.[39]

Gardom translated the Feuz-Aemmer drawings into blueprints calling for a stone building 35 feet long, 19 feet wide and 18 feet high.[40] To Gardom's associates, the plan was absurd. Building a beautiful guide's cottage on the shore of Lake Louise was one thing. This they had already agreed to do. But the guides were going to construct a house on the 2,962 metre knife-edge of Abbot Pass. That was another matter.

Abbot Hut was difficult to build. The only route to the pass from Lake Louise was up the Lower Victoria Glacier and through the Death Trap to the summit of the col, a section on the Mount Victoria side overhung by ice that collapsed on to the route at unpredictable intervals. Above this the way was safer, but very steep.

Construction began in the summer of 1922. The only way materials could be transported was by horse. It took cool wranglers to lead the heavily laden packhorses through the crevasses to the Death Trap. Guides carried everything in a sled that had been rigged to a winch, to haul the materials the final steep distance to the col.

Even though the rock for the building was to be quarried on-site, there were still two tons of materials to be ferried to the pass. Everything – cement, lime, bolts, windows, timbers, a stove, tools, beds, mattresses, bedding, cutlery, along with sufficient food to sustain the workers – had to be carried up the Death Trap on the guide's backs. Trip after trip after trip, guides carried up to 75 pounds (34 kg) per load up the steep defile.[41]

ABBOT HUT

As more and more guests requested the services of mountain guides at Lake Louise, it became apparent that a high hut would make climbs of Mount Lefroy and Mount Victoria less of an endurance contest. Michael Vincent is pictured here at Abbot Hut.

Photograph by R.W. Sandford.

Twenty members of the Appalachian Mountain Club journeyed all the way from Boston to remember Philip Stanley Abbot at the official opening of the hut in 1923. Edward Feuz's remarks at the opening were brief: "Down in the valley, a house, a big house, is just a big house. But up here, in the ice and snow, with all those beautiful peaks everywhere, this simple hut is home."[42]

Feuz proudly maintained throughout his whole life that the stone hut on Abbot Pass was the only true alpine hut in Canada. Feuz had achieved his goal. Abbot Hut made climbing possible and safe at Lake Louise.

For 50 years, until Neil Colgan Hut was constructed above Moraine Lake in 1983, Abbot Hut had the distinction of being the highest permanent building in Canada. It was turned over to Parks Canada in the mid 1960s. In 1985, through the efforts of Peter Fuhrmann, Parks Canada turned the operation and maintenance of Abbot Hut over to the Alpine Club of Canada, whose volunteers have restored the building to its original simple elegance.[43]

From these humble origins has arisen a most remarkable backcountry hut and lodge tradition. In his guidebook to huts and lodges in the Rockies and Columbia Mountains, Jim Scott lists 124 different places

railway's great westbound trains. Almost overnight the lone land of the West, with its stupendous peaks and roaring rivers, became a symbol of the purity of experience that Romantic poets celebrated. Van Horne touched an aesthetic nerve that brought people from all over the world. Locals were stunned when flocks of foreigners started arriving by train to experience the beauty. All that the locals had seen, at first at least, were rocks and trees.

Until the railway was completed in 1885, few painters made their way as far west as the Rockies. The country was simply too remote and dangerous to visit. When the railway was completed, it began to hire artists to interpret the grandeur of the mountain West. Famous early Canadian painters like Lucius O'Brien, F.M. Bell-Smith and Marmaduke Matthews focused artistic attention on the mountains surrounding railway hotels at Banff, Lake Louise, Field and Rogers Pass.[1] While the significance of the work of these painters was immediately recognized within a small circle of Eastern aficionados, most Canadians never saw these early paintings. These works are of great importance to us today, however, because they represent the foundation of Canadian artistic landscape sensibilities especially as they relate to the mountain west.

As cheap colour lithography had yet to be developed, early railway advertising depicted what is now the Mountain Parks by way of black and white engravings. Though advertising engravings were largely based on photographs, many were stunning works of art. Among these best of these early engravings is one entitled *Rocky Mountains, Near Canmore* that appeared in a lavishly illustrated fifty-page Canadian Pacific pamphlet entitled *The New Highway to the East* (1888). The production of this pamphlet was personally supervised by Van Horne himself who was then Vice President of the CPR.

Images for this brochure were made by the Montreal photographic firm, William Notman and Son Photographic Studio, which sent two photographic parties to the Rockies in 1871 and 1884.[2] Led by Alfred Selwyn, Director of the Geological Survey of Canada and CPR chief engineer Sandford Fleming, the 1871 expedition made photographs of the proposed route the tracks would take through the mountains in the west. The resulting brochure was composed of half-tone reproductions of photographs and engravings made from Notman and Son photographs by American Bank Note Company artists.

Remarkable in their detail and accuracy of perspective, these fine reproductions tell us a great deal about ecological state a century ago of what is now this World Heritage Site. A particularly beautiful engraving

based on a Notman photograph of the Three Sisters illustrates what the Bow Valley looked like before the town surrounded the main line of the railway. Though the valley has been burned over, it is still wilderness. A thin steel line snakes coldly through the few remaining spruce while overhead an overcast sky threatens summer rain.

It was not long after these engravings that the exciting new medium of photography began to influence the way people thought about Canada's western mountains. Mary Schäffer was already an accomplished photographer and well established watercolourist when she undertook her first expedition in search of Maligne Lake in 1907. That year, G.P. Putnam and Sons published *Alpine Flora of the Canadian Rockies*. Written by Stewardson Brown, curator of the Herbarium Academy of Natural Sciences in Philadelphia, the book was illustrated with photographs and watercolours by Schäffer. The first artistic images we have of Maligne Lake and the Maligne Valley are the fine hand-tinted photographs that Schäffer made into lantern slides so that she could show her friends the wonders of what local First Nations called Chaba Imne. These, along with images taken by the Vaux family, Walter Wilcox, and later by Byron Harmon, remain among the most cherished historical photographs of the Rockies.

The moment it became possible to print black and white photographs cheaply the world of seeing was utterly transformed. Byron Harmon

was at the forefront of this movement. Harmon explored
and took more photographs of the Mountain Parks region
than any other early photographer.[3]

While a great many other photographers later made
good livings and established enduring reputations in the
mountain West, Harmon was the first to travel widely with
a camera in the region. Like the Vaux family who visited in
the last decade of the nineteenth century, and W.J. Oliver
of Calgary, Harmon made images from very large negatives
that today still yield prints of extraordinary clarity and
quality. Other photographers contributed to local mountain culture in this tradition. These included Harry Rowed
in Jasper and Bruno Engler in Banff.

While a few contemporary photographers like George
Brybycin travel as widely in the backcountry as Harmon
did, only the large format black and white images of Craig
Richards demonstrate today the capacity to represent the same powerful and immediate sense of perspective and place that the Vaux family
and Byron Harmon captured a century ago. It could be argued that
the true sense of mountain place is as well preserved in contemporary
painting as it is in photography. But even painting continues to wrestle
with the scale and nature of Canada's western mountains.

GENERATIONS OF PAINTERS TRYING TO GET THE ROCKIES RIGHT

FORTUNATELY, THE Canadian Pacific Railway didn't exist just to serve
tourists. At the turn of the century, the railway brought settlers west
by the thousands with the promise of a new start in the West. Professional artists were among these immigrants. By the 1920s, a widening
circle of artists were living in a number of Western Canadian cities.
Art societies began pressing for the creation of art schools and galleries
in bigger centres like Edmonton and Calgary. Once established, these
schools attracted well-established Eastern Canadian and European-
trained artists and instructors. Many of these established painters were
reluctant to abandon the European influence that, in their minds, gave
credibility to their work. A few, however, began to adjust their techniques and pictorial approaches to the massive, colourful environments
of the mountain West.

Among the first Canadian artists to allow themselves to be influenced by the unique character of the Canadian landscape was the Group

of Seven. They formed in Toronto in 1914, and included Lawren Harris, J.E.H. MacDonald, A.Y. Jackson, Frederick Varley, Frank Carmichael, Arthur Lismer and Frank Johnston. Though their initial departures from the mainstream of Canadian painting were brutalized by critics, it gradually became apparent that these painters were creating a uniquely Canadian way of seeing. Here, at last, were paintings that mirrored the immensity and loneliness that were foundations of the Canadian spirit. There was no warmth in these paintings and little sentiment or humour. The emotional appeal of these paintings lay in sobriety and austerity that were at the heart of the grandeur of Canada. What the Group of Seven painted was the essence of the sublime – and there was no more sublime a place in all of Canada than the mountain West.

Members of the Group of Seven began employing their bold new styles in representing the Rockies in 1924. In the late summer and early fall of that year Lawren Harris visited Jasper with A.Y. Jackson. They used Jasper Park Lodge as a centre for expeditions to the Colin Range and the Tonquin Valley. Harris and Jackson also explored the Maligne Valley. They painted at Maligne Lake, Opal Hills, and Coronet Creek in what are now called the Queen Elizabeth Ranges. Harris would return again and again to Jasper and to Mount Robson creating some of the finest mountain paintings ever done in Canada.

The Rockies began to establish a national profile in the arts when members of the Group of Seven became summer instructors at the Banff School of Fine Arts (now the Banff Centre for the Arts). One of the most prominent painters on the faculty of the school during the 1930s was A.Y. Jackson. He and J.E.H. Macdonald were the only members of the group to establish a lasting relationship with the communities of Banff and Canmore.

Perhaps the most influential painter and teacher to have come to the Rockies was Walter Phillips. Walter Joseph Phillips was born at Barton-On-Humber, Lincolnshire, England in 1884. At twenty-eight, Phillips was building the reputation for artistic competence that would follow him for the rest of his life. By 1912, however, Phillips was ready to leave England. He and his wife chose Winnipeg by sticking a pin into the centre of a map of Canada. After arriving in June of 1913, Walter was appointed Art Master at St. John's Technical High School in the city's multi-racial North End. Initially, Phillips painted in the European style he had learned in England. Gradually, however, the Canadian landscape began to impose itself. Soon he was painting the prairies as they were, rather than as a European was trained to see them.

In 1947 Phillips illustrated Frederick Niven's *Colour in the Canadian Rockies*.[4] The work in this book was a testament to the artist's remarkable capacity to render rock and water and light into images that radiated an inspired sense of mountain place. It also stands as one of the very best early books about modern travel – particularly on horseback – in the expanded geography of what are now the Mountain Parks.

In the summer of 1940, Phillips began teaching at the Banff School of Fine Arts. In 1941, Walter and Gladys Phillips moved to Calgary where He became an instructor at the Institute of Technology and Art. In 1943, they moved again, this time to St. Julian Road in Banff. Walter painted in their living room.

Phillips spent the next fifteen years in Banff teaching, painting and making woodblocks of the magnificent scenery of the Rockies. During that time, he became a tireless champion of Canadian art and artists. Through his writings, Phillips introduced a generation of artists who made formative contributions to Canadian culture through their painting.

Phillips was irritated by the fact that many artists residing in Canada were slaves to techniques that did not allow them to give themselves to the nature that surrounded them. Phillips admired painters who let the landscape speak for itself. One of his favourite painters was Thomas Fripp. Fripp was a well-trained English watercolourist who immigrated to British Columbia in 1893. Phillips delighted in Fripp's capacity to reproduce the delicate, opalescent harmonies of changing mountain weather. Phillips pointed out that, though the art aristocracy in Toronto found him reactionary, Fripp had been able to get the mountains right. If you knew and understood the alpine, then Fripp's sense of cold drama would stay with you.

Phillips also admired Carl Rungius. Born in Berlin in 1869, Rungius was already an established wildlife artist by the time he immigrated to the United States after a hunting and painting expedition to Wyoming in 1895. In 1910 Rungius was invited to the Canadian Rockies by outfitter and guide Jimmy Simpson. Though Rungius painted in the Rockies every summer for the next twenty-five years, his work was virtually unknown in Canada. In 1933, Phillips drew the attention of the Canadian public to Rungius by proclaiming his mastery in portraying the spirit of Canada's mountains and wildlife.

Phillips also admired Alfred C. Leighton. Leighton was born in Hastings, Sussex, England in 1901. After suffering serious injuries in a plane crash during World War I, Leighton briefly became a toy designer before establishing a studio to make architectural models. A model he built of the port of Liverpool came to the attention of the Canadian Pacific Railway, and in 1924 Leighton became Chief Commercial Artist with the CPR. In this capacity Leighton designed brochures and advertising promotions.

In 1925, Leighton made his first trip to the Canadian West to paint mountain scenes for the railway. In 1929, Leighton decided to move to Canada and became Director of Art at the Institute of Technology and Art in Calgary. It was here that he befriended Walter Phillips, who helped him establish the school as a prominent force in artistic development on the prairies.

Word of the exciting artistic culture associated with painting in the Rockies quickly spread, attracting new talent. Nicholas de Grandmaison was born in southern Russia in 1892. After immigrating to Canada 1927, he began painting the portraits of trappers, traders, Métis and Native peoples in The Pas, Manitoba. When his friend Alfred Leighton fell ill in the fall of 1931, de Grandmaison took over his instruction work at the Institute of Technology and Art. Walter Phillips wrote that de Grandmaison painted Indians in a way that inspired others to see their sophistication and abiding dignity. De Grandmaison's timeless portraits define our relationship to history and place to this day.

One of the great teachers of the Group of Seven tradition was Illingworth Kerr. Kerr was born in Lumsden, Saskatchewan in 1905 and was taught art by his mother before travelling to Toronto to study under Arthur Lismer, J.E.H. Macdonald, Frederick Varley and J.W. Beatty. When Kerr returned to the prairies, he made it his ambition to encompass a complete interpretation of the prairies in his work. He wanted to do for the prairies what the Group of Seven had done for northern Ontario and the Rockies. In 1947, Kerr came to Calgary to direct the Art School of the Provincial Institute of Technology and Art. Under his guidance, this school later became the Alberta College of Art and Design, and influenced and trained hundreds of local painters and sculptors. Somehow, Kerr still found time outside his administrative responsibilities to paint and, later in life, generated impressive results in the Rockies.

The increasing presence of the work of these artists encouraged Canadians to believe in the powerful aesthetic possessed by the landscapes in which they lived. Inspired visual affirmation of the qualities of place contributed to the gradual emergence of a mountain culture in which respect for the landscape was uniquely commensurate with the

you? Could you trust words that betrayed you? Could you continue to tell stories that extinguished the fire among the pines, then carried the dripping forest away?

The earliest writings, like the earliest paintings, were created by visiting foreigners for audiences at home. As Native peoples in the West had no written language of their own, early European exploration accounts served to create a new image of the mountain West that largely excluded local presence and pre-contact history. Native people had no way to defend their interpretations of place from the explosive influence of the popular print media of the day. A few words written in a journal by a hasty traveller had more impact than the oral traditions passed down through thousands of years of Native presence in the West.

Most of the very early Europeans who made their way west to the Rockies were fur traders. As trade was their central focus, theirs is largely a language of commerce. We know how many furs were taken here and there, and we can learn distances between features along the rivers. But for the most part the journals of the fur trade are as spare and empty as the lonely miles that separated the traders' posts.

As has already been noted, the most famous of fur trade explorers was David Thompson. Thompson first came to the Bow Valley near Canmore in the autumn of 1800 and spent the next dozen years cultivating Native knowledge of the mountain passes that crossed the Great Divide. The conditions under which Thompson travelled were often deplorable. At the end of a long day's push into unknown mountains, he must have had difficulty summoning the energy to write. That he was the first to write about many of the places he visited imbues his work not only with historical but literary importance.

As dryly and matter-of-factly as Thompson tried to describe it, the West could hardly be contained by his prose. It is January of 1811. Thompson has found his way to the summit of his second great gap in the spine of the Rockies, Athabasca Pass:

> strange to say, here is a strong belief that the haunt of the mammoth is about this defile, I questioned several, none could positively say, that they had seen him, but their belief I found firm and not to be shaken. I remarked to them, that such an enormous heavy Animal must leave indelible marks of his feet, and his feeding. This they all acknowledged, and that they had never seen any marks of him, and therefore could show me none. All I could say did not shake their belief in its existence.[1]

David Thompson was cautious in his literary creation of the Rockies. Under the sway still of the Church, he is representative of those early generations of explorers who thought mountains abodes of evil remote from the blessings of God. This same attitude prevailed widely among travellers during the fur trade. Ross Cox reports that a "rough-spun, unsophisticated Canadian" in the party, which included Gabriel Franchère, that crossed the Rockies in 1814 spoke for many who crossed the Rockies early in the nineteenth century. "I'll take my oath, my dear friends," he wrote of Athabasca Pass, "that God Almighty never made such a place."[2]

ARTICULATE ADVERTISING ATTRACTS LITERATE TOURISTS

THOUGH THERE WAS A GOOD DEAL of technical writing done on the subject of the Canadian Rockies during the railway survey era, a real literature of place didn't emerge until tourists rode the first trains west. In those heady days before transcontinental train travel became commonplace, surprisingly good writing about the Rockies was even found in advertising. Copywriters in the employ of the Canadian Pacific outdid one another with superlatives describing the scenery surrounding grand new railway hotels.

In 1888, Canadian Pacific published a brochure entitled *The New Highway To The East*, which was a paean to the glories of travelling across Canada as a direct route to the Orient. In it was some highly compelling writing:

> *Passing three emerald lakes, deep set in the mountains, we follow the west-bound stream down through a tortuous rock-ribbed cañon, where the waters are dashed to foam in incessant leaps and whirls. This is Wapta or Kicking Horse pass. Ten miles below the summit we round the base of Mount Stephen, a stupendous mountain rising directly from the railway to a height of more than eight thousand feet, holding on one of its shoulders, and almost over our heads, a glacier, whose shining green ice, five hundred feet thick, is slowly crowded over a sheer precipice ... and crushed to atoms below.*[3]

The railway created our modern image of western mountains and established a new standard for travel writing. The educated and the literate flocked west. For a time the reality of the Rockies was actually equivalent to image portrayed through advertising. Visitors went home wild-eyed with the glory of Canadian peaks.

Walter Dwight Wilcox was an early tourist-explorer who wrote in an enduring way about the Canadian Rockies. After graduating from Yale University, Wilcox spent his summers in the remote wilds of the

Canada's mountain West. In 1893, he and a few companions spent most of the summer camped on the north shore of Lake Louise.

Wilcox wrote two influential books about the Rockies. His earliest work, *Camping in the Canadian Rockies*, was published in 1896 and went through several editions before appearing in an enlarged format entitled *The Rockies of Canada* in 1900.[4] In 1909, Wilcox published his *Guide to the Lake Louise District*, a popular and definitive trail aid that quickly went out of print. Consistent with his time, Wilcox tried hard to be scientific in his descriptions:

> *The lake is little more than a mile long and about one-fourth of a mile wide. The outline is remarkably like that of a human foot. Forests come down nearly to the water's edge on all sides of the lake, but there is a narrow margin of rough angular stones where the ripples from the lake have washed out the soil and even undermined the trees in some places. The water is a blue-green color, so clear that the stones on the bottom and the old water-logged trunks of trees, long since wrested from the shores by storms and avalanches, may be discerned even in several fathoms of water. The lake is 230 feet deep in the centre, and the bottom slopes down very suddenly from the shores.*[5]

The success of Wilcox's books inspired Canadians to begin to think in a new way about their own mountains. If American tourists could write popular books about the Canadian Alps, then surely Canadians could do the same.

The first successful Canadian mountain writer was Arthur Oliver Wheeler. After years of working with the Dominion Land Survey, Wheeler wrote the definitive work on the history of exploration and mountaineering around Rogers Pass. When *The Selkirk Ranges* was published by the Department of the Interior in 1905, it was immediately recognized as Canada's first homegrown mountain classic. As already noted, it was in the following year that Wheeler co-founded the Alpine Club of Canada. Though the club's principal aim was to get Canadians climbing, it also encouraged Canadians to contribute to the *Canadian Alpine Journal*, Canada's first and longest-running mountaineering periodical. The first issue of the CAJ was published in 1907. Mountain writing in Canada hasn't looked back since.

WRITER-MOUNTAINEERS

THE SECOND MAJOR WORK of 1905, *In The Heart of the Canadian Rockies*,[6] was written by a British vicar who had visited Canada over the course of several summers while convalescing from "mental fatigue." While

THE PEAK OF AUTUMN
Visitors often express a sense of experiencing an underlying current at Mount Assiniboine that somehow connects the landscape to the fundamental universal rhythms that unify form and meaning in art, poetry and music.
Photograph by R.W. Sandford.

the state of James Outram's mental health may have at some time been tenuous, there was no doubt about his mountaineering abilities.

Outram first visited the Rockies with his brother in 1900. As has already been indicated, in 1901 he became the first to climb Mount Assiniboine. In 1902, he returned again to make the first ascent of Mount Columbia, then as now one of the most remote peaks in the Rockies. Later in the summer, he and guide Christian Kaufman made the first perilous ascent of Mount Bryce, far and away the most dangerous climb undertaken in the early period of mountaineering in the Rockies.

This book is best accompanied by *Climbs and Explorations in the Canadian Rockies* by Hugh Stutfield and Norman Collie.[7] Collie discovered the Columbia Icefield in 1898 and competed fiercely with Outram to be the first to climb the giant peaks that rose from the silent ice. Skilled naturalists, these early climbers exhibit powers of detailed observation in their writings that surprise and impress even today.

Ontario geologist Arthur Philemon Coleman's explorations are beautifully documented in *The Canadian Rockies, New and Old Trails*, published in 1912.[8] Coleman also published a monogram on the glaciers

JON WHYTE

The scion of the famous Whyte family in Banff, Jon Whyte held court over the literary and artistic life of the Rocky Mountains for more than twenty years. Though he died in 1992, his profound sense of history and geography continue to inspire a generation of writers, poets, musicians and film-makers.
—*Photograph by R.W. Sandford.*

The scion of one of the area's bedrock pioneer families, Jon Whyte was born in Banff, Alberta on the Ides of March 1941. He remained in Banff until 1956 when he moved with his mother to Medicine Hat. After receiving a B.A. and an M.A. in medieval English at the University of Alberta, Jon then advanced to Stanford University in California. While at Stanford, he pursued a second master's degree, this time in communications. As part of his course work for this degree Jon completed a short biographical film on the early horse packer and guide Jimmy Simpson, a film that would later become a local classic in the mountain history genre.

In 1968, Jon returned to Banff permanently where he was able to apply his considerable mental prowess to the writing of poetry and prose that reflected a profound appreciation for life in the Canadian Rockies. As the manager of Banff's famous Book and Art Den, Jon took it upon himself to react productively to the paucity of good natural and human history writing in Western Canada.

Over the next twenty-four years, until his death in 1992, Jon wrote or contributed to more than twenty books on the Rockies. His best known works include, *The Fells of Brightness: Some Fittes and Starts* (1983), *The Fells of Brightness: Wenkchemna* (1985), *Indians in the Rockies* (1984), and his little gem *Tommy and Lawrence: The Ways and the Trails of Lake O'Hara* (1983).[15]

One of the finest of his mountaineering poems, *The Agony of Mrs. Stone*, was written about the death of Winthrop Stone on Mount Eon in July of 1921. It proved that Jon Whyte could tell you stories that were fifty years old and give them the urgency and the drama that made them seem they happened only yesterday.

As the Curator of Heritage Homes at the Whyte Museum of the Canadian Rockies, an institution founded by his aunt, Jon also committed himself to the encouragement of other local writers in their efforts to come to grips with the history and culture of the Rockies. The mountain writers that he influenced included Brian Patton, Bart Robinson, Sid Marty, Peter Christensen and many, many others. He also collaborated with historian Ted Hart in a number of publications, including a masterwork on the life of painter Carl Rungius.

Whyte was also a source of inspiration for some of Canada's best poets, including local intellectual powerhouse Charles Noble. But Jon did not confine his interest in art to the Rockies. Over the twelve years that Jon worked at the Whyte, he held court over an entire generation of visiting Canadian and foreign artists, writers, musicians and thinkers. Jon also knew many of the world's most active mountaineers and guides. Using the Whyte Museum of the Canadian Rockies as a vehicle, he was able to continue to elevate the culture of Banff from that of a transient tourist town to a cosmopolitan centre for landscape and art appreciation. As much as anyone in this area's history, Jon Whyte made good writing a part of our local heritage.

THOMAS WHARTON Thomas Wharton is an Alberta writer and the author of a novel entitled *Icefields*.[16] Spare and simple, like the glaciers and frozen peaks he describes, Wharton's writing mirrors the beauty of the high alpine landscape. Only the important features relating to the nature and character of place stand out.

Wharton's characters are similarly constructed. They are reduced to the elemental spareness of the ice over which they wander. Subject to only the most fundamental emotions, we see them come to grips with themselves by coming to grips with the ice and rock and pure light of the icefield upon which his remarkable story unfolds.

Wharton has chosen historical figures that mean a great deal to the history of Canada's mountain national parks, as the prime movers of his spare but haunting story. One of his prime characters was drawn from the adventure narratives of the Earl of Southesk, who travelled through the remote wilderness of what is now Jasper in 1859. Wharton then superimposed Southesk's narrative on the adventures of Norman Collie, who with Hugh Stutfield and Herman Woolley discovered the Columbia Icefield in the summer of 1898. The narratives of these two figures also overlap with those of a famous woman mountaineer, American climber C.S. Thompson, a poet horseman from England, an entrepreneur who initiated snowmobile rides on the glacier, and the leader of the 1925 Japanese Expedition to Mount Alberta.

The key character in *Icefields* is Dr. Edward Byrne. The story begins when Byrne falls in a crevasse on the Arcturus Glacier and discovers the image of a frozen angel in the ice. He returns to England haunted by his accident and by the remarkable woman who has tended him during his convalescence in a settlement near Jasper. After abandoning everything people search for when they travel, we confirm the valuable role that knowledge and understanding can play in making the world meaningful to others.

We also discovered that in many communities, all of these aspects of heritage are under some sort of threat. Natural landscapes throughout the mountain West are suffering from increased human presence, a number of important wildlife species are having difficulty sustaining themselves, and ecosystem health in many areas is in decline. Strong historic connection to place is also under threat. Where once our mountain communities were artifacts of a time when the dominant force in human life was nature, our communities are becoming more and more like the cities our visitors left behind.

We have more distractions, which means that we have less time to spend in the landscape. Visitors are also becoming more alike in their interests. Many of our visitors are from cities; their expectations are increasingly urban in nature. As their demands change, we change the places in which we live, in order to meet their expectations. We alter place, thereafter place alters us.

Along the entire spine of the Rockies, from Canada to the United States, communities are losing their unique character and becoming more and more like the cities the people who live in them sought to escape. Memory of what the West was like in the past is vanishing. Huge numbers of people are moving into many of our mountain areas either permanently or on a part-time or weekend basis. Most have little understanding of how dramatically these mountain places have changed in the last century.

As we struggle to grow our tourism potential in the wake of declining resource industries, we are beginning to realize that what is now happening cannot be stereotypically characterized as passionate environmentalist versus insensitive developer. The challenge is broader, and in some senses deeper. As American writer Rick Bass put it, "we owe a debt of love and thanks to the country that makes us; and that it is up to us to make sure that the last good parts of it are not divided up into halves and then quarters and then eighths, then further divided into the invisibility of neglect or dishonor."[1] This, however, is easier said than done.

We are struggling now in the mountain West to retain the connection to place upon which our very identity depends, upon which many locals have found their reasons for living here. If we cannot stand up for place, then we may lose what is most essential about ourselves, for when

THE TOWN OF BANFF
Banff's original location, by necessity, was based on the growing popularity of the hot springs on Sulphur Mountain. It wasn't until much later that it was realized the town's location, in combination with roads and train tracks leading into it, posed a serious problem for wildlife movement.
Photograph by R.W. Sandford.

the West is gone there will be no place left for many of us to go. When there is no place for us to go, there will be no place for visitors to go either.

Few Canadians want the myth of our wilderness West to end. Many people are prepared to make real sacrifices and compromises to ensure that creatures such as wolves and bears survive. Through careful consideration of what makes our circumstances unique more and more people who live in communities in and around our mountain national parks can make where and how they live the basis of what distinguishes this region in the world tourism marketplace. At a time when natural habitat loss and species extinction worldwide are occurring at an unprecedented rate, surviving intact ecosystems and cultures closely associated with their perpetuation are rapidly becoming the world's most precious and desired future resources.

In order to sustain our tourism economy, our ecological ethics cannot simply reside in marketing slogans. Hard facts have to be addressed. People will not travel from afar to visit landscapes that are as compromised and crowded as the ones they have at home. They come because they want to experience a world that has not been dramatically altered or disturbed. They come because they want to see wild animals whose existence is an embodiment of functioning natural processes they associate with the Canadian West. Wolves and grizzlies have great value in the world's imagination. But it is not just wolves and bears that must be protected. It is also important to protect enough uncrowded, open space to allow ourselves and our visitors to have meaningful communion with place.

Protection of functioning ecosystems should not be just a national park or World Heritage Site imperative, but one that should apply everywhere people live on this planet. Our mountain national parks are a crystal around which a new sense of long-term economic stability can be established and radiate outward. That stability will be defined in large part by how well our intact ecosystems slow and moderate the effects of landscape change in the West, and the impacts of global climate change. By preserving what is important about our heritage, as it has been defined locally, we protect what is unique about our way of life. By standing up for place, we retain our cultural authenticity at a time when it is being compromised and homogenized worldwide. We also stand up for the natural places that are at the heart of our identity as a people. In so doing we protect the ecosystems that give meaning and provide stability to our culture. By preserving our way of life we are more likely to have tourism on terms that we and our visitors can accept over the long term. By preserving place, and local connection to place, we assure that sustainable tourism is not just a marketing slogan but also a way of life.

In his book, *Becoming Native To This Place,*[2] Wes Jackson argues that, in North America at least, it has never been a goal to become native to where you lived and to establish deep ties to all aspects of place. He claims that now, almost too late, we are beginning to perceive the necessity of establishing such relationships. Jackson argues that due to huge increases in human populations and the profound nature of our cumulative effects, we have to affirm local responsibility and commitment to the places in which we live if we are going to save what is worthwhile and unique about our experience of this amazing continent. Jackson argues that the sense of place to which we might aspire has not only been altered but also severely compromised by substantial change in many of the places in which we live. In order to preserve even the possibility of enduring sense of place, Jackson contends that we have to slow down our aimless, wandering pursuit of upward mobility at any cost and find a home, dig in and aim for some kind of enduring relationship with the ecological realities of the surrounding landscape. Only in this way, according to Jackson, can we cultivate any sort of cultural or environmental sustainability.

Localness was redefined in the West the moment the land was divided and sub-divided into rectangular plots that allowed settlement to proceed in a manner consistent with methods of topographical survey. Until surveyed, all lands were essentially a borderless commons. The division of land into carefully defined rectilinear units facilitated private ownership. Land became a commodity with little connection to the greater space around it or to the ecosystem of which it was formerly part.

One of the reasons our mountain national and provincial parks are important to us is that they have remained a commons. They have not been as subject to the tyranny of the survey grid as other parts of the country. The land is open and expansive as we remember land ought to be. These places remind us of the thrill this continent must have provided to the first Europeans who came west. In our mountain parks, it is not just the peaks that impress us. It is all that geography piled up on itself, unfenced, unowned and unownable. We love our mountains in part because they defy the rectilinear patterns that have crept up the valleys from Europe. We also love these places because they appear undisturbed. The great "shouting, neighing, lowing, grunting, buzzing, barking and meowing invasion"[3] largely by-passed these places. As such, they appear unchanged, pristine somehow in the way they might have been when humans first set eyes upon them.

If the ecological history of this continent teaches us anything, it is that we can no longer afford to be the kinds of people who look upon where they live as a source of mere raw material out of which to fashion our livelihoods and our prosperity. As Wes Jackson has pointed out, we have to be devoted to where we live for its own sake and do whatever we can to protect and restore it.

The preservation of the unique character of where and how we live in and around the Mountain Parks cannot be achieved by just talking about it. It takes careful consideration and clear-decision making to wrestle the direction our history is taking us back into alignment with a vision of the West we want. The days of bold, sudden changes in land-use and other habits ended when our national railways finally succeeded in fulfilling their ambition of settling the West. We have to rely now on small increments of positive change applied over longer periods of time to define progress toward the ideal of creating a culture commensurate with landscape in the Rockies.

Fortunately for the mountain parks and for the Canadian Rocky Mountain Parks World Heritage Site as a whole, there are a growing number of people who understand that the work of building a culture worthy of the grand landscapes of the mountain West is the work of whole generations, and not just the responsibility of land managers responsible for parts of a larger whole. One such person is Ian Syme, who at the time of this writing worked for Parks Canada in Banff National Park.

Though his responsibilities as Chief Park Warden for the Banff Field Unit focus principally on management issues in the south part of Banff National Park, like many others Syme has worked in jobs that have allowed him to be familiar with every part of the Mountain Parks. His experiences are not only typical but also highly representative of those of a generation of men and women who have committed themselves to the protection and understanding of the landscapes and ecological processes we have managed to save in the Rockies.

At a presentation to the Rosenberg International Forum on Water Policy in 2006, Syme explained that in 1980, the year he started with Parks Canada, the population of Calgary was only 650,000. As the mine in Canmore had recently closed, its population was still only 3,100. Banff had a population of barely 4,400 and only a couple of hundred people lived at Lake Louise as its famous railway hotel was still closed in winter. At that time only 2.9 million cars travelled on the Trans-Canada Highway through Banff National Park each year.

Back in the 1980s, however, backpacking was still very popular. Wardens travelled extensively in the backcountry, regulating the impacts associated with 20,000 camper nights a year. Syme remembers also that garbage was not well managed and dumps then were still places where locals and visitors alike could see bears. That also began to change after a series of terrible bear maulings that resulted in a death inside Banff townsite in September of 1980, described by Sid Marty in his book *The Black Grizzly of Whiskey Creek*. The grizzly bear population in the park at the time was estimated to be between fifty and seventy, and some argued the bears were largely concentrated around dumps in Banff and Lake Louise.

One noticeable difference in 1980, Syme recalls, was a greater acceptance of wildlife mortality. At that time there was an average of 100 to 125 automobile collisions with elk every year, mostly on the Trans-Canada Highway. It was also a period during which park wardens still stocked many lakes. At one time or another almost all of the lakes in the

mountain parks were stocked with trout fingerlings reared at a fish hatchery in Banff. The wardens in Jasper had their own hatchery and did the same thing. It was standard practice then to ensure anglers had a material reason to visit backcountry lakes. Not much thought, if any, was given to the impacts such programs might have on natural aquatic ecosystem health. In fact, Syme remembers that very little consideration was given at all to what was happening at that time to water in the mountain parks. Even sewage was poorly treated.

The entire ecosystem, Syme observes, was different in 1980. It could hardly be described as natural. Some 700 to 800 elk lived in the Bow Valley, all descendents of a herd of some 200 introduced from Yellowstone in the 1920s to give visitors some majesty to observe in the lower valleys. This herd, in the absence of wolves that were at the time considered vermin and shot on sight, had grown to nearly 3,000 by the late 1930s but declined in numbers after decimating much of this new range. In 1980, the automobile was effectively performing the predatory role for elk and other ungulates. In reality it was an elk-automobile-caribou ecology that operated in the absence of fire. This, Syme is quick to note, was a great deal different than the buffalo-wolf-caribou-fire-First Nations ecology that predominated in the region now encompassed by the Mountain Parks at the time of European contact. The region had, in fact, been altered dramatically by less than a century of "scientific" management. There were some 2,500 elk along the eastern boundary of Banff Park, which hunters like to encroach upon in the fall. There was also a considerable amount of poaching.

Ten years later, in 1990, Ian Syme was no longer a backcountry warden but an area manager responsible for Parks Canada's Lake Louise operation. By 1990 the population of the city of Calgary had grown by 50,000 people, or about 7.7 percent, to 700,000. The population of Canmore had grown some 71 percent to 5,300 and the town of Banff had grown by 57 percent to 6,900. Car traffic through Banff National Park was up 17 percent, to 3.4 million vehicles a year.

Syme also remembers that it was around this time that wolves returned, all on their own, to the Bow Valley. A small pack suddenly appeared and began preying on elk. Numbers of elk had grown completely out of proportion, and the elk were an easy target for the hungry pack. For their part, the wolves must have thought they had died and gone to heaven, says Syme. But the cars and trains that were also killing the elk, began to take a sizable toll on the wolf population.

While the wolf drama was playing itself out, Parks Canada was busy decommissioning backcountry fire roads that, in essence, effectively expanded the wilderness areas of the mountain national parks by hundreds of square kilometres. This respite for the landscape, however, was brief, lasting only as long as it took mountain bikers to reclaim these areas as front-country that could be accessed in a short time from highway trailheads.

Tangible protection gains were also made between 1980 and 1990 on the park boundary as the Province of Alberta moved toward restricting access along the eastern slopes of the Rockies. This reduced poaching and allowed for easier movement of wildlife throughout the eastern portion of the Mountain Parks and the larger central Rockies ecosystem that extends far beyond national park boundaries. The province also created Kananaskis Country, a multi-use mountain reserve offering recreational opportunities in a protected area adjacent to Banff National Park.

By 1990, Parks Canada had also begun to change its views with respect to the role of fire in the on-going management of mountain ecosystems. Eighty years of almost maniacal fire suppression had led to huge fuel build-ups in many areas of the mountain national parks. In the absence of wildfire, natural plant community succession had slowed to such an extent in parts of the region that concerns were being expressed about the overall vitality of the mountain ecosystem.

Though in its infancy, a prescribed fire program had been established in Banff by 1990. Syme remembers that at the outset of the program the Warden Service had been calling such fires controlled burns even though they knew at the time that lightning fires of even fifty hectares or less generated circumstances that were not always controllable. "So, as they say," Syme quips, "go big or go home." Parks Canada fire specialists began creating burns exceeding a thousand hectares, utilizing landscape and firebreaks to control the spread of the flames. The gamble paid off, in that fire ecologists working with Parks Canada are now recognized as being among the most experienced and respected professionals in this important and rapidly developing field.

Bear problems were also being addressed by 1990. All garbage was now collected in bear-proof containers. Dumps were closed and garbage from towns like Banff was now transferred to landfills outside the park.

Tensions between Parks Canada and national park communities were also being addressed. An agreement was signed in 1990 that allowed the Town of Banff to incorporate itself as a provincial municipality. Most of the municipal government powers were transferred to an elected town council. The first mayor elected was Leslie Taylor, a former acting Banff park superintendent. While the town remained under regulation by Parks Canada, the newly formed town council gained control of tax revenues and re-investment. One of the central controls Parks Canada retained was the need-to-reside clause relating to who could own homes and actually live within the national park community. The premise of this regulation was, and always has been, that only those with a bona fide need to live in the community, based on the work they are doing or have done, will have the right to own and occupy a home inside a national park town. It is this regulation and this regulation

COW MOOSE

Moose populations in the Canadian Rocky Mountain Parks World Heritage Site are slowly recovering from a twenty-year decline, associated with parasite-related diseases, during which moose almost disappeared from many of the mountain parks. The connected nature of this system, however, facilitates recovery of troubled species over time provided their numbers don't become too small.
Photograph by R.W. Sandford.

interesting but very volatile situation in which elk swarmed downtown parks and green spaces, grazed on lawns and established a habit of scaring the hell out of both locals and visitors alike as they defended the space that in their minds marked individual and herd territory.

At the same time, Parks Canada was also addressing at long last the sewage treatment problems created by increased local human populations and exploding visitation in its communities. As a result of significant phosphorous and fecal colliform count reductions, Parks Canada soon learned that you can't do anything without affecting something else. While the new water quality standards did a great deal to restore original pristine aquatic ecosystem conditions in the Bow River, they at the same time reduced the nutrient base of the downstream water to the extent that trout populations in the river at Canmore were reduced.

In the 1990s, the Trans-Canada Highway was twinned as far west as Castle Junction. In order to reduce wildlife mortality on the widened highway, the entire thirty-kilometre stretch was fenced to prevent animals from getting on to the road. The decision was also made to incorporate animal overpasses rather than the underpasses that had been employed in the first stages of the twinning between the park's eastern gate and the Banff townsite.

This decision was made as a result of years of monitoring wildlife movement through the underpasses, research that revealed some very telling trends. The problem that emerged was that predators like wolves were not at all averse to hanging around underpasses to wait for elk driven out of town by park wardens.

Syme pointed out that by 2000 the mitigation toolbox that included fencing, wildlife overpasses and underpasses, and wildlife movement corridors around Banff townsite was now the most comprehensive and advanced in the world. Scientists and engineers, Syme explained, come from all over the world to examine the design and function of the Trans-Canada Highway mitigation system.

Syme concluded his presentation by talking about what the park was like in comparison to when he started as a park warden twenty-five years before. Calgary, he pointed out, had just reached the one million mark in population and five times more people were living in Canmore just outside Banff National Park. A city suddenly exists right on the boundary of Canada's first national park. It makes little difference that 25 percent of Canmore's "residents" are "recreational homeowners." Their numbers are growing and are expected to do so until the population of Canmore doubles again, which is expected to happen by 2030 when there will be no longer be any land left to develop immediately adjacent to the park. The population of Banff, however, has been capped as a result of the Bow Valley Study, at 8,500. Its current population was about 7,800 people, up only 77 percent since 1980, which compared to Canmore was hardly anything at all. The number of vehicles entering Banff National Park was 4.7 million, which represented an increase of 93 percent since 1980.

Perhaps because he has played such an active role in addressing many of Banff Park's problems over the last quarter-century, Ian Syme was proud of the way the Mountain Parks have managed their way through these problems. Syme offered that the elk problem in Banff was resolved by reducing their population in the Bow Valley to between 250 and 300. This was done in part through natural predation, through live capture and relocation to other mountain national park areas and where necessary, through culling. Syme was also justifiably proud of how successful the Trans-Canada Highway wildlife mitigation program had become. Carefully collected data indicated that between 1996 and 2006, there had been over 70,000 wildlife passages under and over the Trans-Canada Highway. Predator use of these pathways was also increasing. In 2005, grizzly bears used the underpasses and overpasses 89 times. Long-term research was now indicating that carnivores such as bears, wolves and cougars need an additional one to two years on average before they use the overpasses.

In part due to this and other management strategies, Syme reported that the grizzly bear population in the mountain parks had stabilized or risen slightly to between fifty and seventy animals. That was the good news. The bad news was that the mountain caribou was in serious trouble throughout its range in both Banff and Jasper National Parks. As far as Syme knew, there were only three left in Banff National Park. Syme's gut feeling was that higher wolf populations associated with artificially high elk populations had resulted in heavier predation on caribou in Banff, but in Jasper the situation was different. It appeared that loss of habitat outside the park combined with various human-use pressures such as forestry and snowmobiling were combining to affect both the range and the food sources of this rare species.

One of Syme's last remarks touched on perhaps the greatest threat presently facing the mountain national parks. Observing that the pine bark beetle had been advancing into Banff National Park, warden service fire specialists modelled "ideal habitats" for these invading pests and proactively used prescribed burns to prevent their advance. Their major achievement was to use the hot dry summer of 2003 to safely burn a large area between Banff and Canmore, to significantly reduce the potential of the pine bark beetle to advance into this highly favourable habitat.

Ian Syme paused before offering his final reflection on his long career in the Mountain Parks. "Yes, there has been a lot of change," he said, "and there is a lot more on the way. But it is still good here – very, very good." With those few words, Syme confirmed that the value of what we saved remains every bit as important as that of what we have built. From the point of view of environmental stability, what we saved might well save us. Syme also said everything that needs to be said about what it was like to commit a lifetime of being shaped by and becoming worthy of place. Life is still good here in these mountains – very, very good. Keeping it that way, however, will require diligence.

10

Countering Dispossession
Saving Our Unique Mountain Culture

WHILE IAN SYME HAS GOOD REASON to be pleased with the long history of achievement of the national parks service in the Canadian Rockies, there are developments occurring on the boundaries of the World Heritage Site that have everyone who lives in the region concerned, at the most fundamental level of relationship to place.

Human population movement has become so rapid and commonplace that it is easy to forget how stationary people used to be and how connected to place we once were. But the lingering attachment we have to where we were born is not something we can easily dismiss. When Europeans first arrived on the Great Plains and in the mountains of the Canadian West, the experience was so alien and the landscape so confronting for many it was as if they were landing on the moon. It took generations for settlers to become at home in this new place. The process required closing a circle of experience, livelihood, and story that resulted in the gradual creation of a history, a specific literature of place, and finally the creation of art that affirmed connection to place. As Ronald Rees suggested in his landmark book *New and Naked Land: Making the Prairies Home*, this creates an ideal past and nostalgia for earlier, less complicated times in our lives and in our history.[1] This nostalgia often has as much to do with an unsatisfactory present as it does with how a former way of life has been idealized in memory. More and more this appears to be true in communities in and around the Canadian Rocky Mountain Parks.

Settlers in the mountain West today must suffer the difficulty of coming to terms with the circumstances and climate of an utterly new place, just as their ancestors did. Fitting in and becoming a local takes time and, just as on the plains, there appears to be a process by which newcomers come to terms with their emerging identity in the Rockies. In a very general way the process is similar to the one Rees describes. Experience of a new and sometimes dangerous landscape, and the trials of making a living, spawn personal stories. Stories coalesce into legend that, in time, becomes the foundation of local history. History in time spawns literature. Literature, in turn, begets art and art confirms the experience of place. It is a clumsy process in which they are many false starts and wrong turns. In time, however, we interlopers gradually apply enough persistence and patience to the project of localness to complete the self-reinforcing cultural circle that allows us to claim the difficult and often dangerous Rockies as home.

Since the Mountain Parks were designated as a World Heritage Site in 1990, we have recognized that we could make our commitment to understanding, appreciating and experiencing where we live the foundation of a sustainable future in the Canadian West. The American philosopher Wendell Berry once claimed that you can't know who you are unless you know where you are. In other words, a sense of belonging to a place matters to our identity as individuals and as communities, and to our economy. In the world of comfort and distraction that has replaced the natural world, however, sense of place is harder to find and harder to keep. Real grounding in place is vanishing from our culture. It is this grounding, however, that we must protect if we are going to make where and how we live the basis of our tourism future.

Though it can help a great deal, you can't acquire or keep a sense of place by just reading about it. To be truly open to the uniqueness of country you have to involve yourself in it physically. Acquiring grace in the mountains is often as much a matter of "letting go" as it is a matter of conquering the country or conquering your own soul. Though he was not a mountaineer, one of the most articulate spokespersons on how we can be transformed by place in the twentieth century was T.E. Lawrence.

A SUNDANCE LODGE
Sacred mountain places still exist for Native peoples. At places like the Kootenay Plains, the Stoneys actively engage in important ceremonies such as the annual Sundance ritual. There is no reason why these places and activities cannot be embraced within an expanded World Heritage Site designation for areas that presently surround the existing mountain parks.
Photograph by R.W. Sandford.

Better known as Lawrence of Arabia, Thomas Edward Lawrence was an Englishman who possessed what he called "an English love of desolate places."[2] In his book *Seven Pillars of Wisdom*, Lawrence describes becoming so exhausted, so thirsty and so sun-baked that he could no longer hold his will on his ambitions or his mission. His ego drained out of him. He became will-less and cultureless with exhaustion and hunger and thirst. And at the moment when he could no longer apply his fierce intellect to his task, something amazing happened to him. In a moment of sublime openness, the desert in all its light and wind, in all its timelessness and unity washed over him. He could no longer resist the eternal beauty of the wind and the sun. In an instant the desert changed – and so did he.

Many people have had similar experiences in the Rockies. You find yourself too physically tired to keep the wilderness at bay. You arrive at a point where all you can hear is your own deep breathing, your heart thumping and the hissing silence of the world. When these sounds subside, you begin to hear again, but you start listening for other things. When the great engine of cultural homogenization we carry around inside us runs out of gas, there is a profound moment when we can be overwhelmed by light and wind and sun. Suddenly we see nature, not as something alien but as a unified whole out of which we have emerged.

You can call the acquisition of a sense of place a mindset change. You could call it a paradigm shift or a transcendence of thought and perceptual form. It has also been called epiphany, or aesthetic arrest. Provided that the great engine of cultural homogenization doesn't start up again too soon, the epiphany can last. If it does, a staggering realization sometimes forms inside us. It is the realization that we are not the centre of everything, that all of nature is holy, too.

It was epiphany of this kind that Aboriginals sought in vision quests. It is this kind of epiphany that today makes ordinary people give up everything they are doing in their lives to move to the mountains and be part of them. It is epiphany of this kind that is at the heart of an inspired sense of place. It is our desire to share such epiphany that makes it worth living in and visiting these mountains.

The American writer Wallace Stegner was among the first in North America to call the nostalgia created in our own minds by the landscapes in which we live "a sense of place." Sense of place, as defined by Stegner, was composed of three essential elements.

The first is unique geography. A person can only appreciate a sense of place where they lived if they see the geography of where they lived as special. As I have said so often, it is hard not to feel that way here. The geography of the Rockies leans in on you, it is hard to ignore. Even unseen in darkness and storm, the mountains exert a presence. This presence is sometimes subtle, but it can be profound. Often people don't know the physical landscape is reaching into them and making them locals, by gradual association if not by choice. But if you stay long enough you see it.

The second is a remembered and celebrated history. This history is most often personal or family in nature. You have to have a history in that place. Perhaps you remember the first time you were overtaken by the smell of pines. Or perhaps you recall the excitement and fear that accompanied your first encounter with a bear. You remember the stream where you caught your first fish. History starts with us as individuals and then radiates outward toward others. We find our place in local history and then become a mooring for others to do the same.

The third step in coming home to place is related to how personal history merges with the larger history of a community and region. It is the application of personal history to contemporary meaning. In reaching this stage in the adoption of place, you suddenly see yourself as part of a continuum in the life and experience of the community in which you have chosen to live. You are part of that continuum and it is part of you. You see how you live reflected in where you live. Suddenly geology and topography have relevance. Suddenly you see why ten thousand years of Native presence matters. You understand the impact of the coming of the railway, not just on your community but also on your life. You see history as a continuum that not only includes you but also affects how you and your neighbours live in your time.

The establishment of this relationship often requires the skilled storytelling of elders, or the informed and enthusiastic interpretation of archaeologists, historians, naturalists and artists. And behind all of these we find the guiding hand of community leaders whose role it is to employ public policy to quietly alter the DNA of place in order to create community adaptability to changing circumstances over time.

It is in recognition of all of these people that I propose a fourth element of a refined appreciation of where we live be added to Stegner's list. Every real place possesses a cast of genuine local characters. These are people steeped in the geography, history and meaning of place, who become crystals around which aesthetics are articulated and passed on through time. It is these people who have made sacrifices that have made them truly worthy and utterly representative of where they live. These are people of such unique character that you immediately want to emulate their sincerity and connection to what is truly meaningful about where they live. In these people, sense of place has become a form of grace. The moment you meet them you want to be like them.

To be truly open to the uniqueness of country you have to involve yourself physically in it. Sense of place is only established when a relationship to a specific landscape or culture captures you and makes you a local by choice. Living in the mountains, we are still close enough to the roots of our past that we may yet hear the siren call of the great lone land. But as urban lifestyles continuously accelerate, people increasingly desire the monumental in nature without having to spend hours or days to find it in the landscape or in themselves. Even a landscape compromised by logging or mining is a relative wilderness for someone who comes from Toronto, Tokyo or New York. People are flocking to natural and semi-natural tourism destinations and resort communities because the urban places they live in are becoming more and more crowded. In many cases, the urban invasion is making the places they flock to uninhabitable, too. Pleasant tourism terms like "amenities migration" do

weather and climate, and therefore in terms of biodiversity. The north slopes of this great continental watershed divide are different again from what we see and experience further south. This leads to the notion that perhaps we should reconsider the way we categorize the individual geographical elements that compose this great World Heritage Site. Instead of simply noting that they are found in either British Columbia or Alberta, we may wish to group the Mountain Parks by commonalities of watershed and direction of river flow, for these criteria more than any others are at the heart of their similarities.

These mountains are the water towers of the entire western half of our continent. If we truly want to understand this place we have to realize that, at its very foundation, the Rockies are all about slopes and divides. With this in mind, one way to re-contextualize the Mountain Parks as a biophysical and cultural unit is to examine it in the context of watershed. In this light, the Magnificent Seven can be reordered into three regions: the North Slope from which waters flow into the Arctic Ocean; the West Slope from which waters pour ultimately into the Pacific; and the East Slope, down which water splashes into rivers that flow into the Atlantic Ocean at Hudson Bay. This ordering has the advantage of mirroring perfectly substantial differences that happen to exist in ecosystem composition on each of these three slopes, and also allowing us to return to perceptions of the mountain West that existed before our direct physical experience of the landscape was interrupted by new forms of straight-line travel like the train and the car.

We may even ultimately wish to extend this idea in the direction of re-thinking the geography and culture of the mountain West, for it is a region defined less by political boundaries than by watersheds. Each of the protected areas that compose the Canadian Rocky Mountain Parks World Heritage Site has been defined by what water is and what water does in its own unique geological and geographical circumstances. This is very easy to see in Banff National Park, where warm water from deep within the earth became the foundation of Canada's national park system.

THE EAST SLOPE

Flowing Toward the Atlantic

11

The Birthplace of Canada's National Park Ideal
Banff National Park

THE ALEXANDRA RIVER VALLEY

Upland areas of the Canadian Rockies are still within the cold grasp of the last Ice Age. Melting glaciers release huge volumes of water, which picks up and transports rock ground into powder by the previous advance of the ice. The Alexandra River Valley is a classic outwash plain. At what is called Graveyard Flats, the river wanders back and forth across the valley floor, depositing debris, and then creating new courses to move around what it has deposited. *Photograph by R.W. Sandford.*

BEYOND BEING THE BIRTHPLACE of Canada's national park system, Banff will always deservedly be famous for the grandeur of its many unique natural features. There is perhaps no place more beautiful on this planet than Moraine Lake. While we have allowed a huge hotel to belly up to the shore of Lake Louise, there are still times of the day when the lake and surrounding peaks radiate the glory that is at the heart of its original fame. Bow Lake is stunning. Peyto Lake is amazing almost beyond imagination. There are places in the backcountry that still hum to the rhythm of an earlier time when humans didn't threaten to overwhelm the world. Banff still has its timeless beauty but at the same time it has its problems. Because this was our first national park, it is here more than anywhere else in the Canadian Rocky Mountain Parks World Heritage Site that what we have built most threatens what we have saved. In many ways that is why it is so interesting to visit, and such an extraordinary place to live and challenging place to work.

The creation of the Canadian Rocky Mountain Parks World Heritage Site allows us to examine Banff in a larger, more interesting context. Within the context of this World Heritage Site's role in protecting a regional mountain culture associated with a regional ecosystem

dynamic, Banff is still important but it does not occupy the privileged place it once reserved for itself as the first and last word in mountain tourism in the Canadian West.

While Banff National Park is historically important to the still-developing notion of national parks, and remains crucially important in terms of how it manages the myriad problems that stardom at an early age has presented in later life, its star no longer outshines the larger accomplishment that is the Canadian Rocky Mountain Parks World Heritage Site. If this book seeks to do anything it is to suggest that the areas surrounding Banff are deserving of equal attention and visitor interest. In many ways this was to be expected. Appreciation of their grandeur and historical significance of the surrounding protected areas

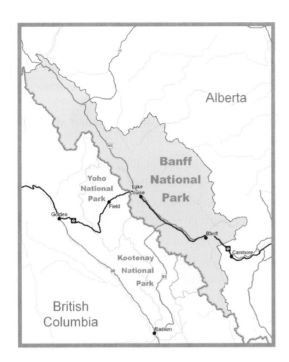

MAP OF BANFF NATIONAL PARK
Courtesy of Ali Buckingham, Parks Canada.

is finally catching up to the reputation Banff spent millions of dollars to cultivate. While the other parks in the World Heritage Site may not have the visitor amenities of Banff, they don't have its headaches either and in the larger scheme of the mountain West they are perhaps more representative of the importance of what we saved as opposed to what we built, in terms of both our material and aesthetic culture.

The world now has the experience to see that Banff was, in many important ways, a founding experiment from which the other national and provincial regions have learned much about what it takes to even contemplate managing a landscape for all time. That said, you can't say you have really been to this World Heritage Site if you have only been to Banff. But this is hardly the end of the story. Banff could be the centre again if it ceases to so desperately and jealously pretend to its former position in the Western Canadian tourism universe and begins to see itself, instead, as the centre of a larger biophysical and cultural region that is of far greater interest to visitors, and of far more importance to the world than the sum of its parks.

Banff is well positioned to be the centre of understanding of the larger World Heritage Site ideal. It is the first national park in the system. It is a place where nationally significant history and grand landscapes have converged to create an icon of Canadian identity. It is also where leading-edge management ideas are tested in difficult and demanding circumstances that mirror less what a national park should be than what the real world outside national parks is actually like. It is a place where history truly matters.

EARLY FIRST NATIONS PRESENCE

THE CONTEMPORARY TRANSIENT nature of the town of Banff suggests an aura of impermanence that is inconsistent with the history of the valley. Due to the disproportionate number of young people who live there, Banff has a reputation for being a party town. Undesirable consequences have followed in the wake of this developing image. Close

CASTLE MOUNTAIN
James Hector named Castle Mountain in the summer of 1860. He was also the first to identify the horizontal strata that compose this huge massif as bedded sea floor sediments laid down over millions of years in an ancient inland ocean. In so doing, Dr. Hector brought "deep time" to the Rocky Mountains.
Photograph by R.W. Sandford.

was attached to the last spike and another to the sledgehammer that was to drive it in. When the Golden Spike was tapped into place, telegraph lines broadcast news of the completion of the line to the entire world.

When you examine the photographs of the event, the completion of the Canadian Pacific Railway didn't generate a lot of smiles. For some, the driving of the last spike on the Canadian Pacific Railway at Craigellachie, British Columbia, Canada, November 7th, 1885, was the end. For others, like railway executive William Cornelius Van Horne, it was just the beginning, the beginning of a nation and the beginning of unlimited possibility in the West. What troubled these men most, however, was the realization that they had built the line in the wrong place.

In order to keep the line far enough south to prevent the Americans from building spur lines into Canadian territory, the CPR had been forced to build its transcontinental line over two impossible passes, Kicking Horse Pass near Lake Louise and Rogers Pass in the Selkirks. Neither of these passes would have been used if Sir Sandford Fleming had had his way. In his mind there was only one reasonable pass through the Rockies and that was Yellowhead Pass. But Fleming didn't get his way – and the story of why he didn't is the story of Canada.

As the country set out to translate a vision into operational fact, the surveying work of three generations of Western explorers became nationally important. As routes through the mountains of the West were the least understood links in the railway, mountain passes drawn by David Thompson and James Hector were pored over with nationalist zeal. Armed with copies of these maps, a route-finding expedition led by railway engineer Sandford Fleming came in 1872. What was required was a pass route of low enough incline to get trains over, yet close enough to the American border to assert strong territorial claim. By 1878, options for routes through the Rockies had been reduced to just four passes: the Kicking Horse, the Kootenay, the Vermilion and the Howse. As it was closest to the United States border, the railway syndicate chose Kicking Horse Pass as the final route through the Rockies. Because it didn't yet know of a route through the Selkirk Mountains to the west, the Canadian Pacific Railway had to wait until 1882, and the discovery of Rogers Pass, to have its choice vindicated.

Once initiated, railway construction advanced with great speed across Canada. By late summer 1883, tracks had advanced up the Bow Valley from Calgary to a railway camp at Padmore on the Kananaskis flats. As the tracks advanced west, a divisional maintenance and refuelling point for the railway was established at Canmore. The relentless advance of the tracks soon brought the railway into the vicinity of Cascade Mountain. It was here that the series of hot springs observed by James Hector was noticed by railway workers, who drew in the sulphurous stink of the therapeutic pools and made a direct link between money and water. It was their claims to these springs that would eventually lead to the creation of Canada's first national park at Banff. In a very real sense, the history of our national parks system is a water story.

IN AND OUT OF HOT WATER

IN THE FALL OF 1883, the main line of the Canadian Pacific Railway had been laid to within a few kilometres of Kicking Horse Pass on the Great Divide. The work was abandoned for the season as winter came on. Some of the workers decided to stay in the valley to prospect and trap for furs. Among them were Frank McCabe, a twenty-six-year-old section foreman, and two friends who worked under him on the railway, William McCardell, also twenty-six, and his younger brother Thomas. While camped below the waterfall on Cascade Mountain, they decided they would like to cross the river to explore Sulphur Mountain, or, as it was unofficially known at that time, Terrace Mountain. As the river was low at that time of the year, they built a crude raft and poled to the other side of the Bow. While moving up a particularly boggy slope on the mountain, they were surprised to find that the water that created the bog was actually warm. At the base of a cliff they found a large basin of steaming water, partially blocked with fallen timber. From the basin there emerged the strong smell of sulphur.

Far to the east another historic moment was passing: the naming of Banff. One interpretation of this event has William Van Horne rising at a meeting of the directors of the Canadian Pacific Railway to name the locale adjacent to the Bow River near the site of Siding 29 Banff, after Banffshire in Scotland, the ancestral home of railway directors George Stephen and Donald Smith. Parks Canada historian Bill Yeo calls this an old wives' tale. He has been arguing for years that Banff Station was named in September of 1883 by the CPR Land Commissioner. Yeo claims that the commissioner used dozens of Scottish names and sprinkled them liberally over stations all the way from Winnipeg to Vancouver. The name Banff, Yeo claims, just happened to be sprinkled, well, on Banff. McCabe and the McCardell brothers built a rough shack at the springs that they allowed other railway workers to use. Though they later argued otherwise, it doesn't appear that it immediately occurred to them to lay legal claim to the hot springs until after other railway workers had built similar shacks at various places along the base of Sulphur Mountain. Later investigation also cast doubt on William McCardell's initial claim that, at the time of their discovery, he and McCabe had cut a statement of ownership on the springs into a nearby tree stump. Details of the discovery of the springs changed as they were told. McCabe later swore that it was January of 1884 before they were able to approach a Calgary surveyor by the name of A.W. McVittie for directions as to how to make an application to the government of the day for recognition of their claim. From McVittie they learned that a legal survey was required to make such a claim and that a survey in that remote part of the country would probably cost a whopping one thousand dollars, which the railway workers could ill afford.

More than a year passed before anything more happened with respect to the claim. On March 20, 1885, the Minister of the Interior received a letter from McCabe, William McCardell, Archie McNeil and C.W.N. Sansom applying for the legal title to the hot springs located 3.2 kilometres southwest of the Banff train station, which, at that time, was located at the base of Cascade Mountain. A few days later another

TAYLOR LAKE
A number of splendid lakes can be reached by trails that lead from the Trans-Canada Highway to the high rim of the Bow River Valley in Banff National Park. Taylor Lake was named for George Herbert Taylor, a horse packer who accompanied Arthur Oliver Wheeler (of Alpine Club of Canada fame) on the Dominion Topographic Survey that mapped the boundary between Alberta and British Columbia between 1913 and 1924.
Photograph by R.W. Sandford.

claimant, Theodore Seebring, applied for the rights to a second spring, now known as the Upper Hot Spring, located a few kilometres south and east of the McCabe claim.

Until these two claims were made, the government had no idea that hot springs even existed in this area of the Rockies. Their potential value, however, was not wasted on the government and it acted quickly to determine the nature of this potential tourism opportunity.

The assistant secretary to the Minister of the Interior instructed a Dominion Land Agent named J.M. Gordon to go to the site and to present a report to his Ottawa superiors, which he did in July 1885. Gordon established the existence of the two springs and observed in his report the improvements made at each of the sites by the claimants. It was at this time that yet another claim, made by one David Keefe, found its way to William Pearce of the Calgary Land Office. Keefe claimed he had discovered the hot springs at the present Cave and Basin on October 16, 1884, and that he had blazed a route to it that still remained. Two weeks later Pearce received another letter from Keefe claiming that McCabe and Seebring were trying to bring his claim into dispute. Pearce advised Ottawa to take no action on the claims until Keefe could authenticate his claim. But other claimants kept coming out of the woodwork. Willard Burrel Younge wrote the government to claim that he had discovered the springs and built a shanty there in the winter of 1875. His claim was supported by affidavits from such historical luminaries as the Rev. John McDougall and Andrew Sibbald of Morley.

As these claims piled up in government offices in Calgary, officials in Ottawa were designing a solution of their own to the hot springs problem. A former Conservative member of parliament visited the springs and recommended to the Prime Minister that this valuable asset be controlled and administered after an American model that saw the federal government recognize the national significance of such resources. By July of 1885, Deputy Minister of the Interior Alexander Burgess was actively seeking information on the process the Americans

LOWER WATERFOWL LAKE

Originally known as the Black Pyramid, Mount Chephren was renamed in deference to its pyramid shape after Chephren, the son and successor of Cheops who built the Great Pyramid at Giza in Egypt. Mount Chephren dominates the view of the Waterfowl Lakes, one of the most pleasant places to camp in all of Banff Park.
Photograph by R.W. Sandford.

impartiality."[4] To Whitcher the title of "vermin" covered a lot of animals we now consider essential to ecological integrity in mountain wilderness. Among vermin, he included wolves, coyotes, foxes, lynxes, weasels, wild cats, porcupines, badgers, eagles, falcons, owls, loons, mergansers, kingfishers and cormorants, all of which he recommended be destroyed wherever possible by park staff. On the aquatic conservation side, Whitcher argued that it was imperative that devices such as dynamite explosions, nets, and "the improvidence of Indian fishing" be outlawed in national reserves.

Whitcher also recommended "improvements" on the natural beauty of Banff, such as the introduction of wild rice in the Vermilion Lakes. He also advocated the construction of dams on selected waters to permit fish restocking. He recommended rainbow trout as the species of preference for introduction of game fish. All of these things Whitcher recommended with the idea of improving the attractiveness of the hot springs reserve to visitors. We now know, however, that many of these proposals did not take into account the realities of natural systems. The elimination of predators in the park, combined with the introduction of exotic elk from Yellowstone in the 1920s, damaged natural environments in the Canadian Rockies far beyond the boundaries of the park.

Impacts of the decision to eliminate park predators still haunt the park today. Whitcher's wild rice can still be found around the Vermilion Lakes and the introduction of game fish destroyed much of the natural aquatic environment. A century later we are confronted with the realization that the natural environments of many national park lakes can now only be restored through the wholesale destruction of introduced species and the reintroduction of natural species taken from lakes and streams outside the park boundaries.

TOWARD A TOWN IN BANFF

ONCE THE ATTRACTION potential of the hot springs was realized, it fell upon the federal government to construct an infrastructure of roads, bridges and services that would make the reserve into a credible national park. The responsibility for developing a townsite in the park fell once again to George Stewart, who in 1886 had undertaken the first survey of the town that would become Banff.

One should never underestimate the power of those who design and build community infrastructure. It was around the first roads, bridges and zoning considerations that the town as we know it today developed. When Stewart came to Banff in February of 1886, what existed in terms of settlement was concentrated at Banff Station at the foot of Cascade Mountain. When Stewart first stopped at Banff Station, the town adjacent to it was called National Park, a name it would keep until 1888. Stewart's immediate tasks were to survey a road from the Banff siding to the Cave and Basin, determine the exact boundaries of the new reserve, and to plot the locations of two townsites. The first of these towns was to be at Devil's Lake or, as it is known now, Lake Minnewanka, which was expected to blossom into a major tourist attraction. The second of these towns, located on the banks of the Bow, was to be the service centre for the hot springs. Stewart completed these preliminary projects by the end of the winter of 1886.

The biggest problem was access to the lower hot springs at the cave and basin. The rough path that connected the train station with the river was difficult even for those in good health and impossible for invalids who were coming in increasing numbers to soak in the pools. Stewart had his men clear a good road to the river and then construct a timber float bridge across the Bow to the springs. This temporary structure was replaced by an iron truss bridge in 1887. It is this bridge that is featured in many of the early photographs of Banff Avenue and Cascade

THAT WHICH WAS LOST IS FOUND
Lost things continue to turn up in the Canadian Rocky Mountain Parks World Heritage Site. This rough cabin, built by pioneer outfitter and early park warden Bill Peyto nearly a century ago was accidently rediscovered during the construction of a wildlife overpass just a few kilometres away from Banff townsite. *Photograph by R.W. Sandford.*

begging Wilson to share his knowledge and expertise. The outfitting business in Banff grew up around him.

Another famous early horseman was Bill Peyto. Ebenezer William Peyto (pronounced Pee-toe) was born in Welling, Kent in 1868. He left England when he was eighteen and after travelling across Canada, found a job working for the railway in Moberly, British Columbia. By the early 1890s Peyto had begun working as an apprentice guide for Tom Wilson in Banff. It wasn't long before Peyto impressed the dudes he took into the backcountry. Petyo's renown as an excellent horseman was rivalled only by his reputation as a character. One of Peyto's most famous Banff escapades involved capturing a live lynx and wandering casually into a Banff bar with it tied to his back. After noting the presence of a few miners with whom he was known to have had certain disagreements, he released the lynx and sat back to enjoy the havoc the cat unleashed upon the bar. The lynx later became a prime attraction at the Banff Zoo located then on the lower slopes of Cascade Mountain. While he was notorious for his local pranks, Peyto was also justifiably famous for his explorations, not the least of which involved a 1895 visit to the lake Walter Wilcox named in his honour the following year.

One of the unsung heroes of the early guiding community was Ralph Edwards. Born in Ramsgate, Kent in 1869, his wanderlust took him to Canada in 1888. Edwards took a mining job in Canmore before coming to work with Tom Wilson in 1894. From then on, Edwards dedicated himself to the trail life. Jimmy Simpson was another famous early horse guide. He came from Lincolnshire, England in 1896 and built his famous lodge on the shores of Bow Lake in 1921. It was through men like these that many visiting explorers were able to put their names, and the names of their friends and loved ones, on the permanent map of the Rockies.[6]

It should also be noted that the great age of horse travel is not over in Banff. You can still hire outfitters and guides to take you into the backcountry. Some of the people who lead these trips are committed to horse travel as away of life. Through them you can relive a vital part of our mountain past. You can travel in a manner that has not changed in two

LAKE LOUISE
A great deal of extraordinary geology comes together in one place at Lake Louise. Above it are the giant peaks of the Great Divide. These peaks are framed by a huge cirque that opens up at the end of the lake to reveal six significant glaciers. The lake glows turquoise in the summer light as a result of the fine glacial flour carried into it by the melting ice. If all this were not enough, the lake is small and protected enough from the wind to become a perfect morning mirror.
Photograph by R.W. Sandford.

hundred years. You can know what it was to be a local in these mountains then and now and for all time.

LAYING THE FOUNDATION FOR MODERN TOURISM

THE DEMOCRATIZATION of automobile use changed visitor patterns in Banff National Park. While wealthy foreigners financed the age of train tourism in the Rockies, regional visitors powered the age of the car. Instead of the international trans-continental train clientele that Banff was used to, the car brought motorists from Manitoba, Saskatchewan and Alberta who did not have the means to stay at expensive railway hotels in towns like Banff. Moreover, this new class of visitor was as interested in driving as it was in stopping to see the sights. A new concept of travel was born and with it a need for a new kind of place to stay. Enter the bungalow camp, inexpensive roadside accommodation that became the precursor of the "motor hotel" or "motel." These camps, fashioned after an American model, were usually composed of from ten to twenty-four small cabins, a store, a service station and a lunch counter, designed to serve the needs of families travelling by car. Rates usually ranged from one to four dollars per night, depending on where the camp was located and on market demand. Seeing patterns of visitation change, the Canadian Pacific Railway built bungalow camps at Lake Windermere, Radium Hot Springs, Vermilion Crossing and Castle Mountain. By 1936, other private bungalow camps had been established at Tunnel Mountain near Banff, Johnston Canyon, Storm Mountain, Lake Louise and Moraine Lake. For motorists who wished to sleep in tents, the government constructed the first campgrounds.

SENTINEL PASS
Some of the most rewarding trails in all of Banff National Park begin at the shores of Moraine Lake. Rising smartly from the valley floor, the trail to Larch Valley offers grand views of Moraine Lake and access to switchbacks leading up Sentinel Pass, a high col separating the Valley of Ten Peaks from Paradise Valley. *Photograph by R.W. Sandford.*

The growing North American fascination with the automobile soon changed visitor demands. As bungalow camps spread all over the Rockies, visitation increased and the length of visitor stays dropped. While the average stay in the Banff Rockies might have been as long as two weeks in the 1890s, automobile travellers often only stayed overnight. While visitors were obviously seeing a lot more geography during their visits to the mountains, they were doing it more superficially, from inside their cars. Protracted journeys into the wilderness began to decline. The wilderness began to shrink back from roads that soon reached into even the remotest of valleys.

The Depression caused an extended period of involuntary restraint for the federal government during which it had to find innovative ways to further its mandate and finance its operations. By putting thousands of relief workers on large public works projects, the government was able to help the country through its desperate times. Some of the largest of the nation's relief projects involved road construction in Canada's mountain national parks. Much of the infrastructure of Banff National Park as we see it today was created during the Great Depression. The list of relief projects and Public Works Construction Act projects for 1931 alone numbered sixteen different major initiatives. The Banff–Calgary road was improved, a new building was constructed at the Upper Hot Springs and the Cave and Basin, extensive new trail systems were developed in the park, enthusiasm for skiing resulted in the completion of the Norquay Road, and an airstrip was built outside of Banff townsite. The Banff–Jasper Highway was built from 1933 to 1939, and officially opened in 1940. By 1936, a new park administration building and gardens had been constructed on the site of the old Bretton Hall, which had burned down in 1933. Between 1939 and 1940, when the depression came to an end, visitation to the park tripled due to better economic times as well as better roads and facilities in the park.

When World War II came to an end, Banff could, at last, take advantage of these investments. The expansion and improvement of the park's road system and a growing post-war prosperity led to unprecedented annual visitation. Encouraged by aggressive and highly targeted government publicity focused on the value of outdoor recreation, visitors came from all over Western Canada and the United States to enjoy the wonders of Banff. For a decade the park held the recreational needs of visitors above the interests of landscape preservation. Though this focus would change gradually through the 1960s in response to a growing environmental lobby, the next five decades would still see spectacular development in Banff. In 1945, the population of Banff was about 2,000 with tourist accommodation for 5,600. If one wanted to add Tunnel Mountain Campground to the formula, Banff townsite could accommodate about 7,500 people at any given time during the summer season. Five decades later, the town's resident population had grown to the level of its former total visitor capacity. To put it another way, the number of people you would have found in Banff on a crowded weekend in 1945 were now living in the town permanently. Other changes had taken place, too. In 1994, the total visitation to Banff National Park was a whopping 4.6 million per year. But only two-thirds of these people were using the park. A total of 1.4 million of these visitors didn't even stop in Banff or anywhere else in the park. In 1994, that still left 3.2 million to visit the town and park every year. At that time 76 percent were Canadian, 58 percent were from Alberta, and 17 percent were American, while the remaining 7 percent came from overseas. In that year there were 650 licensed businesses in Banff Park. Visitors spent roughly $750 million a year staying in Banff's 3,600 hotel rooms, 125 restaurants, 220 retail outlets and three ski areas. In high season during the summer, there were often 25,000 people in Banff, qualifying it as a small city by provincial standards.

While visitation to Banff and to the Canadian Rockies continued to grow through the final years of the twentieth century, the numbers of visitors declined dramatically throughout the first decade of the new millennium as terrorism threats, high fuel prices and economic uncertainty eroded tourism globally. Despite these problems, Banff remains a very popular tourist destination for one very good reason: the town is a centre for the enjoyment of some of the most interesting and aesthetically rewarding experiences that people can have in mountains anywhere in the world. Banff also remains interesting and important due to the sustained and largely successful effort that continues to be made to perpetuate the park's natural ecosystem functions in the midst of a rapidly changing West.

KEEPING BANFF NATIONAL Park in some sort of wild condition and in good ecological health is no easy task. It requires a great deal of knowledge, dedication and no small amount of good technical and scientific skill. It also requires political will and the committed cooperation of locals. Unfortunately, park management is no longer just a matter of leaving Banff as it is and allowing nature to take care of itself. So much has happened in Canada's first national park that it is now impossible to allow some natural ecological processes to unfold on their own.

Anyone living and working in Banff will soon become aware of a number of apparent contradictions in the way the park has been developed and operates. On one hand, the contemporary mandate of the national parks of Canada argues that the preservation of wilderness is the central reason for the existence of parks like Banff. On the other hand, we find a city inside the park, wholesale development at Lake Louise, and a railway and a national highway right through the heart of the park's most ecologically productive valley. Even Parks Canada itself has declared "visitor experience" its highest priority. One might rightly ask, "How can all this be?"

The fact of the matter is that Banff National Park did not come to be what it is today overnight. The Banff we see and experience today has its roots in the past. As a culture we have not always held natural landscape to be as valuable as we do today. We have not always had the scientific understanding we now have of the ecological elements that make up the living framework of a wilderness. Different views of why parks exist and how they should be managed and used divide us still today. We are also living with the consequences of well-meaning but ultimately serious mistakes made in park management in the past. Lest one be unduly surprised and alarmed by this, it is important to understand just how much we have learned from Banff. It was our first national park. It was created at a time when no other national parks existed as models upon which we could base appropriate management and care. We had to learn by doing. We now have in this country one of the finest national parks systems anywhere in the world. Much of that is due to hard lessons we learned in Banff. Many of these lessons have to do with boundaries and how boundaries affect jurisdiction that ultimately affects ecosystem function.

SASKATCHEWAN GLACIER

At six kilometres in length, the Saskatchewan is the largest glacier that flows out of the Columbia Icefield. This massive valley glacier can be seen in its entirety from the top of Parker Ridge. The viewpoint is accessible by way of a short, gentle trail from the Icefields Parkway, and begins just south of Banff's boundary with Jasper National Park. Many consider the Parker Ridge Trail the best short hike within the Canadian Rocky Mountain Parks World Heritage Site.
Photograph by R.W. Sandford.

KEEPING THINGS IN THEIR PLACE: SHIFTING POLITICAL BOUNDARIES

As the twentieth century dawned, a conservation ethic gradually began to inform the consciousness of a growing Canadian professional class. As this occurred, increasing political pressure was applied to the challenge of defining and evolving the national park ideal in Canada. It took years for this issue to finally erupt into government action. This is not to say that nothing had been done since 1887 to forward the national park concept as it relates to Banff. Yoho and Glacier parks were created in 1886, and in 1892 a reserve around Lake Louise was established. But the issue of wildlife conservation had yet to be resolved. In 1902, the federal government responded to concerns about the disappearance of "big game" in the Northwest Territories by extending the boundaries of Rocky Mountains National Park, as Banff was known then, to 11,396 square kilometres, nearly twice its current size. The expanded park area now included the reserve at Lake Louise and the watersheds of the Bow, Red Deer, Kananaskis and Spray rivers. In other words, the park then extended from the current boundary of Banff National Park past the town of Canmore right to the Kananaskis River.

12

The Birthplace of Western and Northern Rivers

The Columbia Icefield and Jasper National Park

THE HEADWALL OF THE ATHABASCA GLACIER
If it were not already classic by virtue of its elegant form, the Athabasca Glacier possesses another feature that makes it a very interesting and beautiful study. The ice descending from the icefield from which this outlet valley glacier is derived also falls over a series of three spectacular cliff faces, causing the tumbling ice to shatter and fracture into awesome icefalls. The vertical distance from the top of the first icefall to where the glacier finally flattens out is around 1,000 metres.
Photograph by R.W. Sandford.

JASPER HAS ALWAYS SEEMED different and special to me. For a very long time I thought it was the many friends I had there, but then I realized there was even more to it than that. The people in Jasper, as everyone in Banff will attest, are, well, different. I have been wondering how they are so and why this came to be.

It took me twenty-five years and hundreds of journeys over Sunwapta Pass to realize that, if you concentrate hard, you can actually sense a difference in what the landscape feels like when you cross the divide from Banff to Jasper National Park. While you see the same high mountains in the area of Sunwapta Pass that you see in Banff, there is a perceptible sense that the valleys that radiate out from them will open into an immensity that is different from what you experience further south in the Rockies. It is then that one is struck by the realization that Sunwapta Pass is, in fact, a Great Divide in its own right, quite different from the one that has paralleled the road all the way from Lake Louise. From the summit of Sunwapta Pass, the continent slopes down to tidewater. But this is not an east-west divide. From the Columbia Icefield to the town of Jasper, the Icefields Parkway drops down from the north slopes of the Rockies into one of the greatest watersheds on Earth. The waters that

It was a most unlikely group of people who undertook the first explorations of the great stone divide that formed the spine of the continent in Canada. For the most part, they could be considered tourists. They took the train West on their holidays and explored the country as time and money permitted. While they were competent and inspired, it was their wealth and leisure that granted them the opportunity to do what locals could not do, given the demands of a pioneer culture that insisted that the most practical things related to basic survival be done first.

The three adventurers associated with the discovery of the Columbia Icefield were Hugh Millington Stutfield, Hermann Woolley and John Norman Collie. Stutfield was a wealthy British stockbroker who through careful and considered investment was able to retire early from the London Stock Exchange and pursue his interest in travel. He was also a crack shot with a rifle and shotgun, a talent that later allowed him to save his fellow climbers from a difficult predicament in Canada with respect to supplies. It was this same talent, however, that caused him to be hunting instead of climbing when the full extent of the Columbia Icefield was discovered in 1898.

Woolley was a pharmaceutical chemist and the head of a large Manchester drug firm. He was also an amateur boxer of note and a strong climber. Collie was best known as a chemist. He also had a fine reputation as a climber. A biography of Collie[1] records that he made a total of seventy-seven first ascents in Skye, the Scottish mainland, the Lake District, the Himalaya and the Canadian Rockies.

Fortunately for us, however, Collie was as good a geographer as he was a scientist. Over four visits to the Canadian Rockies between 1897 and 1902, he mapped more than three thousand square miles (7,770 square km) of Canada's mountain West. He was also a climber of note in the Rockies a decade before mountaineering became popular in the region. While Stutfield and Woolley deserve to be remembered for the parts they played in finding the Columbia Icefield, a hundred years after this historic discovery it is Collie we remember best.

Collie first heard about the Canadian Rockies as a result of Philip Stanley Abbot's 1896 accident at Lake Louise. Collie participated in the Anglo-American expedition that climbed Mount Lefroy on the anniversary of Abbot's death. Two days later Collie and Sarbach made the first ascent of Mount Victoria with Charles Fay and Arthur Michael. The climbers then went to the Bow Lake area where, on August 11,

**BREWSTER'S ICE
EXPLORERS**

The Athabasca Glacier is
the most accessible glacier
in the Rocky Mountains.
Brewster offers visitors safe
and convenient access to
the surface of the Athabasca
Glacier on specially built
"Ice Explorers." The fully
commentated hour-long
excursion also allows
passengers to get off the giant
snow machines to walk on the
surface of the glacier itself.
As the Ice Explorers also
accommodate wheelchairs, it
is possible for almost anyone
to have an Ice Age experience
at the Columbia Icefield.
Photograph by R.W. Sandford.

they made the first ascent of Mount Gordon. With three new ascents to
celebrate, the Americans had run out of time and had to go home.

Following the departure of part of the team, Collie, George Baker and
Swiss guide Peter Sarbach planned to visit Mount Assiniboine, which
had acquired the reputation of being the Matterhorn of the Rockies.
Collie changed these plans, however, on the basis of some thing he had
seen to the north from the summit of Mount Gordon: a fine double-
headed snow peak with large glaciers pouring down its east face. They
also looked upon a giant that loomed cold and sharp into the clear
August skies further north. This peak, they surmised, was Mount Forbes,
which they guessed to be somewhere near 14,000 feet (4,267 m) in
height. The sight of this mountain triggered something in Collie that
would change his plans for the remainder of the summer of 1897 and
bring him back the following year.

The image of Mount Forbes brought an old legend to life in Collie's
mind. It was a legend that grew from the journals of David Douglas
who, in 1827, had been the first man to climb a major mountain in North
America. Douglas had told the story of two giants that guarded Athabasca Pass in what is now Jasper National Park. These stone monsters,

COLUMBIA GLACIER OGIVES

When viewed from the icefield above it, the Columbia Glacier looks very much like any of the other major glaciers that flow from the neve, or high snowfield, that creates them. The Columbia Glacier is unique, however, in that it falls into the neighbouring valley so steeply that the ice forms concentric pressure ridges called ogives.

Photograph by R.W. Sandford.

which Douglas had named Mount Hooker and Mount Brown, were said to be Himalayan-sized peaks that lay to the north, beyond Mount Forbes. Collie decided to find and then climb them. During the winter of 1897–98, Collie could not get the Hooker-Brown problem out of his mind. Through careful research, Collie learned that many competent explorers had already applied themselves to the mystery of the two mountains and had published excellent accounts of their findings.

The entire issue surrounding the legendary heights of Hooker and Brown began with the explorer and mapmaker David Thompson, who was the first European to traverse Athabasca Pass in 1811. Thompson, perhaps from an incorrect boiling-point determination, estimated the 5,735 foot (1,748 m) summit of the pass to be about 11,000 feet (3,353 m). Ross Cox and Thomas Drummond, who crossed the pass in 1814, compounded Thompson's mistake by calculating the summits of the two major peaks in the area of the pass at 16,000 to 18,000 feet (4,877 to 5,486 m). When botanist David Douglas crossed the pass in 1827, he recorded in his journal that he became desirous of climbing one of the two peaks at the crest of the pass and set out to climb the mountain on the left or west side that appeared the taller. In his journals he did not identify any peak by name or elevation. Nor did he claim that the peak he had climbed was the tallest in North America. Quite contrary to what he claimed when he got home, his journals clearly admit that there were many other mountains in the area of the pass that were higher than the one he climbed.

Douglas returned to England in 1828 and began the transcription of his journal notes into an account he hoped to present before the Royal Horticultural Society. It is at this point that the account begins to diverge from his notes and from fact. His published transcriptions argue that, instead of climbing the mountain on the left or west side of the pass, he climbed the one on the north side of Committee's Punch Bowl, the small lake at the summit of the famous trade route. He claimed the mountain to be 17,000 feet (5,182 m) instead of his original estimate of 18,000 feet (5,486 m), and for some unknown reason claimed this peak to be "the highest yet known in the Northern Continent of America." He then named the two Athabasca Pass mountains for botanist colleagues William Hooker and Robert Brown. With a few strokes of a pen, Douglas sent three generations of geographers and mountaineers on a wild goose chase searching for these two fabled peaks. Though Collie probably sensed that the mystery of Hooker and Brown had already been solved, he decided to take up the adventure.

On July 31, 1898, Collie and company left Laggan with a large pack string organized by local outfitter Bill Peyto. The expedition decided to follow Peyto's 1897 suggestion of reaching the drainage of the Saskatchewan by way of the Pipestone and Siffleur valleys, which permitted them to avoid the timber jams and bogs of the lower Bow Valley.

On August 17, their nineteenth day out from Laggan, the expedition was camped on the watershed that separated the Saskatchewan and Athabasca rivers. Opposite their camp, a huge glacier-clad peak beckoned to them. Late in the morning on August 18, 1898, Collie and Woolley started for the summit of Mount Athabasca. Soon they were on the east side of the peak and climbing. The ridge gave them little trouble until it gave way to rotten, eroded rock. They then took to the glacier and made their way up to a large basin just below the summit. Then they cut steps for two hours along a line that was so steep they couldn't change places to relieve the tedium of step cutting. Finally, they arrived at a small platform just below the summit where a chimney led them to a very trying pitch that allowed them access to the summit ridge. The peak itself would have been reward enough, but the view slowed their minds. Collie later described what he saw:

up the Bush River only to find themselves a full fifteen miles (twenty-four km) away from the Columbia Icefield.

Disappointed by their failure to climb even one decent mountain during the summer of 1900, Collie gave the Rockies a miss in 1901 and went instead to climb in the Lofoten Islands in Norway. In the meantime, however, the Canadian Pacific Railway advanced their plans to turn the Canadian Rockies into the Canadian Alps. In 1901, the railway brought Edward Whymper, the conqueror of the Matterhorn, to the Rockies to promote mountaineering in Canada. This angered Collie, who wrote to Charles Thompson to complain that Whymper was going to hog all the first ascents.

Though Whymper did not prove a threat to Collie's first-ascent plans in the Columbia Icefield area, another British climber did. After teaming up with Edward Whymper briefly, James Outram made headlines in Canada and abroad with the first ascent of Mount Assiniboine in September of 1901. Collie resented Outram as much as he did Whymper if only because he had played no role in the exhausting early exploration of the Rockies, but was managing simply to make first ascents of mountains already found and mapped by others. When Collie returned to the Rockies in 1902, he was no longer interested in exploration. He wanted to make first ascents in the icefield he had discovered. Competition between these two climbers would lead to full exploration of the Columbia Icefield and first ascents of many of its most prominent peaks.

In the summer of 1902, Outram got into the field two weeks before Collie. Realizing he had only a short time before Collie arrived, Outram advanced immediately up the main branch of the Saskatchewan to the Alexandra Valley with the intent of stealing the first ascent of Mount Columbia, the giant of the Columbia Icefield. Near the base of Mount Alexandra, which dominates the head of the valley, Outram and his guide Christian Kaufmann ascended a high ridge to survey the surrounding peaks. There they saw before them the edge of the great icefield discovered by Collie and Woolley four years before. They saw also the narrow, three-pointed ridge of Mount Bryce and, as the clouds parted, the exquisite summit of Mount Columbia. They saw, too, that they were still a difficult and trying distance away from both.

On July 19, 1902, Outram and Kaufmann set out from their camp at 2:20 a.m., in just enough light to see the shadows of the trees in the valley. In an hour they felt the coldness of the glacial ice. At 5:00 a.m. they roped together to thread their way through the maze of crevasses and soon looked out over the eternity of ice and snow that forms the windswept névé of the icefield. The mountain looked no closer than it had from the valley floor. It took the climbers nearly four hours of continuous walking to reach the bergschrund out of which the peak of Mount Columbia rose into the cold, indifferent sky. They made their gradual way up the arête to a sheer and icy escarpment that was the last obstacle to the summit. At just after 2:00 p.m., Outram "planted the Union Jack on the broad, white platform that crowns the summit, the highest point in Canada from which the British flag has ever floated."[3] Then they faced the careful descent and the long slog back over the ice to camp. Just after midnight, after 22 hours of strenuous walking and climbing, they at last stumbled into their tents.

Between 1902 and 1919, there was virtually no exploration done in the area of the Columbia Icefield. During that time, the efforts of mountaineers were concentrated further south at Lake Louise and beyond. While a few expeditions made their way north from Lake Louise to Jasper, they avoided the difficult Columbia Icefield section. In time, however, civilization began to catch up with the remoteness of the West. In 1913, a survey to delineate the boundary between Alberta and British Columbia was initiated by the Office of the Surveyor General in Ottawa. During the first three years, the survey concentrated on the southern Rockies between Akamina Pass and Mount Assiniboine. By 1918, the survey had advanced past Thompson Pass to within sight of the Columbia Icefield. In July 1919, a climbing party ascended to the Columbia Icefield and began to survey a line across it to Mount Columbia. The survey was undertaken by R.W. Cautley of the Alberta Land Survey and Arthur Oliver Wheeler of the British Columbia Land Survey.

The next major expedition to the Columbia Icefield was led by the prominent American ophthalmologist James Monroe Thorington, and his friend Dr. William S. Ladd. Their guide was an Austrian named Conrad Kain, who was already famous for leading the first recognized ascent of Mount Robson.

A 1922 expedition to the Freshfields had whetted James Thorington's appetite for the northlands. Throughout the following winter Thorington and Ladd spent hours pouring over the few available maps and photographs of the region they called the "Alexandra Angle." This country that they considered "a land lost behind the ranges" included the peaks along the Continental Divide between Howse Pass and Mount Columbia, all of which were encompassed by the uppermost drainages at the headwaters of the North Saskatchewan River. Though some of the earliest expeditions had made brief incursions into this blank space on

COLUMBIA GLACIER
The Columbia Glacier terminates in a lake created by its own melt. In summer the glacier's forward motion results in ice calving off the snout of the glacier into the lake. The icebergs float in the water until they melt.
Photograph by R.W. Sandford.

the map, it was still to a very large extent unexplored.

After visiting the East and West Alexandra Glaciers and the north basin of Mount Lyell, the expedition reached Castleguard Camp on the 5th of July. The next day, the entire expedition climbed Mount Castleguard.

On July 9, while William Ladd unsuccessfully tried his luck fishing in the Castleguard River, Conrad Kain and James Thorington made the first ascent of Terrace Mountain. The following day they were ready for their first big ascent. At 3:20 a.m., they set out for the North Twin. As Thorington later explained, they came to know the scale of the Columbia Icefield on that day. At 6:00 a.m., the climbers were at last able to leave the shoulder of Mount Castleguard at the head of the Saskatchewan Glacier and begin their long tramp over the icefield proper. Though it looked only half that distance to the Thorington party, the North Twin is a full twelve miles by air (nineteen km) from the shoulder of Mount Castleguard. It took them several hours just to reach the head of the Athabasca Glacier and the base of Snow Dome. They were still only half way to the North Twin. After circling widely to avoid crevasses at the head of the Columbia Glacier, Thorington began to see things that weren't there:

> *Fatigue mirages – momentary illusions – began to appear; for an instant I was convinced that the dark line of a distant crevasse was a staff planted on the summit of North Twin; and I berated Conrad for bringing us so far only to let us be cheated of a first-ascent.*[4]

Thorington's observations of mirages on the immense plateau give an idea of just how big the Columbia Icefield really is. It is big enough to create its own weather and optical effects. His observations were confirmed the following year by the Field expedition and have, from time to time, been reported by climbers right up until the present. Bushes and trees constantly seem to present themselves at various places all over the icefield as climbers pitilessly observe their own slow progress over the eternal snows.

Only after the party stopped at 2:00 p.m. for lunch, after nearly eleven hours of walking across the ice, had they reached their mountain. Before them was a stunning scene. Framed by the North Twin and ice-deep summit bulges of Mount Stutfield, the climbers peered in silent awe at the unclimbed, cliff-walled summit of giant Mount Alberta. They reached the summit of the North Twin at about 4:20 p.m. But as too often happens in mountaineering, the climbers had reached the summit only to be greeted by dense cloud. Robbed of the view, they had to be satisfied with the first ascent, the last of the unclimbed 12,000 foot peaks in the Columbia Icefield area, and the first traverse of the Columbia Icefield from the Castleguard Valley to the head of Habel Creek. As any climber will tell you, the summit is only halfway to the goal. The arduous return journey from the North Twin is one of the epics of early mountaineering in Canada. Thorington described it as if it were a dream:

> Someone, following in our track, may one day understand that journey back across the icefield's vastness. For an analytical mind, it will at least afford insight of the psychology of fatigue: the half-hour in a blizzard, obscuring the trail and exhausting us; the clearing at sunset, with crimson and orange light banded against masses of lead-blue storm clouds behind The Twins; mist and snow-banners wreathed about and trailing from Columbia and catching up the light – we three mortals in the middle of the field, in all its immensity, struggling on in insufficiently crusted snow until the light failed.[5]

Twenty-three hours after leaving camp, the climbers fell on the grass beside the campfire and ate breakfast as the sun rose on the peaks surrounding the Castleguard meadows. This had been the longest mountaineering ordeal to date in the Canadian Rockies.

In 1923, Thorington had, in effect, dropped a gauntlet to other climbers by announcing that Kain, Ladd and he had set a "new long-distance and altitude record in Canadian mountaineering." Their claim had been established by climbing, in five successive days, the North Twin (the first ascent and a journey of 54 kilometres, or more than 30 miles), Mount Saskatchewan (another first ascent and a journey of 27 kilometres,

THE TRIPLE HYDROLOGICAL APEX

A rare and very interesting hydrological feature also exists at the Columbia Icefield. Mount Snow Dome, near the Athabasca Glacier, is buried deeply in snow and ice. The mountain, however, is located such that meltwaters from its top flow to three different oceans, west to the Pacific, east to Hudson Bay and the Atlantic, and north by way of the Athabasca River to the Arctic. In this photograph Jasper Park Superintendent Ron Hooper, the author, and the Mayor of Jasper Dick Ireland send water to each of the great oceans from the summit of Snow Dome, in celebration of the United Nations International Year of Fresh Water.

Photograph by Ward Cameron.

about 16 miles) and Mount Columbia (a second ascent and a journey of 42 kilometres, nearly 25 miles). There exists in the climbing tradition a myth that mountaineering is not supposed to be a competitive sport. Not everyone subscribes to that myth.

Harvard glaciologist William Field came to the Rockies in 1924 due to a talk given by James Thorington to the American Alpine Club in Boston about his 1923 Columbia Icefield expedition. This group wished to make the first ascent of the South Twin.

Guide Edward Feuz led them first to the Castleguard Meadows where they camped. As the South Twin was a good 25 kilometres (about 15.5 miles) away, Feuz instructed the party to leave at 8:00 p.m. one evening and to walk across the icefield by moonlight to the base of the 11,700 foot peak (3,556-m peak). It was only lunchtime when the team of very strong climbers made their way to the summit of the South Twin. Relishing the stimulating physical exercise and the grand views, William Field proposed that the party climb the North Twin while they were in the vicinity. Feuz agreed, suggesting that since they were going to be late getting back to camp anyway, they might as well make a full day of it. Fred Field complained that he'd already had enough but was overruled. William Field and Feuz had their way.

The return trip from the North Twin was something of an exercise in masochism. As had happened to the Thorington party the year before, the climbers had to return over the icefield during the hot part of the summer day. The usual mirages began to appear, just as they had to the eyes of Thorington and his party. Lawren Harris saw bushes and trees growing out of the ice and claims to have seen groups of people watching their "piteously slow progress on that interminable march."[6] In just over twenty-four hours the climbers had walked 58 kilometres (about 36 miles) and climbed two of the highest peaks in the Columbia Icefield group. They were clearly worthy of an additional and most remarkable discovery they made just inside what is now the northern boundary of Banff National Park, just on the edge of the Columbia Icefield: a

THE CASTLEGUARD CAVES

Underlying the Castleguard Meadows is the longest cave system in Canada. Beginning in 1967, Derek Ford of McMaster University led a series of winter mapping explorations, which ultimately revealed the extent and character of the 20-kilometre-long Castleguard system. Ford and his colleagues discovered that the Castleguard Caves actually terminate under the Columbia Icefield. Because of the extreme hazard, the cave system is now closed to public access.

Photograph courtesy of Dr. Derek Ford and Parks Canada.

discovery that in its own right would have later qualified the region to become a World Heritage Site.

THE DISCOVERY OF THE CASTLEGUARD CAVES

THOUGH MANY OTHER outfits had camped in the Castleguard area and observed how meltwater disappeared through cracks and fissures in the bedrock of the meadows, none had hitherto discovered where that water went. Exploring the timbered slope below their camp late one afternoon, two members of the 1924 William Field party heard a rumbling underground, then a river burst forth from the side of the mountain below them. Further exploration revealed a substantial cave mouth out of which the water was issuing in torrents. Two days later the water subsided, at least for a time, and the party was able to explore the cave for some two hundred metres until the cave floor dropped into an abyss. The mystery of the Castleguard Cave system would haunt scientists and cave explorers for more than fifty years until research initiated by McMaster University geologist and caver Derek Ford led to the realization that the twelve-kilometre-long cave system ended under the Columbia Icefield itself. It is one of the longest cave systems in Canada.

The cave system is now closed to the public for reasons of safety. Even the entrance to the cave system can only be accessed by experienced and well-equipped mountaineers. Travelling within the system itself can be extraordinarily dangerous as flooding is common and unpredictable. The Castleguard Caves remain one of these places we are happy to know exists and pleased to have protected within a World Heritage Site. It is not, however, a place that will ever be visited by many people.[7]

With the Field expedition, the great days of pioneering mountaineering expeditions in the Columbia Icefield area came to an end. While they discovered much else as well, what the early explorers and mountaineers essentially discovered was the birthplace of western rivers. The organizing principle of this World Heritage Site is watershed. We see a century later that almost every aspect of the mountain landscape is an expression of what water does in upwardly tilted geological circumstances. All of the rest of the wonder – the shapes of the peaks, the colour of the lakes, the rich forest and alpine ecosystems – all follow from the fact

supported glaciers in the Columbia Icefield area for as long as three million years, ice movement at the Columbia Icefield has also been linked to more widespread climatic coolings, which have resulted in major glacial advances throughout the Rockies. What appears to be the most extensive of all modern ice ages began roughly 240,000 years ago. The Illinoian or Great Glaciation covered most of the northern regions of the upper hemisphere, fashioning much of the geography as we know it today in North America. The Great Glaciation was a spectacular geological event that lasted a hundred thousand years. Though the glaciers of the Columbia Icefield would have grown dramatically during this continental cooling, the dynamics of the icefield itself would have changed little. The only difference would be that the major alpine glaciers could have been hundreds of kilometres long and as much as two kilometres deep as they left the Rockies and joined the even greater ice masses flowing southward from the direction of the pole.

Other notable but lesser glacial advances took place in the Rockies seventy-five thousand and twenty thousand years ago and did much to give these mountains the contours that make them so dramatic today. Another climatic cooling took place around eleven thousand years ago and initiated what is called the Crowfoot Advance, a smaller but still measurable glacial growth period still represented in the surface geology of the Columbia Icefield area. The last glacial advance to have taken place in the Canadian Rockies is so recent that early travellers were able to document its close. The Cavell Advance, often call the Little Ice Age likely began near the year 1200. At the peak of this advance, in about 1750, the Athabasca Glacier was two kilometres longer than it is now.

CLIMATE AND MICROCLIMATE: THE LITTLE ICE AGE

History tells us that Anthony Henday was likely the first European to look upon the Rocky Mountains in Canada, an act he is said to have performed in the summer of 1754 from a hilltop vantage near the present site of Gull Lake, Alberta. So dazzling was the panorama of the distant snow-clad peaks, that he called the Rockies the Shining Mountains. Today, from the same summer vista on the Great Plains, the Rockies would not likely appear as quite the wall of white Henday witnessed before he packed his canoes with furs and headed east again for Montreal. Henday looked upon the Rockies while they were buried deep beneath the throes of the most recent time of glacial advances,

TRACKING THE GLACIER'S RECESSION
Markers along the road to the terminus of the glacier indicate the location of the snout in recent years. The markers indicate rapid recent and accelerating recession of the glacier, which is associated with natural climate change and, more recently, to anthropogenic influences on the composition of the Earth's atmosphere.
Photograph by R.W. Sandford.

the Little Ice Age. But since then the climate of the West has changed. By the beginning of the twentieth century, the climate of the Rockies had warmed considerably. Since then most of the glaciers of the Rockies have retreated.

It is very difficult to predict what will happen next in terms of glacial advance and retreat in the Rockies. Though much of what happens in terms of ice dynamics at the Columbia Icefield depends upon local or micro-climatic conditions, even this great mass of ice is not immune to the larger influences of planetary climatic change. Due to the way glacial ice is accumulated and endures, glaciers offer an excellent and reliable source of information about the earth's past climates. Glacial cores from the ancient ice of the poles tell us that, before 1900, natural atmospheric pollutants overwhelmingly outnumbered human-generated pollutants. This is no longer true.

Human activity is now an important factor in the evolving climate. One cumulative result of all of these atmospheric changes is the greenhouse effect we have heard so much about, which is causing warmer temperatures worldwide. It is clear that such warming could have a substantial impact on the planet's inter-connected ecosystems and on patterns of human settlement. The ultimate effect of these atmospheric changes on the Columbia Icefield is unclear. Even if the climate does warm, however, it may not mean the end of the ice in these mountains any time soon. The glaciers may shrink back into the icefield that formed them. The decreased surface of the ice will likely accelerate melt.

But that may not be the end. There is something to be said for glacial patience. Shrunken but by no means defeated, protected by the cold heights of the Great Divide, the ice will simply wait and wait. Provided the warming is not too great of course, it will survive.

Current evidence suggests, however, that our glaciers are in trouble. One quarter of the glacial mass in the cordillera has disappeared in the last century. Rapid glacial recession and dramatically lower stream flows have also been recorded at the headwaters and downstream on all major rivers that have their origins in the mountain national parks.

As the mountain glaciers continue to melt, water availability will diminish on the Great Plains. As hydropower generation becomes less reliable, more coal-fired generation will be required which will likely result in greater greenhouse emissions. The kinds of life that live in the river will change as the temperature of the water rises in the wake of decreased introduction of cold water from glacial melt. If the climate continues to warm as expected and stream flows are reduced as projected then the water needs of projects like Alberta's oil sands could reach a critical proportion of winter low flows.

According to Dr. David Schindler of the University of Alberta, both Alberta and Saskatchewan have already recorded a warming trend of 1 °C to 4 °C, mostly after 1970. Regional climate models predict that the average temperature could further increase by as much as 4.8 °C to 8 °C by 2100. This range is outside our society's current willingness or capacity to adapt.

Reduced river flows, reduced glacial melt contributions, and other climate-related changes in precipitation patterns and timing are converging to create a new hydrological regime on the eastern slopes and on the prairies. And yet we continue to develop heavily in our headwater regions. We are writing cheques our landscapes may not be able to cash. One does not think of such things, however, when heading down-valley from the Columbia Icefield toward Jasper. One thinks about water because it is everywhere, falling from the mountains surrounding the valleys and, in the case of the Maligne Valley, flowing invisibly beneath our feet.

NORTH SLOPE WONDER: THE MALIGNE VALLEY

LEGENDS HAVE ALWAYS EXISTED of sacred places deep in the mountains where nature is said to exist in the most extravagantly pristine state. For hundreds of years, Native peoples in the mountain West knew

ANGEL GLACIER
The glaciers that are disappearing most rapidly in the Rocky Mountains are those that are already small in size and located at lower elevations. Despite its altitude and north-facing aspect, the Angel Glacier on Mount Edith Cavell will not last long if current warming trends persist.
Photograph by R.W. Sandford.

about a remarkable lake in a stunning valley enclosed by the most beautiful of mountains. Even though few actually visited the lake, for it was remote and difficult to reach, word slowly found its way to the outside. In order that the secret not fall into uncaring hands, stories of this almost mythical place were told only to the most inquiring of early European explorers. These adventurers longed to search out this magical valley, but few had the time or the resources for an extended expedition. The wilderness through which they would have to travel was trackless and wild, and the only maps that existed were images lodged in the fading memories of Native elders.

It was the lower reaches of this fabled valley that Europeans found first. As if to protect the upper reaches of this sacred place from vandals, the river that roared from this valley proved difficult and dangerous to cross. Naming the river *Maligne* for the curse they uttered on its banks, the Europeans carried on westward across the mountains, to the Columbia, to the sea. Only as the map of the West filled was the legend of the primeval valley heard again. There was a remarkable lake deep in the wilderness, back of beyond.

The first European to stumble on the lake at the head of the magical valley was not looking for it. Henry McLeod was looking for something else – a way out perhaps – and did not see what he was looking at. Walled inside himself by private misery, he named the lake for his sore feet and wandered on. The noisy rustling that passes for silence in the wilderness descended again. More than thirty years went by. In summer, water lapped on ancient shores. Ice groaned on the peaks. Loons called. In winter, the lake froze deep and hard. Then only wolf-howl could be heard above the hiss of the falling snow.

BACKCOUNTRY SOPHISTICATES

In the Rockies, rail tracks were laid through Lake Louise in the south and, later, through Jasper in the north. Tough, hard-cussing bush-whackers made their summer living by cutting crude trails through the burnt forests and muskeg in order to take American pilgrims into the wilderness along the Great Divide. The trips often took weeks. Climbers and adventurers had the time to leave the city behind. As long days passed beneath the sparkling glaciers, travellers slowed to the pace of the land. Even the most single-minded were then visited by a sense of well-being that often changed their lives. Captured by the unutterable beauty of the Rockies, some never went home. One such traveller, Mary

**ALPINE
FORGET-ME-NOT**
In terms of climatic
conditions, the mountains of
the Canadian West act as a
southward extension of arctic
ecosystems. Many arctic
plant species find their way
southward along the spine of
the Rockies. Alpine Forget-
me-not *(Myosotis alpestris)*
is one of the most colourful
alpine flower species.
Photograph by R.W. Sandford.

Schäffer, (see Chapter 10) spoke eloquently but softly of a "wonder trail," a difficult but rewarding path through the primeval peaks from Lake Louise to Jasper that possessed an extraordinary charm. Before this "wonder trail" became "the wonder road" and, later, the Icefields Parkway, she marked this relatively blank space on the map as one of the most remarkable places on Earth.

Mary Townsend Sharples (pronounced Sharp-less) was born into no small amount of Quaker family wealth in West Chester, Pennsylvania on October 4, 1861. Though thoroughly educated in all the usual skills and graces appropriate to a young lady of her station, Sharples also inherited an intense interest in natural history bequeathed to her by her father, whose passionate interest in mineralogy was cultivated through regular contact with some of the most prominent scientists of the day. Sharples' interests led to a study of botany that, combined with natural talent in art, later permitted her to contribute significantly to the field identification of North American wildflowers. Taken by the notion of the Wild West, in her mid teens Sharples realized the dream of travelling by train to see the Indians of the American southwest.

A second trip west also included a steamer voyage up the West Coast to Alaska where her desire to acquaint herself with aboriginal cultures seemed to be satisfied. What wasn't satisfied, however, was what was to become an abiding interest in travel, an obsession that further expressed itself in an extended rail journey from Montreal to Vancouver in the summer of 1889. This journey was inspired by the encouragement of family friend Mary Vaux, who had become interested in the glaciers and deeply carved valleys of the Selkirk Mountains when her family first visited Rogers Pass two summers before. The Vaux family was, in fact, so taken by the Selkirk landscapes they began formal studies of the movement of both the Illecillewaet and Asulkan Glaciers and continued this research on an annual basis after 1894. The enthusiasm of the Vaux family toward Canadian mountains was to infect Mary Sharples, too.

THE TONQUIN VALLEY
It would take a lifetime to explore all the glory of the Jasper part of the Canadian Rocky Mountain Parks World Heritage Site. The Tonquin Valley is accessible only by trail. Its stunning beauty, however, makes it one of the most popular backpacking destinations in the Canadian Rockies.
Photograph by R.W. Sandford.

When Jasper National Park came into existence, it was thought that simply protecting landscapes from logging and mining would permit natural processes to sustain the wilderness. It is now realized that the park is part of a much larger ecosystem that extends far beyond Jasper's boundaries – and that distant events can have profound impacts on natural ecological processes inside the park. Within this context, the natural character of the Maligne Valley has been recognized for its true uniqueness. We now know that of all the spectacular places in Canada's mountain national parks, this is one of the most remarkable. The variety of its amazing natural features, its exotic wildlife, the healthy nature of its intact ecosystems and the long history of human presence in the Maligne Valley could qualify it, in its own right, as a United Nations World Heritage Site. Early travellers were right to marvel about this valley.

It is now the challenge of our generation to give value to the experiences we have in this remarkable place. Though we cannot be the first to visit the valley, we can still feel a measure of the awe and wonder early visitors felt in this most sacred of natural places. We are not pioneers, as James Monroe Thorington noted, but we can journey over old trails that are new to us, with hearts open.

THE AGE OF ADVENTURE TOURISM

EVEN AS IT WAS BEING CREATED, the Canadian National Park system embraced a new notion of wilderness. Mountains became summer sanctuaries to which pilgrims would return again and again for the solace of so much open and often unmapped space. Grand railway hotels offered elegant living in the midst of the staggering beauty of Canada's suddenly accessible peaks. Edwardian adventurers took full advantage of this unique opportunity to make history while drawing spiritual and physical refreshment from the wilderness. The world was new and bright to them. The winter of misunderstanding mountains was over. The demons and alpine dragons that had populated the evil peaks were gone, leaving only trails bright with wildflowers.

But even in the twentieth century, that most urban of human epochs, there was still a place in the Canadian Rockies for explorers. Though physical toughness and unstinting commitment to the task at hand were useful attributes, you didn't have to be a mountaineer to open up the remaining blank spaces on the map of mountain Canada.

Among the climbers and explorers of the early twentieth century, the last giants were very much a mixed lot. Pampered socialites, rugged cowboys, Austrian peasants, ambitious clergymen, fur trappers and a diverse host of other unlikely heroes and heroines left deep marks on the then impressionable history of Canadian mountains. Though some major work was to be done in the Purcells, the bulk of the exploration would be done north of the main line of the Canadian Pacific Railway. Through their photographs and, later, their writings they were able to contribute to the unique sense of place that characterized the Canadian alpine as possessing high aesthetic and adventure appeal. Some of these were packers and horse guides like Sid Unwin, Billy Warren and Curly Phillips. Others were often clients of these horsemen who were so deeply affected by the experiences they had in the Canadian West that their lives were changed for good by what they saw and did. Some of the most important of this latter group were young women from prominent families who used the privilege of their family wealth to fashion highly individual lifestyles in a time when women were not expected to rise out of the stations into which they were placed by their families and husbands.

MALIGNE CANYON
Until alternate access to the upper reaches of the Maligne Valley were developed, most visitors saw only the canyon located just above where the Maligne River joins the Athabasca. The canyon is a stunning introduction to the wonders of the region. *Photograph by Virginia Penny.*

that the limestone bedrock dips gently westward and that the stream follows the dip. As it does so, it creates a gentle bank on one side and a steep and deeply undercut bank on the other. Then it disappears. Though you can hear it, you have to look a long way down to find the water. At fifty-five metres, this is the deepest part of the canyon. The spray is lit by the occasional ray of morning light that falls at just the right angle to penetrate the dark chasm of the narrow canyon.

We see a huge waterfall that drops twenty-three metres to the base of the slit. Here we see that the upper layers of the rock that compose the canyon walls are thicker, harder and more resistant to the force of the cascade than those below. The narrow canyon suddenly widens at the falls and its walls expand into a huge stone amphitheatre out of which wells the canyon's ceaseless song.

Wind-blown dust and fine debris from frost shattering have combined to create isolated pockets of soil on ledges in the walls of the deepening canyon. Here in the shade and the spray, mosses grow in lush carpets out of which spring species of ferns that have likely occupied such places for a quarter of the age of the earth. On the canyon's lip, wild roses grow, adding their delicate fragrance to that of the pines and the scent of dusty spray wafting up from the booming water below.

The big rocks on the far side of the bridge are as worn by people climbing on them as the steps of some old European cathedrals. Yet, while I am standing on the bridge in the warm light, two large tour groups come and go, pausing only long enough to peer into the abyss and wander aimlessly on. I wonder what they are experiencing. It occurs to me that in their hurry they are missing something. Our shadows are like those the clouds cast on the canyon walls. A place like this canyon needs time to speak to you. How long do you have to spend in nature to begin to hear it? A minute? An hour? A week? Nature speaks in long sentences. We appear before the stage in the midst of a soliloquy a million years long. Even in a lifetime we hear only a few words and are gone.

As the trail nears the Third Bridge, it approaches the canyon again. We discover that the canyon has widened and is less deep. The canyon narrows again just as it approaches the bridge. The Parks Canada sign indicates that the canyon is only ten metres deep at this point. But the river is still roaring below as it cascades down a spray-alive falls and disappears again into a gloom of moss and stunted trees that cling to the crumbling walls of the canyon. The Maligne is intent on making its relentless way down to the valley floor and its union with the Athabasca River just upstream from Jasper Park Lodge.

At the Fourth Bridge the canyon is twelve metres deep and narrow. Here the river makes a sensuous green and white right turn through a knot of birch trees and is joined by a small stream nearly hidden by the moss and the bleached skeletons of fallen pines.

Below the Fourth Bridge there is no one. Here the canyon has only one wall and the trail drops to near the river's edge. The green water froths around rocks and down stone spillways toward the Fifth Bridge. En route I come upon the first evidence of the underground river that makes the Maligne Valley so remarkable. A stream of water issues from a grotto on the far side of the river. A sign explains that this is one of the larger seepages from Medicine Lake, which is located fifteen kilometres upvalley.

Over time, cracks in the limestone bottom of Medicine Lake have been dissolved and have opened and expanded to create an underground drainage system. Water takes seventy hours to flow through the fifteen-kilometre underground channel from Medicine Lake to where it joins the Maligne just below the Fourth Bridge on the canyon. Water from this same underground network also surfaces at Lac Beauvert and Lake Annette near Jasper Park Lodge. Though this system carries a great deal of water, it is not likely big enough for a man to walk through.

For most visitors to Jasper National Park, Maligne Canyon is all they see of the Maligne Valley. Spectacular as it is, the canyon is only part of a larger wonder that is the seventy-kilometre-long, sixteen-kilometre-wide valley.

THE DISAPPEARING WATERS OF THE MALIGNE VALLEY

ONE OF THE MOST AMAZING features in the valley, indeed in the whole park, is Medicine Lake. Early visitors to the Maligne Valley noticed that Medicine Lake filled up in the summer and then emptied in the fall and winter. It soon became apparent that the waters in the lake were draining off through an immense undiscovered underground outlet. The Native peoples were impressed enough by the phenomenon to suggest supernatural causes. Many people believe that this is the origin of the lake's name.

Later residents were also baffled by the disappearing waters. Throughout the 1930s, a park warden named Micky McGuire experimented with ways to determine the location of the outlet. He began by dumping two truckloads of *Saturday Evening Post* into the sinkholes to determine if they could be blocked. Later he experimented with a truckload of mattresses. Nothing seemed to work. Park officials, concerned with the impact of the disappearing waters on potential fish stocks, went so far as to propose the construction of a dam on the lake. The idea foundered, however, when it was realized that the sinkholes were immense and that a huge amount of fill would be necessary to stop the water from disappearing.

It was not until 1956 that the true extent of the underground river system that drained Medicine Lake began to be understood. In that year a French scientist named Jean Corbel concluded that a sinking river system had probably been created in the Maligne Valley before the last ice age. Corbel's hypothesis was confirmed in 1965 by research teams from McMaster University. They emptied special dyes into the lake and traced the water from Medicine Lake to the outlet stream that surfaces in Maligne Canyon and to Lac Beauvert and Lake Annette. During high water, the lake drains at a rate of fifteen to forty-two cubic metres per second. The water disappearing from the north end of the lake takes nearly three days to surface again sixteen kilometres away in Maligne Canyon.

The Maligne River has been proclaimed one of the largest known sinking river systems in the western hemisphere. Some scientists have gone so far as to suggest that the valley may contain one of the largest inaccessible cave systems on the planet. But nobody knows for sure. No one has found the entrance.

Though unsuccessful to date, the intensive search for the outlet system on Medicine Lake has led to the discovery of other cave systems in the Maligne Valley. Mouse Hole Cave and Log Hole were discovered

MALIGNE LAKE
Because of their widespread use in tourism promotion, Spirit Island and Maligne Lake are icons of how the rest of the world views Canada. Places like these are the reason Canadians are seen by others as living in one of the most desirable places on the planet.
Photograph by R.W. Sandford.

by Mike Goodchild in 1967. Maligne Canyon cave, 373 metres in length, was discovered by Chris Smart of McMaster University in 1974. Located close to the Third Bridge in Maligne Canyon, this "tight and unpleasant cave" features a spring at its entrance in the summer and a thick layer of icicles in winter.

In his classic book on Rocky Mountain caving, caver Jon Rollins also notes how fragile the underground drainage systems can be and how difficult it can be to predict human impacts on these subterranean resources.[8] A recent attempt to drill a well for the Maligne Canyon Tea House resulted in the mixing of sulphur-laden underground waters with the spring waters of the Maligne Valley. Hydrological accidents of this kind can have unpredictable effects on entire underground systems, making it very difficult to predict the impacts of development in areas where the bedrock is water-soluble limestone.

As has already been noted, the jewel of the Maligne Valley is the lake at its head. Maligne Lake is the largest glacier-fed lake in the Canadian Rockies and one of the most impressively beautiful places in all of Canada. Famous for its unique geological features which include the largest icefield in the Front Ranges of the Rockies, the largest known active karst drainage system in the western hemisphere, the largest glacier-fed lake in the Rockies and one of the largest gorges in the cordillera, the Maligne Valley meets the criteria for World Heritage Site designation on its own merit. The Maligne Valley and Maligne Lake are natural wonders of global significance. While one could dwell for a lifetime on the hydrological anomalies of the Maligne Valley system, another element of wonder is the natural systems that overlay the geology of the basin.

MALIGNE LAKE AND THE BIODIVERSITY OF THE MALIGNE VALLEY

THE ECOLOGICAL SYSTEMS found on the surface of the Maligne Valley are just as complex as the subterranean systems below. The biodiversity of the Maligne Valley can be broken down into four distinct regimes. The first is the aquatic ecosystem of Maligne Lake itself. Even to this day, not much is known about the natural systems that support life in the lake. We know that Maligne Lake can be found at an altitude of 1,676 metres. We also know that, at twenty-two kilometres, it is the longest lake in the Canadian Rockies. We know that the lake lies in a glacially carved sedimentary rock basin and that the length and depth of the lake have been extended by a natural rockslide dam at its northern end. We also know that at its deepest point, Maligne Lake is ninety-seven metres deep, making it the third deepest lake in the Canadian Rockies. There is not a great deal more we know about it. Cold and deep, this lake has historically been inhospitable to life.

Although it is the largest body of water in the Canadian Rockies, fish are not native to Maligne Lake. The towering waterfalls and turbulent waters of Maligne Canyon proved too great an obstacle for fish that re-colonized the rivers of the Rockies at the end of the last ice age. Fish did not become a part of the aquatic ecosystem of Maligne Lake until the lake was stocked with brook trout in 1928. The idea at the time was to have only one species of fish in the fragile Maligne watershed. Later rainbow trout were introduced without authorization. These more aggressive trout have come to dominate the aquatic ecosystems of both the lake and the river. Though Maligne Lake has become famous for its fishing, stocking no longer occurs and the populations of trout in both the lake and the river are stabilizing around natural conditions and food supply.

Some sixty-seven species of resident or breeding birds and more than fifty species of migrants and accidentals can be found in the Maligne Valley. Many of these, including the stunningly beautiful Harlequin duck, can be found in the shoreline ecosystem that surrounds the lake and along the banks of the Maligne River. The moist shoreline of the lake and river banks provide habitat for shrubs and plants that harbour a huge range of insect species which are the preferred food of wading birds and ducks like the goldeneye, bufflehead and mallard. Loons are also found on the lake, as are bald eagles and ospreys.

Spirit Island is part of this shoreline ecosystem. Formerly known simply as Sampson Narrows or The Narrows, Spirit Island was named by renowned Jasper photographer Harry Rowed. During the 1960s, Rowed canoed frequently to the Narrows where his spirit was moved by the islet and the grand backdrop of peaks that rose up around it. He named the tiny islet after that spirit. His stunning photographs of the islet were soon used to promote Maligne Lake in Canada and abroad, and the islet is now known as Spirit Island.

The valley ecosystem of the Maligne area is composed mainly of forests of lodgepole pine, Engelmann Spruce and subalpine fir. This ecosystem is similar to forest ecosystems everywhere in this region of the Rockies with the exception of one key inhabitant. These forests, and the meadows of the alpine ecosystem above it, are the home of one of the most rare and most spectacular of all the creatures that exist in the Canadian West, the mountain caribou.

THE MOUNTAIN CARIBOU

ELK, DEER AND MOOSE are common in Jasper National Park and are often seen in the Maligne Valley. Caribou, however, are rare. Creatures of the arctic tundra, the mountain caribou that exist in the Maligne Valley and in the neighbouring White Goat Wilderness are a remnant of what must have been large herds of caribou that moved into this area of the Rockies as the glaciers retreated twelve thousand years ago. At that time, treeline was much lower and much of the Canadian Rockies would have resembled habitat caribou occupied in the arctic.

You can often see mountain caribou on the alluvial fan at the head of Medicine Lake in the spring. Later in the summer they are up high in the alpine meadows along the Skyline Trail and in the area surrounding Maligne Pass. Mountain caribou are about the size of a mule deer but are more heavily built. Adult bulls weigh up to 120 kilograms. They are distinguishable from deer by way of a number of interesting features. Caribou are the only members of the deer family in which females have antlers. The antlers of the male are like nothing else on the planet.

All of Jasper National Park is amazing; including many of the day hikes, it offers the grand prize in wilderness travel in Jasper in the North Boundary Trail. This 179-kilometre trail begins at Celestine Lake, thirty-six kilometres north of Jasper, and ends in Mount Robson Provincial Park. The hiking options on this trail are endless. Blue Creek is one of the most interesting side trips that hikers can take on the North Boundary Trail. It allows access into the adjacent Willmore Wilderness in Alberta. Created in 1959, Willmore Wilderness Park protects 4,600 square kilometres of stunning foothill and mountain terrain. It also protects traditional packtrails that were used by Aboriginal peoples, trappers, guides and outfitters. The Wilmore is unique in that long-standing hunting and guiding traditions are still sustainably maintained within protected area boundaries. The management of the Willmore is informed by a strong local culture that holds that people should never consider themselves separate from place, a view that is changing the way we manage protected areas elsewhere in the Rockies.

THE WEST SLOPE

Flowing Toward the Pacific

13

The Roof of the Canadian Rockies
Mount Robson Provincial Park

LOCATED A HUNDRED KILOMETRES west of Jasper, Mount Robson Provincial Park is the second oldest of British Columbia's parks. At 3,954 metres, Mount Robson is the highest peak in the Canadian Rockies. The mountain is so big it creates its own weather. When it is not in cloud, it dominates the skyline.

Mount Robson Provincial Park provides everything from developed, vehicle-accessible camping to remote valleys that seldom see a human footprint. More importantly, it also protects the headwaters of the Fraser River, one of the great salmon rivers of the West and one of the few major rivers in southern Canada that has not been dammed.

Flora and fauna are typical of the wetter western-slope climate, with trees like cedar and hemlock. The park also exhibits a great deal of vertical diversity. On some trails one is able to travel between three different vegetation zones during a day hike. Over 182 species of birds have been recorded in the park. All wildlife indigenous in the Rocky Mountain can be found here. Mule and whitetail deer, moose, elk and black bears are found through the lower valleys of this 2,170-square-kilometre protected area. Higher-elevation species include the grizzly bear, mountain goat, bighorn sheep and, for the moment at least, the mountain caribou.

**MAP OF MOUNT ROBSON
PROVINCIAL PARK**
*Courtesy of Ali Buckingham,
Parks Canada.*

The human history of the park area is as interesting as its geography. Most of that history is associated with attempts to reach the daunting summit of Mount Robson. The value in looking at that history resides in the knowledge it presents of what altitude does to landscape, especially in more northerly latitudes in Canada. A vertical kilometre or two above our heads, it is possible to experience a completely different planet than the one we take for granted living in the valley floor. Mount Robson provides an object lesson in understanding the ecology of cold that defines the identity of those who live in the mountain West.

One of the most celebrated figures in the history of Jasper National Park and adjacent Mount Robson Provincial Park is Donald "Curly" Phillips who came from Ontario to live in the Rockies in 1908. The legend of Phillips begins with an odd association with an eccentric mountaineer who became the centre of a decades-long debate over who made the first ascent of Mount Robson.

George Rex Boyer Kinney was born in New Brunswick in 1872. Like his father, Kinney joined the clergy, and during temporary postings in Banff and Field he developed an interest in geology and the mountains. In 1900 he received a permanent posting in James Bay, near Victoria, B.C., and began mountaineering during his long summer vacations.

In 1907 he accompanied the brothers Arthur and Lucius Coleman to Mount Robson. The expedition was largely unsuccessful. The party, unfortunately, arrived very late in the season and was driven from the flanks of the mountain by heavy snows. Despite these hardships, Arthur Coleman made plans to return with Kinney the next year, but with an experienced outfitter and guide. The 1908 expedition set out from the Yates ranch on the west side on Lac Ste. Anne near Edmonton on August 4 and camped at the foot of the Robson Glacier on August 28. In the three weeks they spent in the cold shadow of Mount Robson, only twice were there two days in succession when the weather was good enough for climbing. But even when the weather was good, the mountain was in no condition to be climbed. In the face of these horrendous conditions, only Reverend Kinney seemed anxious to apply his energies to the

AT BERG LAKE
Because it is so close and so big, Mount Robson is difficult to photograph from Berg Lake. For those who walk the twenty or so kilometres in to the lake, the biggest reward is to simply contemplate the glory. This image suggests why many early travellers maintained that it was impossible to go to Mount Robson and not come back changed.
Photograph by Vi Sandford.

mountain. For Kinney, the summit of the highest peak in the Rockies was becoming an obsession. Kinney set out alone. Bad weather ensued. The snow-squalls became fierce tempests that nearly swept him from his footing and hid everything above, so that advance was impossible. Finally, in a howling blizzard at a point well above 10,000 feet (3,048 m) as shown by an aneroid barometer he carried, he decided that to go farther would be madness, and turned back.

Over the winter of 1908–1909, Kinney made plans to climb the mountain without the Colemans. At the same time he received word that a substantial "foreign expedition" composed of Europeans had set its sights on Mount Robson and were planning to attempt the first ascent as soon as the Alpine Club of Canada camp was completed at Lake O'Hara in the summer of 1909. A.O. Wheeler had invited to the camp some very competent members of the British Alpine Club: Arnold Mumm, scion of the famous family of Champagne makers, Leopold Amery, a Member of the British Parliament, and climber Geoffrey Hastings. Hastings had also brought along a friend, A.G. Priestly, and Mumm had furnished to backpack you can walk to Berg Lake below the towering Mount Robson in less than a day. From Berg Lake you can walk all the way back to Jasper via the North Boundary Trail. And everywhere you look there will be water or evidence of what water is and does in the headwaters of the mountain West.

Few are those who come back from such places unchanged. Local culture was defined initially in the mountain West by what experience of the peaks does to human sense of time and timelessness. Today, however, the focus of experience is gravitating toward ecosystem understanding that revolves around concerns related to how global warming will affect the high altitudes and latitudes of the world. Because they are largely defined by the alpine tundra zones that compose them, parks like Mount Assiniboine figure largely in these concerns.

MARMOTS IN THE ROCKIES: CLIMATE CHANGE EFFECTS ON NATURAL ECOSYSTEM FUNCTION

IN 2009 A NEW BOOK appeared on the subject of what was happening to nature in a warming world.[4] Written by a highly respected American scientist named Anthony Barnosky, *Heatstroke* is of particular interest to those with a passion for the natural history of the mountain West due to Barnosky's extraordinarily revealing research on climate change impacts on marmots and other high-altitude species that are common also in Mount Robson Provincial Park, and in the Canadian Rockies.

Barnosky holds that, because the species has survived many earlier changes in climate, alpine species such as the marmot are climate-change bellwethers. Fossil evidence gathered by Barnosky suggests that marmots have been part of North American mountain ecosystems for close to a million years. He observes that if there was any species that ought to be adaptable enough to persevere through climate change events it should be the marmot.

Marmots emerge from hibernation sometime in the spring, usually in April or May, just as the fat reserves laid down during the previous summer are exhausted. The environmental cue for them to come out of hibernation and leave their burrows is air temperature, which in ideal circumstances has been melting the snow outside the marmot's burrow while at the same time stimulating the growth of fresh new shoots of plants marmots thrive upon.

Barnosky's research in Colorado indicates that in 1999, marmots in Colorado were emerging from their burrows about twenty-three days

HOARY MARMOT
The delicately tuned evolutionary mechanism that has been genetically coded into the climate-control survival strategy of marmots – a mechanism that has allowed them to survive recurring ice ages and warming periods in the past – is under siege. Due to changing climate, the environmental circumstances marmots are presently experiencing are different from what they have had to face in the past. Mountains are ecological islands. To keep pace with change, marmots have no place to go but up. Some ecologists fear that marmots are going to be forced upward and northward into extinction.
Photograph by R.W. Sandford.

– the better part of a month – earlier than they were in the 1970s. Meanwhile, in Colorado at least, more winter snow is falling each year and even increasing spring temperatures cannot melt the snow fast enough to permit plant growth to occur before the marmots end their annual hibernation. Starving marmots are coming out of hibernation, finding no food, and they are dying.

As Barnosky explains, the delicately tuned evolutionary mechanism that had been genetically coded into the climate-control survival strategy of marmots – a mechanism that has allowed them to survive recurring ice ages and warming periods in the past – no longer works. The climate change circumstance marmots are presently facing is different from what has occurred in the past. This may also be the case for other hibernating animals, including bears.

Barnosky, who is a fine storyteller, introduces the reader to an Idaho hunter named Jim Martell who in April of 2006 paid fifty thousand dollars for an opportunity to shoot a polar bear on Banks Island in the Canadian central high arctic. Martell was lucky in that he spotted a bear and was able to shoot it. But when he and his guide-outfitter examined the kill they found something completely amazing. The bear he had killed had the cream-coloured fur typical of a polar bear, but it also had a hump on its back, long claws, a shallow face, and brown patches

ARTHUR PHILEMON COLEMAN

Though virtually unknown outside of mountaineering circles, A.P. Coleman explored a great deal of what is now the Canadian Rocky Mountain Parks World Heritage Site. Born in Lachute, Quebec in 1852, Coleman later became a professor of geology at the University of Toronto. An expert in glaciation, Coleman helped bring Canada into the modern world of geological thought. Coleman was also a founding member of the Alpine Club of Canada.

Photograph Courtesy of the Alpine Club of Canada.

to be transformed when he stood up before his students, who would often remember his teaching and his enthusiasm for the rest of their lives. But like many academics, teaching was only one element of Coleman's university life. It was research that inspired Coleman most. That research required time in the field. With a secure position, Dr. Coleman could at last focus his energies on expanding the field of geology in Canada. His student days were over. He had a regular job, a stable income and holidays in the summer. There was an entire country waiting to be explored – and finally with the arrival of the railway in the mountain West there was a means for exploring it.

In the years during which Coleman was a student in Germany, Canada was undergoing substantial change. The notion of a transcontinental railway had transformed the idea of nationhood. With the line finally reaching the prairies in 1882, it appeared that the Articles of Confederation, which had induced British Columbia to join Canada in 1871, were about to be fulfilled. In the summer of 1883, the tracks reached the Rockies. Coleman couldn't wait for the line to be complete. The fabled mountains of the west were calling to him. As soon as classes were over in the spring of 1884, Coleman boarded a Canadian Pacific passenger train bound for the west. It is with the account of this journey that his famous book *The Canadian Rockies: New & Old Trails* begins.

COLEMAN'S FIRST VISIT TO THE MOUNTAIN WEST, 1884

IN THE SPRING OF 1884, the rails ended west of Laggan siding, near the summit of Kicking Horse Pass. (Today Laggan is the hamlet of Lake Louise.) After a brief visit to Lake Louise, which had received its first non-Native visitor in the person of Tom Wilson only two years before, Coleman was joined by Messrs. Grier and Severin, whom he had hired at Morley. Soon their pack train was heading west into British Columbia. After reaching the Columbia River, Coleman spent three weeks exploring rugged, unnamed valleys in what is now part of western Yoho National Park before completing a big loop through the remote North Fork of the Spillimacheen River back to the Columbia.

After a brief visit with his brother Lucius, who ranched near Morley, Coleman went home to begin another academic year at the University of Toronto. Throughout the long winter he couldn't stop thinking about

FORTRESS LAKE

One of the largest natural bodies of water in the mountain West, Fortress Lake is the signature natural feature of Hamber Provincial Park. Unfortunately, few get to see this enormous lake because of its remoteness. Float plane charters take visitors to a tourist fishing camp open in summer, but for the most part Fortress Lake is as wild as it was when it was first visited by Arthur Philemon Coleman in 1892. *Photograph by R.W. Sandford.*

the mountain West. He began to read about the mountains of the west and even bought a camera in preparation for his next expedition. When classes ended in the spring of 1885, Coleman was ready to return to the Columbia River to explore the Selkirk Ranges.

COLEMAN'S SECOND VISIT TO THE MOUNTAIN WEST, 1885

BY THE TIME THE academic year came to a close in the spring of 1885, the Canadian Pacific Railway had crossed the Rockies and was reaching up into the Rogers Pass area of the Selkirks. It was possible to take the train as far west as Donald, British Columbia, a town that had sprouted up, entirely complete, in less than one year. At the end of track, Coleman once again hired his own pack train, an expensive proposition even for those days, and headed west toward the glacier-clad summits of the Selkirks.

As Coleman reports, the excursion to the goldfields was not particularly successful. Rain and delays of all kinds cut down on the actual time Coleman could commit to geological study. Coleman did conclude, however, that his visit to the placer mining operations in the Mount Sir Sandford area was interesting from a "geological as well as human side." The scientist in Coleman was fascinated by how gold could have appeared in these remote British Columbia valleys. From a human perspective, however, Coleman was appalled by what happened to these valleys once they were discovered by gold-crazed prospectors. Their invasions, Coleman wrote, were "like a bad dream." Slowly, after the departure of the miners, the bushes grew over the shacks and the creeks returned to their former channels. Only then did peace return to these valleys.

Coleman did not return to the West for three years. During this time, it is clear that he read a great deal about early exploration in the Rockies and had become anxious to put his own name on a corner of the blank map of the mountain West. It is also apparent that Coleman, like Norman Collie after him, had been tantalized by the rumour of Himalayan-sized peaks in the area of Athabasca Pass. The problem was that, though many competent explorers and surveyors had gone looking, no one could find these mountains.

IN SEARCH OF THE DAVID DOUGLAS GIANTS: A.P. COLEMAN'S THIRD EXPEDITION TO THE MOUNTAIN WEST, 1888

AS HAS ALREADY BEEN NOTED, the legend of Himalayan-sized giants at the summit of Athabasca Pass owes its existence to David Douglas. Enthusiastic and able, the young Scottish botanist had been sent by Sir William Hooker and the Royal Horticultural Society to collect plant specimens on the Pacific Coast of North America in 1824. Intending to spend only one year on the coast, the small and frail redhead developed rheumatism during the winter. Though he was certain he was going to die amid the dripping forests, he survived and, revived by the luxuriant plant life, resolved to spend two further years in Canada and make his way across the entire continent with one of the spring fur brigades.

In the spring of 1827, Douglas joined Hudson's Bay Company traders and voyageurs as they paddled their fur-laden canoes up the Columbia toward Boat Encampment at the top of the Big Bend of the river. Leaving their canoes behind, the expedition made its slow way toward Athabasca Pass, the summit spine of the continent's rivers. After exhausting himself floundering in the deep spring snow, he halted below the pass on April 30, 1827. By ten the next morning a circling raven would have found him resting at Committee's Punch Bowl, a small pool that marked the divide between the Pacific and Atlantic watersheds at the summit of the pass. His journals do not explain what compulsions led to his next actions; they only indicate the course he took in the next few hours that would become the foundation of mountaineering history in Canada for the next seventy-five years. We join Douglas as he reflects on the experiences as they were portrayed in *Botanical Magazine* published in England after his death:

> *Being well rested by 1 o'clock, I set out with the view of ascending what seemed to be the highest peak on the N. Its height does not appear to be less than 16,000 to 17,000 ft. above the level of the sea. After passing the lower ridge I came to about 1,200 feet of by far the most difficult and fatiguing walking I have ever experienced, and the utmost care was required to tread safely over the crust of snow.... The view from the summit is of too awful a cast to afford pleasure. Nothing can be seen in every direction, as far as the eye can reach, except mountains towering above each other, rugged beyond description.*[2]

Mounts Hooker and Brown were impossibly high mountains. Perhaps only Douglas's poor eyesight made it possible for him not to see that other higher mountains existed in the main ranges that surrounded Athabasca Pass. It was a great story, though, and even if it wasn't true it would later bring some important climbers and explorers to the Rockies to look for the fabled Mounts Hooker and Brown. Arthur Philemon Coleman would now join this select company.

By the time that Coleman read the story of the Athabasca Pass giants, there was already a lot of doubt about the veracity of Douglas's 1827 claim. Supported by the university's excellent library, Coleman had begun to ask some pressing questions about Douglas's story. In examining Douglas's own account, Coleman was dismayed that the great botanist had made no scientific observations to support his estimated height of Mount Brown at between 16,000 and 17,000 feet (4,877 and 5,182 m). Coleman conceded that it was possible that Douglas had calculated the heights of Hooker and Brown based on a faulty survey by Lieutenant Aermilius Simpson undertaken from Jasper House in the winter of 1825–26, which placed the altitude of Athabasca Pass at 11,000 feet (3,353 m). But even if this had been so, how could the presence of these giants have eluded later visitors to the pass? How, for example, could an artist of the stature of Paul Kane fail to notice and paint these huge peaks during his visit to the pass in 1847? Why was it that none of the highly competent surveyors in the employ of Sir Sandford Fleming's later railway survey ever mentioned high peaks in the Athabasca Pass area? The mystery of Mount Brown gave Coleman a reason for returning to the Rockies.

BY HORSE TO ATHABASCA PASS: A.P. COLEMAN'S FOURTH
EXPEDITION TO THE MOUNTAIN WEST, 1892

ADMITTING THAT HIS 1888 attempt to reach Athabasca Pass by canoe from the west was a fiasco, Coleman grew more and more eager to come to close quarters with the Douglas giants. Though not fond of horses, Coleman realized his only hope of reaching Athabasca Pass and solving the mystery of Douglas's giants lay in a horse expedition that would approach the pass from the east. "If the camel is the 'ship of the desert,'" he concluded, "the cayuse should be the 'canoe of the mountains.'"[3]

Coleman's 1892 horse trip to Athabasca Pass was an ambitious and well-planned expedition. As he, his brother and three friends would be travelling extensively through the Native hunting grounds, Coleman also hired two Stoneys, Mark Two-Young-Men and Jimmy Jacob, as guides.

Departing on the evening of July 6th, 1892, the large expedition set out from Morley for Athabasca Pass by way of the Ghost and Red Deer rivers to Mountain Park. Throughout this part of the journey, Coleman continued to remark on the sedimentary geology that was exposed on each peak they passed. They then followed the Clearwater and White Rabbit valleys to the upper reaches of the North Saskatchewan River. Ten days after departing, they arrived at the Kootenay Plains. Long a meeting place of Native peoples, the Kootenay Plains remain a place where there is grass for horses, clear water and good hunting. It is the kind of place that deserves to be added to the Canadian Rocky Mountain Parks World Heritage Site. Certainly, Coleman was impressed:

> The Kootenay Plains were once in a small way the high-road of nations, and full of picturesque life, when the Kootenay tribe from southern British Columbia came across Howse Pass at one of the head streams of the Saskatchewan to hunt the buffalo and trade horses with the Stonies. That traffic ended many years ago, and Howse Pass is now seldom crossed by white men and never by the Indians; but the plains are still lively once a year when the Stonies come north from Morley before scattering into their special hunting grounds.[4]

As Jacob had little experience beyond these sacred plains, the expedition now had to rely on Two-Young-Men to guide them north to the Brazeau River by way of the Cataract River. On August 1, more than three weeks after setting out, the party camped near the forks of the Brazeau where Coleman and a fellow professor from the University of Toronto, L.B. Stewart, made the first ascent of a small and as yet unnamed mountain, their third ascent on the expedition. Though the

peak was insignificant in height compared with the much taller mountains along the Great Divide, Coleman observed that he could see "a spotless dome of snow twenty or twenty-five miles away." This, he surmised, upon reflection later in his life, was probably the Dome shown on Norman Collie's map as the central point of the Columbia Icefield. The inference here is important. What Coleman is telling us is that he likely saw the Columbia Icefield a full six years before it was formally discovered by Norman Collie and Hermann Woolley in 1898. Coleman and

After passing Sunwapta and Athabasca Falls, the Coleman party went on to Jasper, where they met Lewis Swift, the legendary prospector and explorer who lived at a farm on the Athabasca River. After procuring supplies from Swift, Coleman wasted three days scrambling through the wrong valley looking for the Whirlpool River. On the second day of their journey up the Whirlpool, a sharp sapling drove through Coleman's stirrup right into his horse's side. In the ensuing melee, Coleman smashed into a tree and was thrown from the saddle. The next day his left knee hurt so badly that he could only walk with the aid of crutches. It was the end of climbing on this expedition – and for many years after. Though in excruciating pain, Coleman did not want to abandon the expedition so close to its goal. On August 18, 1893, Coleman and his party at last reached the Committee's Punch Bowl and the summit of Athabasca Pass. They looked everywhere but there were no giants.

Even though it was clear that Coleman had solved the mystery of Mount Hooker and Mount Brown, not everyone was willing to accept that Himalayan-sized giants could not exist in the Rockies. When the celebrated British climber John Norman Collie was invited to the Rockies four years later to make the first ascent of Mount Lefroy, he used his visit to Lake Louise as an opportunity to search to the north for Douglas's fabled giants. Years after Coleman had proved Douglas a fraud, Collie still questioned aloud if Coleman hadn't reached the wrong pass and whether further explorations weren't warranted to validate Douglas's claim. Gentlemen, and especially English gentlemen, didn't lie. Finally Collie, writing in 1903, vindicated Coleman:

> If Douglas climbed a seventeen-thousand-feet peak alone on a May afternoon, when the snow must have been pretty deep on the ground, all one can say is that he must have been an uncommonly active person. What, of course, he really did was to ascend the Mount Brown of Professor Coleman, which is about nine thousand feet high. These two fabulous Titans, therefore, which for nearly seventy years have been masquerading as the monarchs of the Canadian Rockies, must now be finally deposed.[11]

Coleman made many other trips to the Rockies and was later instrumental in the creation of the Alpine Club of Canada. His most recognized exploration achievement, however, remains his discovery of Fortress Lake.

Standing on the shores of Fortress Lake you can still feel Coleman's presence. The lake has changed little if at all since he first visited it and one cannot escape the feeling that the wild mountains that surround the sparkling water still harbour the ghosts of Hooker and Brown.

15

The Geography of Wonder

Yoho National Park

FOR THE CREE, "YOHO!" was an expression of profoundest awe. Suggesting the sacred and the mysterious, *Yoho* was first applied by the Cree to those rare and powerful natural places that could induce a mind-slowing sense of aesthetic arrest. *Yoho* is a word describing reverence tinged with fear inspired by the sublime. In its simplest contemporary translation, *Yoho* means wonder. The name Yoho was applied first to the river and then to the valley through which the river runs, and later applied to the national park as a whole.

Yoho became a national park in 1886. On the official maps of the Rocky Mountain National Parks, Yoho is a small, irregular diamond tucked between Banff National Park on the east and Kootenay National Park on the south.

As has been explained, Dr. James Hector of the Palliser Expedition certainly had his problems here. It was August of 1858. After a year of travelling across Canada, Hector was well accustomed to long days in the saddle in unfamiliar country, and was looking forward to the new discoveries he was going to make in what were locally called the Shining Mountains. As planned, the other members of the Palliser party had already set out on separate, independent expeditions looking for new build a national railway, it could too. The building of Canada's first national railway was as much a political coup as it was a feat of remarkable engineering. The history of Yoho National Park is inextricably linked to this history.

At Confederation, settlement was concentrated in Upper Canada in Ontario and Quebec; the only other large concentration of people was along the Pacific coast, where most trade was with the western United States. To achieve greatness, Central Canada had to embrace the west coast by way of the almost limitless lands that formed the interior of the continent. Four years after Confederation, the Dominion of Canada made a rash promise to the Colony of British Columbia, offering a railway in exchange for political union. The area that is now Yoho played a huge role in this story and if you don't get off the highway or away from the train tracks in this national park, it would be easy to think that what we built here is more important than what we saved. In Yoho, however, both matter to our history and our future.

SURVEYING THE WONDER

THE BUILDERS OF CANADA'S national railway knew where they wanted to go, but they didn't know what lay between them and their goal. In April 1871 an engineer named Sandford Fleming was hired to solve the problem of locating the railway over its nearly six-thousand-kilometre route across Canada. A number of very proficient surveyors were assigned to the Rockies. Since Kicking Horse Pass had already been noted and mapped by James Hector, surveying efforts by Walter Moberly and others were concentrated on other sections of the Great Divide. Their efforts were halted by a scandal in 1873 that led to the fall of the country's Conservative government under John A. Macdonald. Once in power, the Liberals, under Alexander Mackenzie, put a temporary halt to the railway.

Surveying in Western Canada continued sporadically throughout the next five years. During that time, British Columbia became restless over the Dominion's lack of progress toward the fulfillment of its promise and threatened to leave Confederation. By 1878, however, Macdonald's Conservatives were back in power and the dream of a railway once again gathered steam. A new syndicate was established, arguments over where the Pacific terminus would be located were finally resolved, and as the railway began to snake westward from Montreal, contracts were let to begin laying the rails inland from the Pacific toward the

Great Divide. It did not seem to matter that a route across the prairies
and through the Rockies had yet to be firmly chosen; the Great Railway
had finally been started and the rest would take care of itself.

Uncertainty over which pass the railway should use in the Rockies
was complicated by a number of factors. Although Yellowhead Pass was
the preferred route of Sir Sandford Fleming, it was argued that a line that
far north of the international border would require more trackage and
would therefore be more expensive to build. A more southerly route
would not only cost less but might also open up the Canadian prairies
for agricultural development. When the decision was made to lay the
track in the south, two obstacles remained. No known route existed
through the Selkirks and an acceptable pass through the Rockies had yet
to be identified. The responsibility of solving these two problems was
given to an American engineer named Albert Bowman Rogers.

THE BISHOP OF BLUE THUNDER

MAJOR A.B. ROGERS WAS born in Orleans, Massachusetts, on May 28,
1829. A Yale graduate, Rogers quickly developed a reputation as both
an outrageous character and one of the best railway and civil engineers on the continent. While working on the Erie Canal, the Chicago,

Milwaukee and St. Paul, and a number of other, lesser railway projects, Rogers mastered most of the obscenities in the English language. By the time he went to work for the Canadian Pacific in 1880, Rogers was already well-known by the nickname of "the Bishop." He also possessed a respected reputation for almost superhuman physical endurance.

Many of Rogers's explorations followed leads on potential routes left behind by earlier surveying parties. Following an eagle up a remote valley on the western edge of the Selkirk Mountains in 1865, Walter Moberly had discovered Eagle Pass. In the spring of 1881, Rogers advanced past Eagle Pass to the head of the valley and, by way of a fork that Moberly had not visited, discovered the glacial headwaters of the Illecillewaet River. There he was certain he had found the pass through the Selkirks that was the key to southern route of the railway. Now that Rogers Pass had been discovered, it would not take long to pick a logical route through the Rockies, the next and last mountain obstacle in British Columbia. But Rogers had only travelled to the west side of his pass and did not know what its descent would be like. Rogers charged himself with further investigation and rushed back to the Rockies to organize the tracing of the rail route east from the Great Plains to the Great Divide and over Kicking Horse Pass, which had scarcely been examined since James Hector last saw it in September of 1858. In so doing, the Bishop would come into contact with a man who could see past his gruff facade and to the sincerity and kindness that were at the centre of Rogers's being. That man was Tom Wilson. This quiet cowboy would put the next grand human stamp on Yoho.

Tom Wilson began his career in the West as an officer in the service of the North-West Mounted Police at Fort Walsh in the Northwest Territory. Thinking a change of career would suit him, Wilson hired on at Fort Benton, Montana, to assist in surveying a route through the Rockies. In 1881 found himself employed as a packer by P.K. Hyndman, Chief Engineer for Major A.B. Rogers, Engineer-in-Charge of the Mountain Section of the Canadian Pacific Railway.

On July 5, 1881, Wilson departed Fort Calgary as part of a large movement of supplies, including eighty packhorses to freight supplies into the mountains. The party was to await Major Rogers on the Bow River at the entrance to the Rockies. Wilson did not have to wait long to meet the great engineer, and when he met him, he understood immediately what kind of work it was going to take to make this railway plan work. Tom Wilson did not leave behind extensive journals. What he wrote about A.B. Rogers, however, is pure Canadiana. His accounts also tell us that travel in Yoho had not become any safer since James Hector had travelled there twenty-three years before:

> On the 15th of July I had strolled a short distance west of the camp and was sitting smoking alongside the narrow Indian trail when suddenly a mottled roan cayuse, carrying a rider, appeared round a curve. Behind it came two packhorses then two other animals ridden by Shuswap Indians. The leader, whom I instantly sensed was Major Rogers, wore an old white helmet and a brown canvas suit. His condition, well, dirty doesn't begin to describe it.
>
> His voluminous sideburns waved like flags in a breeze; his piercing eyes seemed to look at and see through everything at once. I had heard that Major Rogers was famous for his tobacco chewing ability and may have doubted the stories I had heard. Such doubts, if I had any, were dispelled during the first few minutes I was with him. Every few minutes a stream of tobacco juice erupted from between his sideburns; I'll bet there were not many trees alongside the trail that had escaped his deadly tobacco juice aim.
>
> Someone once said of him, "Give him six plugs of chewing tobacco and five bacon rinds, and he will travel for two weeks." The man who said that was no exaggerator. Despite his fifty-odd years he leapt from his horse in a manner that many a younger man could have envied.[2]

When Wilson met the famous surveyor, Major Rogers was accompanied by his twenty-one-year-old nephew, A.L. Rogers, better known as "Al," who had travelled from St. Paul to meet his uncle in Kamloops, B.C., where the Hudson's Bay Company had a trading post. Rogers arranged for his nephew to begin exploration of Kicking Horse Pass from the west while he rounded to begin an assault from the east.

The party, with Wilson included, worked its way slowly up the Bow River Valley toward the Great Divide. In his gruff way Rogers was living up to his reputation. The men were already complaining. Only Tom Wilson sympathized with Rogers:

> [Major Rogers] called for a volunteer to accompany him and act as his special attendant. Silence greeted his request; there were good reasons for it. Every man present had learned in three days to hate the Major with a real hatred. He had no mercy on horses or men; he had none on himself. The labourers hated him for the way he drove them and the packers, for the way he abused the horses; he never gave their needs a thought. When no one volunteered I thought I might as well take a chance and so took him up.[3]

This invitation from Rogers was, in fact, an invitation to become part of history. There were a good dozen other men there who could have easily decided to participate in the discovery of many of the most significant natural features the Rockies, but they simply hated Rogers too much to do so.

Wilson knew that James Hector had not travelled the entire length of the Kicking Horse. Hector had come upon the Kicking Horse River by way of the Beaverfoot, thereby missing the section of the river between Wapta Falls and the Columbia where it enters Kicking Horse Canyon, a long, deep, sunless gorge where even Native peoples declined to travel. During the summer of 1881, Wilson discovered why the two European parties that travelled through the valley of the Kicking Horse had both suffered from starvation and acute exhaustion. This was difficult country to explore. There were dues to be paid before the landscape would reveal its greater splendour – and Wilson did not mind paying them.

TOM WILSON FINDS EMERALD LAKE

FOR WILSON, THE SUMMER of 1882 began in much the same way as the previous summer. He began ferrying loads of equipment and supplies from Padmore, now called Kananaskis, to Rogers's main surveying camp at the summit of Kicking Horse Pass. While returning from his second trip for supplies, Wilson camped at the junction of the Pipestone River and the Bow. The next day, a small band of Stoneys camped at the same site. It was raining and soon everyone was gathered around a big fire. In the mist they heard the thunder of avalanches falling from above. One of the Stoneys in the party indicated to Wilson that the thunder was coming from "snow mountains above the lake of the little fishes." The following morning, Wilson invited the man to take him to the lake. They had little trouble reaching it by horse. Wilson named the stunning sheet of water Emerald Lake, and it appeared as such on the first geological map made of the area, drawn by George Dawson. Before the map was published in 1886, the Geographical Society of Canada had changed the name to Lake Louise, in honour of Princess Louise Caroline Alberta, the fourth daughter of Queen Victoria. By the time the map was published, however, Wilson had already found another Emerald Lake, in Yoho.

The day after first visiting Lake Louise, Wilson ran into Major Rogers, who, as Wilson's story goes, made a prophetic announcement about Wilson's future in the mountains, an announcement that has been made for more than a century since to those who have been captured by the mountains: "'Blue', he roared, 'I knew you'd be back. I knew you'd be back. You'll never leave these mountains again as long as you live. They've got you now.'"[4]

MOUNT STEPHEN
Mount Stephen towers over the town of Field, the administrative centre of Yoho National Park. It was named for George Stephen who became the President of the Bank of Montreal in 1876. The mountain was first climbed by surveyor J.J. McArthur in 1892. *Photograph by R.W. Sandford.*

It did not take long for Rogers to confide to Wilson his growing doubts about what route the railway should take through the Rockies. Rogers was now more certain than ever that Rogers Pass was the right route through the Selkirks, but he did not know whether Howse Pass or Kicking Horse Pass was the most economical route over the Great Divide. Rogers wanted more information about the Howse area and offered Wilson a fifty-dollar bonus if he would go to Howse Pass to get it. Since a lone, lightly equipped traveller could move with greater speed, Wilson agreed to go alone and on foot.

Although the going was harder than Rogers had predicted, Wilson encountered few problems on his journey up the Bow River and down the north side of Bow Pass to the Saskatchewan River and the mouth of the Howse. He got lost a few times on the ascent of the pass, but his problems did not really begin until he began his descent from the Great Divide into the valley of the Blaeberry River. The deadfall was nearly three metres deep and his progress slow and exhausting. Rogers had predicted that the journey would be brief, so Wilson only carried food for ten days; by the time he reached the Blaeberry he was starving. He soon became so weakened that he doubted he could make it to

Cline had a special trail cut up the Maligne River to Maligne Lake, over Cataract Pass, then down what is known today as Cline River, to the big plains of the Saskatchewan. There he met the Kootenays and Shuswaps with his packtrain of trade goods and received from them their furs, etc. in exchange. That annual trade meeting gave the locality the name Kootenay Plains, a name that has often puzzled people when trying to discover its origin.

The Kootenays and Shuswaps had many enemies therefore, when setting out for their annual trade, they dared not leave their families and chattels to fall prey to those enemies. A whole tribe with its belongings travelled until well on the route, then encamped their families, old men and extra horses, in "hidden valleys" to await the braves' return from the Kootenay Plains. This system of trade ceased during the early 70's and was followed by the British Columbia Indians and the Stonies paying alternate annual visits to each other for the purposes of feasting, dancing and trading.

EMERALD LAKE
Another of the startlingly beautiful places in Yoho is Emerald Lake. With Mount Burgess as a backdrop, Emerald Lake ranks as one of the most spectacular places in the entire Canadian Rocky Mountain Parks World Heritage Site. Visitors can look up from the lakeshore and see where the famous Burgess Shale is being quarried for its amazing fossils.
Photograph by R.W. Sandford.

Some of the horses that we had purchased from the Stonies carried Kootenay or Shuswap brands; they proved that the Stonies had obtained the horses from their original owners at some of the annual festive-trading meets. It was evident that the pasture where I found them was one of the B.C. Indians' "hidden valleys" and the natural conclusion was that one, if not more of our horses had, when belonging to Shuswap or Kootenay, been left there for safety. While hunting food in the Kicking Horse sloughs, the horses had remembered the good feed in the "hidden valley" and with unerring instinct had led the rest of the bunch to there. That is the conclusion I arrived at and, right or wrong, it is certain that the incident resulted in the discovery of Emerald Lake.[7]

After confessing that Indian horses knew the local geography better than visiting European explorers, Wilson stayed in the Kananaskis area that winter instead of heading south. In the spring of 1883, Wilson returned to the summit of Kicking Horse Pass. The railway was advancing rapidly past Maple Creek in Saskatchewan and was expected to reach Calgary in the summer. By the end of the season, after further doubts about the superiority of Kicking Horse Pass over Howse Pass were finally resolved, the steel advanced as far as Silver City, below Castle Mountain. The next season the tracks would reach the Great Divide and cross Kicking Horse Pass into British Columbia.

Tom Wilson's surveying work with the railway came to an end. He became a prospector and later joined the Steele Scouts and fought in the Riel Rebellion. At the conclusion of his military service, Wilson returned to Morley to visit friends. While he was there a train arrived and a conductor who knew him asked if he was coming along on the ride to Craigellachie to watch the driving of the last spike. After the ceremony, Wilson shook hands and bade Major Rogers a fond farewell.

"Tom," the Major said, "One day we'll take a holiday and ride ocean to ocean on this railroad."[8] But Wilson never saw Rogers again. While working with the Great Northern Railway in the Coeur d'Alene Mountains in Idaho in 1889, Rogers fell from a horse and in May of that year, died from his injuries. Just as Rogers had predicted, Tom Wilson went on to live in the mountains for the rest of his life. In time, he became the most famous outfitter and guide in the Rockies, the man to see if you wanted access to the wonder of the western wilderness.

OVERCOMING OBSTACLES

YOHO'S LATER HUMAN HISTORY is tied directly to the railway and the problem of the steep descent from Kicking Horse Pass into the valley below. By the fall of 1883, the tracks had been laid from the east as far as the approach to Kicking Horse Pass. From the west the tracks had been advanced as far as the western slopes of the Gold Range. Less than three hundred kilometres of railroad remained to be built between the two advancing lines of Canada's national railway. That relatively short section would take two years to build. There were a number of serious obstacles. On the western side of the Selkirks there was Notch Hill, Eagle Pass, and finally the spine of the Selkirks at Rogers Pass. Along the Great Divide was the difficult passage down the west side of Kicking Horse Pass, as well as the gorge of Kicking Horse Canyon farther west.

Work on the railway was slow to begin in that wet spring of 1884. Deep snow lingered long into the spring, making work difficult and dangerous. By May 25, the tracks at last crested the divide, a cause for some celebration. The steep descent down the pass delayed further progress until July. After tote roads were built, the grading slowly continued in advance of the laying of the track. Deciding that the originally surveyed route would take years to build, the contracting company proposed constructing a "temporary" line that would descend from the summit of the pass to the valley floor at twice the slope proposed by Rogers and Hurd. Critics of the plan argued that such a slope would make the Kicking Horse Pass section of the Canadian Pacific Railway the steepest main line in the western hemisphere.

Undaunted as ever, William Van Horne arrived on the scene to survey the problem. After much analysis, Van Horne argued that the cost of maintaining special locomotives for a short, steep push up the pass made for less expense and delay than a slow, more gradual climb up a lesser grade. Van Horne's argument pivoted around the idea that the construction of a temporary line could permit the Canadian Pacific a number of years in which to observe weather patterns, stream flows, glacial activity, and the frequency of avalanches before a final decision about the route needed to be made. The fact of the matter was that the railway could afford to do little else. The "Big Hill" was part of the political cost of moving the main line 250 kilometres south from Yellowhead Pass to be closer to the American border. At this crucial stage in the railway's construction, the cost of reducing the grade at the Great Divide was beyond the means of the railway because it was beyond the means of the nation.

The entire Big Hill project was labour-intensive. The line required continuous maintenance, as did the pusher trains and the standard locomotives that pulled the regular service trains. It was clear that a railway service centre was going to be necessary to keep the Big Hill open even in summer. A small yard and engine facility was laid out on the valley floor at the foot of Mount Stephen, and a stone roundhouse was constructed to service the locomotives. For a number of months this burgeoning community was simply called Third Siding. In December 1884, Donald Smith, the railway syndicate's great financier, came to the end of the tracks. A few months earlier he had encouraged Cyrus West Field, a wealthy Chicago businessman and the promoter of the first Atlantic communications cable, to come and see the potential of the railway for himself. In an attempt to persuade Field to invest in the financially troubled railway, Smith, with a sweep of his hand, named the little railway community and the mountain across the valley from it in Field's honour. Despite the honour, Field did not commit any money to the venture. The little town grew anyway.

GRAVE OF AN UNKNOWN RAILWAY WORKER
Though no one knows the exact number, it is thought that a railway worker died for each mile of track laid through the mountains of the Canadian West. Many of these workers were Chinese. A quietly maintained grave marker at the summit of Kicking Horse Pass commemorates those who lost their lives supporting their families and dreaming of a better life in Canada.
Photograph by R.W. Sandford.

In 1884, a 4.5 percent railway grade was a serious matter. Steam locomotives going up such hills had to be full of water to prevent their boilers from exploding, and even a passenger train of only a few cars would need pusher engines to help it up the Big Hill. Such a steep grade also pushed contemporary brake technology to its very limits. To prevent runaways on the Big Hill, three runaway tracks were built. The switches leading to the runaway lanes were always open. Every train had to come to a complete stop above of each switch before it would be turned to allow the train to continue downhill. As early Big Hill railroader Roxy Hamilton commented, there was a big difference of opinion as to how well this system worked. He argued that the first siding saved some trains because at that point on the descent the downward speed was not great enough to make the siding impossible to take: "As for the other two, about all you did was to pile up a train in the siding instead of down the mountain."[9]

The Big Hill saved money and time, but at the expense of overall safety. There were some terrible wrecks. Early in 1884, a construction train steamed out of Hector, near the top of Kicking Horse Pass pulling flatcars loaded with heavy bridge timbers. One hundred and twenty men were on board. Suddenly the train began to pick up speed. With brake shoes screaming, the train began to thunder down the grade. Men started jumping for their lives. The train reached nearly 130 kilometres an hour before it telescoped into a mountainside, where the huge

square kilometres (828.5 square miles) and its name was changed to Yoho National Park. In 1902, architect Francis Rattenbury designed a massive expansion to the hotel. Mount Stephen House became a luxurious and elegant entranceway to the glorious scenery of the Rockies. Emerald Lake Lodge also opened for business in 1902.

Located between Banff National Park with its famous hot springs and the dramatic scenery of Rogers Pass, Yoho was in the very centre of what the railway promoted as the Canadian Alps. The Canadian Pacific compressed all the ranges of mountains in the west into "Fifty Switzerlands in One; a mountain playground for the world." Mount Stephen House would soon become one of the earliest centres of alpinism in Canada's mountain West and would remain so for more than fifty years.

SENSE OF PLACE IN A MOUNTAIN TOWN

FIELD IS THE CAPITAL of Yoho National Park. It is a real place in that to live there one must make ritual and actual sacrifices to survive and to be worthy of the honour of living in one of the world's most remarkable places. We arrived there to live in May. Most of the snow had disappeared in town but still lingered in deep drifts in the trees that rose like green surf up the nearly vertical walls of the surrounding mountains. The dark, just-thawed earth smelled of mud, grass and pine needles. The potholes in the dirt streets were filled with still brown water that reflected the bruised blue of the sky. It was silent save for the rising and falling thrum of the traffic on the Trans-Canada Highway across the river.

We had been warned about Field. Field distinguishes itself from other mountain towns by the fact that due to its location tight in the valley at the headwaters of the Kicking Horse River it can be a difficult place in which to live. In the other mountain park towns there is plenty to do if you do not like to hike, climb or ski. Life in Field, however, demands that one really does love the mountains. The landscape demands nothing less of you.

Living in Field is like living in the bottom of the Grand Canyon. It is two kilometres, more than a vertical mile, from the river that slides along the bottom of the valley to the summits of the peaks that loom over the town. We moved into an old saltbox next to the train tracks. Without the need of binoculars we could sit on the front porch and watch mountain goats as they picked their way along ledges on the cliffs of Mount Burgess. The mountains were a presence one could not escape. They exerted themselves on the imagination even in darkness

WINTER IN YOHO
You have to love the mountains if you want to experience Yoho year-round. Because its valleys are so deep, places like Field can be gloomy in winter. Heavy snowfalls also create high avalanche hazards in most years. However, the light regime improves late in winter, creating the backcountry skiing conditions that are a growing part of the Yoho legend.
Photograph by R.W. Sandford.

or when they were obscured in storm.

In summer it rained. In winter it snowed and snowed and snowed. There were often blizzards called Yoho Blows that buried our one-storey house in drifted snow. The very harshness of the country could get to you, and if it didn't, the highway would. Driving in and out of the valley, locals faced two serious hazards. Ice, snow, avalanche, and mud- and rockslides constituted one hazard. The most serious hazard was other drivers. Most Fielders had either seen a fatal highway crash or had had a life-threatening experience of their own on the Trans-Canada. The highway and all its terrors were part of life in the mountains and part of living in Yoho. So it was that people came and went from this town, staying as long as it took to solidify a job with the government or the railway and leaving when the weather, the isolation, or the highway made living in Field unbearable. The people who stayed were invariably characters – dyed-in-the-wool mountain people.

When I moved to Field I did not have all the life skills needed to live successfully there. I was taught a great deal by my neighbours who, I discovered later, had viewed me as something of a rehabilitation project. Under their guidance I learned to clean a chimney, shovel a roof and even fell a tree if need be. Though at no point was I ever beyond accidentally throwing a log through the back window of my pickup truck, I gradually became accomplished enough to cut my own firewood. Although none of my neighbours ever liked to watch me split this wood, I was slowly accepted into the community of Field. Over the time it took to accomplish this, I gradually realized that many of my attitudes and much of the behaviour of locals had in some subtle way been shaped by the mountains around them. This, I discovered, had even begun to happen to me.

Given time, the mountains shape us. Native North Americans know that. All the old-time park wardens understood this fact. So did early horse guides and packers. In Field we were all subjects of the weather and the season. Even our moods were shaped by the kinds of clouds that obscured the narrow slit of sky above the town. Houses in Field were

After World War II, Italian immigrants came to Canada in large numbers. Many found work with the Canadian Pacific Railway. Grandma Colonna was the matriarch of one of the large Italian families that has defined the friendly and neighbourly character of the town of Field for more than two generations.
Photograph by R.W. Sandford.

small so that they would be easier and cheaper to heat. Almost all of them had wood heaters to augment propane furnaces. Since fuel was very expensive, people put on more clothes when it got cold, rather than just turning up the heat. There was no such thing as fashion in Field. Everyone wore roughly the same kinds of wool shirts, winter jackets and boots, warm hats and gloves, often even in summer. The same practical attitude applied to transportation. Very few people in Field bought expensive, luxurious cars. A practical vehicle bought at a reasonable price was a sign of common sense. I remember being teased relentlessly for buying a two-year-old station wagon because, well, it was simply too new.

The object of these compromises was to allow you to create a self-reinforcing lifestyle. Living in Field could be relatively cheap if you adopted a simple way of life. The less it cost to live, the more time you had to travel in the mountains inside and outside of the park. The more places you visited, the more the country could grow in you. The more the country grew in you, the fewer your material needs and the more simply you could live. It was a way of living that fed positively upon itself.

There were a good number of locals who had mastered this mountain way of life. They lived simply but very elegantly. They read widely in winter and walked or biked or climbed just as widely in summer. They had time for the country and the country had time for them. Unlike harried visitors who raised their frustrated fists to the wet skies, locals seldom got very excited about the weather. There were always just enough clear and perfect days to travel in, and if there weren't, you just dressed for the rain. It was with this enlightenment that my inquiry after wonder, which is the foundation of this book, began.

Although it was easy to see who had mastered a simple way of life, it was more difficult to measure how many any of my neighbours had been affected by the wonder that is the basis of the park's name and spirit. It is my experience that a deep, carefully nurtured appreciation of place is not something worn as a badge. It is not a degree you can get or a trophy you can win. Nor is it something you can directly ask about. For the people I met in Field who most certainly had a keenly developed relationship with the landscape, sense of place expressed itself more as an attitude than a habit. There was in Field, while we lived there, for example, a park warden named Glen Brook who had developed a remarkable sense of place a good forty years before I met him. The wonder he possessed manifested itself quietly in a keen naturalist's eye, an almost photographic knowledge of the park's backcountry and a gentleness and unselfish charm that easily made him the town's most respected local. His wife, Irene, had the same charm. Their wrangler friend Slim Haugen had it, too – a timeless, fluid grace instilled by a lifetime of exposure to the land.

Gordon Rutherford, another park warden who was born and raised in Field, had this same gentleness and profound sense of place. He, too, possessed an astounding memory of important things that had happened, it seemed, on every peak and in every valley in the park. In explaining the history of Yoho, Rutherford was simply retelling the events of his life as it had unfolded among these peaks. This was also true for Bev, his wife. Randall Robertson, who had spent most of his working life in Yoho, had the same easy grace. So did Sid Brook and his brother Alex. So did Men Camastral. So do Pierre Lemire and forty others who lived in that small town. Each of these people in their own way demonstrated that sense of place is a form of grace. It is a way of refining yourself by giving yourself up to the land in which you live.

I also learned in Yoho that a deep sense of place can only be acquired in increments. To truly see wonder in any place, one has to experience it through the seasons, through years of subtle learning that comes only from cumulative observation. One has to bathe in the country, in its spring creeks, in its summer lakes, in its autumn larches and in the howling winds of its bitter winters. The legend and legacy of a place like Yoho are derived only partly from the rock walls and the waterfalls. The ways of properly and fully experiencing the country are passed on from generation to generation by those who have known and cared about where they lived. If there is wonder in Yoho, it is in part because people put it there. As the poet Sid Marty once said, these mountains are special because those who have lived in them have made them so and because they would not have them any other way. Our lives are shaped and given value by our experience of place. "It is wonderful," the Native peoples proclaimed. Yoho, the name for wonder.

WONDER CONCENTRATED: LAKE O'HARA

THERE ARE A HANDFUL of places in the Canadian West where time and rock and water come together in such profoundly pleasing and overwhelming ways that one cannot spend an hour in the presence of such concentrated wonder without being overcome by awe and reverence for the world that preceded ours. Lake O'Hara is one such place.

Although the main peaks of the Great Divide were explored from the east by way of Lake Louise much earlier, one of Yoho's special delights, Lake O'Hara, was not "discovered" by Europeans until James Joseph McArthur found his way to it via Cataract Creek in the summer of 1890. The lake was later named for retired Colonel Robert O'Hara, who was among the earliest visitors to the lake. During his surveying explorations, J.J. McArthur also crossed a nearby pass and climbed into the amphitheatre occupied by the lake that was eventually to bear his name.

When people say that they have been to Lake O'Hara they could mean a number of things. They could mean that they rode the bus from the parking lot at the junction of Highway 1A and the Trans-Canada near the Great Divide up the twelve kilometres of gravel and potholes following Cataract Brook to the lake to visit the lodge that sits on its shore. Here one may spend hours just taking in the view of the dazzling teal-green lake, which in mornings and evenings is often still enough to reflect Mounts Victoria and Lefroy, the giants on the boundary separating British Columbia from Alberta. Together these two towering peaks form the back wall of a great stone bowl, with Seven Veil Falls spilling over it to form the lake.

But what locals call "O'Hara" encompasses more than just the lake. Lake O'Hara is wonder concentrated. It is the gentle trail that circles the lake. It is also the steep switchbacks that lead up to grand views at Wiwaxy Gap. Wiwaxy Gap is the starting point for an even greater adventure, for here begins the mountaineering route up the Huber Ledges to the west shoulder of Mount Victoria. "Lake O'Hara" is also the elegant, moderately graded stone walkway past rumbling waterfalls and a series of tiny lakelets to Lake Oesa. Due to its high altitude, Lake Oesa used to be covered with ice well into the summer. "Lake O'Hara" also includes the high alpine route from Oesa over the impressive ledges on the shoulder of Mount Yukness to Opabin Lake and the Opabin Plateau. At the head of the Opabin Plateau is the alpine route to Opabin Pass, a glacier-shrouded shoulder from which mountaineers make their way down to the Eagle's Aerie and up Wenkchemna Pass to Moraine Lake in Banff National Park.

"O'Hara" is much more than even the remarkable stillness of Opabin Lake set ablaze in the oblique light with the green fire of spring larches. Yet another trail leads, again by way of carefully laid flagstones, to the lip of the plateau. From a viewpoint on this lip, known as Opabin

LAKE O'HARA
There are places in the Canadian Rockies where time and rock and water come together in such profoundly overwhelming ways that one cannot spend an hour in the presence of such concentrated wonder without being overcome by awe. Lake O'Hara is one of those places. *Photograph by R.W. Sandford.*

Prospect, one can see that there are other lakes in the upper Cataract Brook valley other than Lake O'Hara. A whole other domain can be seen to the west. Odaray Plateau is a great swatch of larch that glows faint green in the spring, then burns yellow-gold where touched by the frost in the fall. In a small meadow in the midst of this larch forest is a small cabin that belongs to the Alpine Club of Canada. Constructed in 1919 and named for the feisty co-founder of the club, this famous log cabin is known as Elizabeth Parker Hut. It is from this hut that generations of Canadians and their guests have explored and been transformed by the glory of Lake O'Hara.

A trail wanders past Elizabeth Parker Hut and then forks south toward McArthur Pass and west toward the head of Odaray Plateau. The McArthur Pass trail is also considered part of the Lake O'Hara area. Past the hut, the trail winds through the wildflowers and huge larches and past a line of shallow pools, before climbing gently to the boulder-strewn pass. From the summit of the pass the trail forks again. One fork leads down McArthur Creek into some of Yoho's wildest backcountry, an area often closed to visitors. The other fork leads upward through some interesting cliff bands to the lip of a cirque that cradles Lake

McArthur, easily one of the most beautiful places on all of the West Slope of the Canadian Rocky Mountain Parks World Heritage Site.

THE CANADIAN YOSEMITE

IT ONLY TAKES ONE VISIT to Lake O'Hara and the Yoho Valley to know that the natural history of Yoho National Park is fundamentally about water. Due to its spectacular waterfalls, roaring rivers and the concentrated abundance of ice-and-water shaped features, it is often referred to as our "Canadian Yosemite."

Glaciers and icefields form Yoho's northeast boundary, which it shares with Banff. In this area, amidst the Waputik Mountains, lie the Waputik and Wapta Icefields. *Waputik* is a Stoney word meaning mountain goat. It is out of this icefield that the Daly Glacier flows. The Daly Glacier and nearby Mount Daly were named in 1916 by the American climber Charles Fay for his friend Joseph Francis Daley, who had served as President of the American Geographical Society in New York. Melt from the Daly forms Takakkaw Falls, the second highest waterfall in Canada. *Takakkaw* is another Native expression of wonderment. It was how the Cree said, "Wow!"

Yoho National Park is roughly divided into three geographical regions. Forested valley floors at the lowest altitudes comprise a little less than half of the park's 1,313 square kilometres, or 507 square miles. Large mountain regions composed mostly of bare, frost-shattered rock comprise another half. It is in this domain of high plateaus of accumulating icefield snows and living but rapidly shrinking glaciers that the water of the West accumulates as snow each winter. The presence of glacier ice, the altitude and relief of the peaks, the proximity of the continental divide and the number of watercourses draining the area imply regular precipitation in summer and heavy snow in winter. Yoho contains a total of ten completely pristine rivers which all feed into the Kicking Horse River. What we saved in Yoho was one of the most important watersheds in British Columbia.

THE BURGESS SHALE AND YOHO

CAMBRIAN, ORDOVICIAN, Silurian, Devonian, Mississippian, Pennsylvanian, Permian. Campbell's Ordinary Soup Does Make Peter Pale. I am sitting in the famous Truffle Pigs Restaurant in Field, trying to use Stephen Jay Gould's mnemonic device for remembering the geological periods of the Paleozoic Epoch of the earth's history.[11] It is 2002, the International Year of Mountains, and I have returned to the town of Field to take a course offered by the Yoho-Burgess Shale Foundation on the most famous fossils in the world. Over a quiet lunch, I am beginning to make sense of Gould's geological soup. Campbell's Ordinary Soup Does Make Peter Pale.

The Burgess Shale course is offered that year in the Yoho Brothers Trading Post. A number of national institutions are working to create a major centre around the UNESCO Nations World Heritage Site on the slopes between Mount Field and Mount Wapta, high above town. A freight train rumbling through town reminds me it was here that Charles Doolittle Walcott discovered these remarkably complete Cambrian-era fossils at roughly the same time as the Spiral Tunnels were completed on the Big Hill up Kicking Horse Pass in 1909.

The course was taught by Dr. Desmond Collins of the Royal Ontario Museum. Between 1972 and 1992, Dr. Collins spent ten field seasons in the Burgess Shale. As Dr. Collins was a world expert on these fossils and on life in the Cambrian seas, it was not surprising that people from all over Western Canada came to Field to hear him speak, and to join his field trips to the quarry he and his students were excavating in the Burgess Shale.

The lecture began with lots of coffee and a detailed introduction to the fossil discoveries made in Yoho National Park. Collins recounted that during the construction of Mount Stephen House in Field in 1886, one of the construction workers went prospecting on Mount Stephen and returned with what he called "stone bugs" trapped in the rock. He showed them to surveyor Otto Klotz, who later showed them to geologist R.G. McConnell of the Geological Survey of Canada and to State of Michigan geologist Karl Rominger, who published the first descriptions of these ancient life forms in a technical journal in 1887. Charles Walcott, who was an unschooled but avid collector of fossils, read Rominger's article. In 1907, Walcott, who had advanced to the prestigious position of Secretary of the Smithsonian in Washington, D.C., came to Yoho to collect some of the stone-frozen creatures that had been discovered on the slopes of Mount Stephen just above Field. While he was in Field, Arthur Wheeler, the President of the Alpine Club of Canada, invited Walcott to write an article on his finds. In 1909, Walcott and his wife Helen came to the Rockies on a working holiday. While traversing the trail across Mount Wapta, they discovered a second great fossil bed now known as the Burgess Shale.

Collins identified Walcott's major fossil discoveries and traced the interpretation of these discoveries through much upheaval of thought to the present. He then subtly placed before his audience a professional point of view about the significance of the fossils based on his own work. It soon became clear that his considered analysis of the importance of the Burgess Shale was at some variance with the interpretations of Stephen Jay Gould in his book *Wonderful Life: The Burgess Shale and the Nature of History*. Lively debate ensued on the subject. Collins then concluded his lecture with Gould's major point about the importance of the Burgess fossils to our understanding of evolution. Gould was right, according to Collins, in that contingency or accident was a powerful evolutionary force.

The Burgess Shale tells us that evolution did not cascade toward the perfection of humans, but toward any channel it could. History may well be contingent upon itself rather than subject to any formal laws of nature. We are, as Gould explains, in awe of these "grubby little creatures of a seafloor 530 million years old." We are in awe because they are the Old Ones and they are trying to tell us something.[12] It was only an accident of contingency that humans evolved. The "stone bugs" of the Burgess Shale have dethroned us from the centre of meaning in the world. Like the Chicxulub Crater in the Yucatan created by the meteorite that likely destroyed the dinosaurs, these fossils teach us that evolution is not simply progress, but the constant adaptation to circumstance and change. As Gould went on to explain in the book he finished just before he died in 2002, the emergence of *Homo sapiens* as a small population in Africa some 200,000 years ago cannot be explained meaningfully without emphasizing the formative role of contingencies that, in principle, do not flow predictably from the laws of nature.[13] Chance plays a huge role in nature, which suggests that human actions matter. This is a fact we need to bear constantly and positively in mind as we work to preserve and enhance the mutual relationship between and landscape and culture that makes living in, and visiting, the Rocky Mountains so worthwhile.

16

The Road to Radium
Kootenay National Park

FOR MOST PEOPLE, VISITORS and locals alike, 1,406-square-kilometre Kootenay National Park is defined not by what we saved but by what we built. The best-known feature in Kootenay is the 94-kilometre-long highway that slices right through its heart. Highway 93 branches off the Trans-Canada and enters the headwaters of the Kootenay River at Vermilion Pass, where it crosses the Great Divide into British Columbia. After tracing the footsteps of James Hector to and along the Kootenay River, the blacktop then cuts up Sinclair Pass and right through Sinclair Canyon to Radium and the Columbia River. Many Albertans, in their great hurry to reach their condominiums in Invermere and Fairmont Hot Springs, have to a large extent lost their capacity to see anything of interest in the landscape blur that separates them from all their weekend fun. It is a perfect place, therefore, to contemplate how the automobile has shaped our experience of the mountain West, and how it threatens the very experiences it made accessible. Only by understanding the impact of the automobile in our national parks can we save ourselves from negative effects of its impacts.

MAP OF KOOTENAY NATIONAL PARK
Courtesy of Ali Buckingham, Parks Canada.

THE ROLE OF THE ROAD IN LANDSCAPE PERCEPTION

IT IS VERY DIFFICULT to imagine today the impact that the automobile had on the way of life enjoyed in the Canadian West in the nineteenth century. The automobile was perfected at about the same time the Prairie provinces were created, and it soon affected almost every aspect of the developing economy and society in the West. The car almost instantly increased individual mobility and became closely associated with status. It defined fashion. It increased social mobility and opportunity. It reformed the experience of travel and refigured rural life. The automobile stimulated the migration of farm families to cities, which in turn were transformed by their need to accommodate this new and highly demanding transportation technology.

The car had huge impacts on urban design, architecture and community. The automobile created a petroleum industry in the Canadian West and linked it to a consumer-based economy. It revolutionized the delivery of goods and services and accelerated our way of life. No other modern technology has so defined who and what we are. To understand the magnitude of these impacts, we have to know what our culture was like before the car.

Before the car, there was the train. Before the train, there was the horse. Before the horse, people travelled on foot in the Canadian West. For perhaps fourteen thousand years, walking was the only mode of travel. Confronted with the immense scale of the West, the limitations of foot travel are obvious. It is slow. The limit of what you can own is defined by how much you can carry. The limits of your carrying capacity then become limits to the complexity of the society you can create. Simple societies are often small. While travelling on foot allowed one to experience landscape more intimately, this means of travel ultimately limited one's sense of place. It was hard to appreciate where you were, because there was no way to leave it so that it could be witnessed comparatively from without.

The horse appeared in the Canadian West in about 1730. The horse accelerated First Nations way of life and tied people into other advances

EARLY CAR TRAVEL
Kootenay National Park was, in effect, created around a vision of a road that would permit the use of the revolutionary new technology of the automobile to transport people from Banff to Radium Hot Springs and on to Windermere. Here we see an early Ford Model T at Sinclair Canyon just north of Radium, just after the road was finished in 1923.
Photograph from the Byron Harmon Collection, courtesy of the Whyte Museum of the Canadian Rockies, Banff, Alberta.

that would eventually alter their way of life forever. One of those advances was the train. The age of the train was heralded as the new Age of Speed. The earliest steam locomotives were capable of smooth travel at over thirty miles per hour (more than forty-eight kilometres per hour). A whole new geometry created itself around the train and the level track it rode upon. The train had a profound capacity to move materials and people. Communities grew up around the tracks. Within only two years of the completion of the Canadian Pacific Railway in 1885, an entire new, non-native material culture was transported and then deposited in the West. Instead of following the sinuous paths of rivers, the train cut straight lines through the West. Through the establishment of regular schedules, the train brought time into play. It was the advent of public transit. Just as the horse had done, it made us dependent upon it and tied us into further technological innovations that would further accelerate our way of life in its wake.

The scientific and manufacturing breakthroughs that permitted the widespread application of train technology were a product of a larger industrial revolution that swept the globe. These breakthroughs included revolutions in the understanding of metallurgy, the wide-spread availability of rubber and glass, a new understanding of how to create and control electricity, and the birth of the internal combustion engine. Invention fed upon invention. It was only a matter of time before the mass production technology and affordable distribution would lead to a self-propelled vehicle that would replace the horse as a means of personal transport.

Because they are directly linked to patents, the steps toward the invention and perfection of the automobile have been well documented.[1] The first internal combustion gasoline engines appeared in Europe as early as 1860. A four-cylinder engine was invented by Nicholas Otto in 1878. In 1885, a German engineer named Carl Benz created the first commercially feasible vehicle, a 0.8 horsepower tricycle car. There was an explosion in interest in development of the new technology. The first front-mounted engines appeared in 1890. Shortly after, car racing became a popular means of drawing public attention to the new technology as it was tested and improved in demanding driving situations on early tracks and roads.

By 1905, the year the provinces of Alberta and Saskatchewan came into existence, the automobile industry even in Canada was well enough established to offer reliable and affordable cars to the public. Soon Henry Ford's assembly line technology dramatically reduced the cost of a car and democratized its use. But creating a car was one thing; operating it was quite another. An entirely new infrastructure was required to fuel, service and repair this exciting new technology. Then, there was the problem of roads. In understanding the huge impact of the automobile on the horse-driven society that preceded it, one must appreciate the importance of roads to settlement and commerce in the prairie and mountain West.

As historian John Nicks reported, there was no such thing as public works in the West before 1870. Rivers were the primary transportation routes. Except in the mountains, where formal routes had been established and marked to prevent travellers from losing their way among the peaks, the few trails that existed on the prairies led to the easiest and safest river fords. As fur trade posts were established, trails between centres began to be cleared and maintained.

When missionaries began to establish permanent settlements, trail networks emerged to connect them. By the mid-nineteenth century, many of the early trails were maintained to a level that would allow regular passage in dry weather by horse-drawn carts and wagons. With the formal passage of these lands from the hands of the Hudson's Bay Company to the Dominion of Canada in 1870, responsibility for maintenance of these primitive roads fell to the federal government and its territorial administrations.

The primitive nature of road development in the West was put into relief in 1874 with the arrival of the North West Mounted Police. By the time the main force arrived in southern Alberta, it had left behind a trail of crippled and dead horses, oxen, abandoned carts and footsore Mounties. A second troop with a larger number of wagons followed the "well-established" Carlton Trail but found the conditions along it so difficult that they had to virtually remake the road in order to pass over it.

Steps to improve trails had to wait ten more years until 1884, when major routes in the West were designated as public highways and orders were given by the Department of the Interior for them to be surveyed with the right of way to be vested with the Crown. This did not mean,

SINCLAIR CANYON
Sinclair Canyon is a great
slit composed of bright red
rock, through which the
traveller gains both physical
and ceremonial access to the
Columbia River Valley. The
Columbia is the Great River of
the West in North American
historical mythology.
Photograph by R.W. Sandford.

however, that the roads were to be improved. Any construction, J.S. Dennis reported in 1898, tended to be "of a light and inexpensive character suited to the then sparsely settled condition of the country."[2]

With the exception of a few steel spans over the larger, permanent watercourses, road improvements in the pre-automobile days were generally limited to wooden bridges, bridge and ferry approaches, a few culverts, stretches of log corduroy through boggy areas, and occasional grade improvements on steep hills. Road improvements during this time were paid for through set allocations assigned to each electoral division. The work was usually carried out by local contractors using their own primitive equipment.

As settlement advanced, villages appeared along the CPR tracks in newly opened agricultural areas. As these villages grew into towns, local government expanded the basis upon which public works could be funded and carried out. As agricultural development intensified and expanded, the need for better roads for farmers to carry their products to market became apparent and electoral districts began to take over responsibility for their own road systems. The work was usually low-cost and the quality marginal due to inadequate supervision over the design and execution of projects.

A major change in government structure in 1897 created a Federal Department of Public Works that was directly responsible for the construction and maintenance of roads and bridges in what was then the North West Territory. The latest earth-moving equipment was purchased and road building began slowly but in earnest in the West.

When Alberta became a province in 1905, all government functions including road building and maintenance were transferred to new provincial departments. The new Alberta Department of Public Works took on the responsibility for the construction and improvement of main roads while secondary roads became the responsibility of local improvement districts. These districts were often small and poorly funded. Many of these districts allowed local farmers to work on roads in lieu of paying taxes, which meant that little was done in spring and fall when it was most needed.

Such was the environment the automobile entered when it suddenly became a viable means of transportation. The train was still the principal means of transportation and distribution. There were few roads, even fewer good roads and the population of the west was too low to support accelerated road development. This, however, did not stop a growing number of enthusiasts from pursuing their interests in better roads.

KEEPING THE CAR OUT OF THE NATIONAL PARKS

THOUGH SOME DISPUTE the claim because the vehicle used the train track and not a road, the first automobile is said to have arrived in the Rockies in the summer of 1904. Its arrival in Banff was not met with enthusiasm. Even the least environmentally-conscious local residents expressed fears of the impact of the automobile on game animals and on the wagon roads that had been developed around the town. These arguments were, of course, simply convenient excuses for resisting new technology. Under pressure from local liverymen, outfitters, hoteliers and the railway, the government passed an order-in-council in 1905 prohibiting the use of automobiles of any kind in the park.

The banning of automobiles from national parks, however, did nothing to stop their westward advance. In 1907, construction began on the Banff Coach road from Calgary and, when it was finished in 1909, the first cars started to arrive in numbers in Banff. On August 14, 1909, Norman Lougheed, uncle of a later premier, and a party of young friends made the first run over the route in a big touring car belonging to his father. Lougheed and his pals made the trip in just nine hours, with only one flat tire. No mention was made of whether they broke any laws in entering Banff.

In the face of the growing popularity and efficiency of the automobile, Ottawa brooded and then, two years later, ruled in favour of the car. In the summer of 1913, locals were disturbed by the news that the government had suddenly permitted automobiles to travel on all of the town's streets and to the Banff Springs Hotel. In 1914 automobiles were allowed to travel anywhere in the park, except to the Upper Hot Springs and on Tunnel Mountain.

THE FIRST AUTO CLUBS

TO DRIVE A CAR IN THE early years, you needed to have a great deal of money, be mechanically inclined and enthusiastic and adaptable enough in your interests to put up with the "new-fangled contraptions" that passed as early cars. Since mud holes, breakdowns and flat tires were common, you also needed the help of like-minded others to keep from being stranded. Driving meant that you belonged to a fraternity that shared the spirit of a new age. Motor enthusiasts gathered into groups for sport and then kept together to apply political pressure for new roads.

Early auto clubs were informally organized and seldom lasted more than a summer. The reason for this was that "automobiling" was a seasonal activity not unlike "snowmobiling" is today. Nor should it be perceived that everyone was in love with the car. Despite the boosters who owned a growing number of dealerships and car enthusiasts who often joined auto clubs, there were many Westerners who resisted this new technology. Some of the resistance came from institutionalized interests such as the railway and horse-based businesses. There was also resistance from those who thought automobile ownership was simply an amusement of the moneyed classes. There were others, however, who had begun to envision the impact the automobile might have on their lives. Some did not like what they saw.

The pushy way in which the Calgary Automobile Club had invaded places like Banff did not win a lot of friends. Many felt that the impacts of this new technology ought to have been examined more fully before motorists were offered carte blanche access to all the special places that were formerly the exclusive domain of hikers and horsemen.

The car also began to threaten the way of life in one of the province's founding cultures. In March of 1912, a car full of Calgary automobile lovers, out for a night spin across the foothills, was attacked by a pack of what historian Tony Cashman described as "hootin' shootin' cowboys." The cowpokes apparently appeared suddenly out of the darkness with guns blasting. They shot a hole through the roof of the iron invader, and then raced their horses away over the foothills on which horses had once been supreme.

Despite antipathy toward the automobile among circles of people who couldn't afford them or who had affection for horses, there was no denying that those who owned cars were enjoying them. There was something about the noise and power and speed of the car that was instantly intoxicating. It was fun to ride in one and a thrill to drive – provided, of course, there was a road to drive on. Alberta automotive interests persisted and it soon became clear they wouldn't be satisfied with a road that ended in Banff. What they really wanted was a road that went to Radium and then south into the United States.

The first challenge to ensuring proper road development in Canada was jurisdictional. As is often the case in Canada, there was a lively argument over whether road construction and maintenance were provincial or federal responsibility. Influential politicians, including William Lyon Mackenzie King, held that road construction was a pro-vincial matter. There were many who held that promoting the interest of the car-owner was one thing, and that promoting good roads was another and somewhat larger but separate matter. It became obvious that interests had to unite in order to resolve these issues.

Despite the outbreak of the World War I, in 1916 another four thou-sand cars hit the road in Alberta. A few trucks also appeared. The coal mines of the Drumheller valley were booming with war orders. It was said of Drumheller that the mines there depended on the Three Ms: men, mules and Model Ts. The tribute to the Model T was an appre-ciation of its ability to "skitter" up the steep mine roads even in wet weather. The car was beginning to prove itself as a practical, working technology.

By 1919, there were thirty-four thousand motor vehicles in Alberta. That same year, the federal government passed the Canada Highways Act, which made $20 million available to the provinces for cost-shared road building projects. Auto clubs across the country and the Cana-dian Automobile Association supported the idea of main highways. A concept known as the King's International Highway proposed that a road from Montreal to Vancouver be identified and improved. This route was to be known as the King's Canadian Highway as soon as the governments of Ontario and British Columbia were able to build enough roads north of the border to contain the highway within Cana-dian boundaries. In 1920, the Vancouver Auto Club sponsored a trip by its president, Percy Gomery, to demonstrate that it was possible to drive

HIGHWAY 93 TODAY
Today the Banff-Radium road is a modern highway along which today's travellers can move at a speed incomprehensible to early motorists. While the highway offers convenience and quick access from Calgary and Banff to the Columbia Valley, motorists do not always appreciate they are in a national park, which results in high wildlife mortality and diminished appreciation of a globally significant resource. *Photograph by R.W. Sandford.*

a car from Montreal to Vancouver in thirty days, averaging nine hours a day at the wheel. The King's International Highway concept would eventually become our first truly national road, the Trans-Canada Highway. But long before the Trans-Canada, the Rockies were first traversed by the Banff-Windermere Highway through Kootenay National Park, the park the federal government got not for a song, but for a road.

THE BANFF-WINDERMERE HIGHWAY

UNTIL THE END OF World War I, almost all traffic in the Columbia River Valley followed the Canadian Pacific Railway line connecting Golden to the Crowsnest by way of the Columbia River Trench. Well before the war, local Columbia Valley businessmen had already begun to press for direct highway connections to the trade centres of Banff and Calgary. The idea was also put forward that a highway that went directly north from Radium would open up a burgeoning automobile tourism market in the United States. The attraction for Canadians driving south and Americans driving north would of course be Radium Hot Springs. Construction started on the road in 1911, but was stalled by the war and provincial funding limitations. Post-war federal support for highway development, however, reignited enthusiasm for the road. In exchange for federal support for the road, the province of British Columbia gave up five miles (about eight kilometres) of mountain landscapes on either side of the right-of-way to federal government in support of the creation of a national park. In retrospect this was a good deal for everyone. The mountain West got its first highway across the Rocky Mountains and in 1920 the people of Canada got a stunningly beautiful national park that provided a crucial ecological link between Yoho and Mount Assiniboine Provincial Park. This link was not created, however, without costs.

THE AUTOMOBILE TODAY

THE AUTOMOBILE CAUSED and continues to cause a lot of problems, especially in and around our national parks. With the advent of the automobile, people began for the first time to feel safe, comfortable and superior around bears. This made people bold. They also carried food, which in turn made bears bold. This mutual boldness led to some ridiculous and dangerous situations. With the creation of what is affectionately known today as the "bear jam," locals and visitors alike competed with each other to publicly demonstrate how thoughtless they could be around wild animals. The consequences were manifold and continue to plague us decades later.

The automobile is by far the most dangerous thing that exists in our mountain national parks. Its toll on wildlife is astounding. Speed and comfort are often the enemy of experience and respect for place. Yet what we saved still has the potential to inspire a different way of thinking about the highway route to Radium.

Kootenay National Park is every bit as amazing and possesses as many remarkable features as other mountain national parks. Kootenay is the only national park in this country in which one can find both cactus and glaciers.[3] But you have to work to see extraordinary features like Helmet Falls, Floe Lake and the Great Rockwall because they are only accessible by trail. Though you can drive to popular Radium Hot Springs, you have to walk uphill to Tumbling Glacier and Kindersley Pass. It is a long haul up the Kaufmann Creek Valley to Fay Hut. Only a committed few experience these marvels. Most will be satisfied with a drive through Kootenay National Park on Highway 93, which is beautiful enough to make it a contender as one of the most spectacular drives in the world. It is a drive that parallels some of most important watercourses in British Columbia before converging upon the Great River of the West.

RADIUM HOT SPRINGS
In the late nineteenth century, when hot baths were still considered by many to be a luxury, hot springs were natural bath houses where you didn't need to heat your own water. They were also held to be of great therapeutic value, especially for those with arthritic and related complaints. Because of its stunning setting and wonderfully warm waters, Radium Hot Springs remains one of the most popular attractions in the Canadian Rocky Mountain Parks World Heritage Site.
Photograph by R.W. Sandford.

I HAVE ALWAYS HAD the same feeling crossing Vermilion Pass in Kootenay National Park as I have when crossing Kicking Horse Pass into Yoho, but once again it took decades before I understood why the sense of destination was the same even though the passes feel so very different. The similarity between the two passes resides in the fact that both lead essentially to the same extraordinary geophysical feature. Though it is so immense and manifests itself in many different ways in response to altitude and latitude, it is the feature that essentially defines sense of place between the continental divide of the Rocky Mountains and the Coast Ranges in this part of the North American West. That feature, of course, is the Columbia River.

The difference in "feel" between the two main passes through the Rockies in Canada resides less in their topography and history than in the fact that each accesses the Columbia Basin at a different point along the course of the great river. These points are different enough in character that it takes a number of visits or even an extended stay in the basin itself to discover that both of these mountain regions are in fact but different expressions of the same great watershed.

As the route parallels one of the Columbia's greatest tributaries, the Kootenay, before dropping like a stone into the Columbia River Valley, the road to Radium provides the traveller with a particularly engaging sense that there is something monumental just beyond, the scale of the landscape that one can't quite grasp. It happens often that visitors pass over the divide and right through the entire basin fully cognizant that there is something utterly stupendous they are feeling but unable to ground their awe in any one feature that would permit them to articulate the overwhelming nature of place in any satisfactory way. Not only is the scale of the Columbia Basin simply to large to grasp as a feature in itself, the great river expresses itself in far too many ways – from the bold exclamation of water and ice-carved mountain peaks, immense forests and the course of the great river itself, to the subtle nuances of the unique species of wildflowers that grow right up to the edge of the road.

While the great basin continues to repeat its story over the ages, we are able to catch only a few phrases in that telling. We can tell from what we see through the windshield that it is an epic tale, as old perhaps as the earth itself, and we'd love to hear more but we just don't have time. As a result we aren't able to connect the part of the story we hear when we cross Vermilion Pass with the part of the story we hear when we reach the Columbia Valley. The story of the Columbia River below Vermilion Pass is one of origins, of the birth of the great river's tributaries; it is the story of the lake at its headwaters, of two hundred kilometres of wetlands, and of the tales water tells in the making of river.

But there is another reason travellers have difficulty comprehending the Columbia River story. The parts of the epic explained by the upper reaches that contribute to the great river have been told in the same way and in the same language for ten thousand years. That language is stone, receding ice and running water. But now we speak a new dialect composed of a whole new vocabulary of roads and rails, ranches and farms, mines, mills and towns. We have almost forgotten our mother tongue. Fortunately, the words that came into existence at the beginning of the world are still spoken in Kootenay National Park. The language of water is one of the things we saved.

THE ROAD TO RADIUM

THOUGH OUR PROTECTED area networks are not presently taking full advantage of growing national interest in water resources, there is no reason why that could not change very quickly in service of the common good. The headwaters that is the Rocky Mountains is a vast and relatively wild domain in which only a single agency has jurisdiction over both land use and watershed management. Imagine that: one agency responsible for both water resources and land use. It is a model situation, really. This is what the rest of the world is trying to work back toward.

It has been widely identified that in the face of a growing global water crisis, what we need in this country is a new water ethic that harmonizes federal and provincial water resource management aspirations under a multi-disciplinary scientific umbrella. Under the aegis of such an ethic, we need to ensure formal representation for the environment itself and ways to advocate for nature's own need for water. This will perpetuate bio-diversity and ecosystem productivity, which are central to long-term perpetuation of favourable hydrological circumstances in the Canadian West. Some think that such an ethic could direct us toward everything else we need to do, including addressing climate change and achieving sustainability.

Such an ethic can be born here in the western mountain parks. To create this ethic, however, there are things we need to know that only

THE VERENDRYE FIRE OF 2003
A series of lightning strikes in Kootenay National Park in 2003 started a huge fire in very dry conditions, which burned a significant area of the Vermilion and Kootenay River Valleys. The fire came very close to burning down historic Kootenay Park Lodge.
Photograph by Gord Irwin.

science can tell us. We know the hydrology of the mountain West is on the move, and that long before global warming takes out our glaciers it will play havoc with snow pack and snow cover and in so doing profoundly change the amount and timing of water availability. From this we recognize an obvious and immediate need for additional monitoring and interpretation of expanded hydro-meteorological data, for enhanced understanding of present and future surface and groundwater flow regimes, and support for aquatic ecosystem research, especially at higher altitudes. We need to further develop techniques that will allow us to more effectively predict and act upon landscape and climate change effects on mountain ecosystems and western water availability. Two avenues are worthy of exploration in this domain.

Firstly it is important to acknowledge the role of upland lakes, wetlands, forests and rivers in capturing and slowly releasing water, as a foundation of downstream water supply security and human settlement stability. It is important to remember, however, that natural and aquatic ecosystems do not exist just to supply and purify water for human use. Natural systems perform many other functions, and when natural ecosystems are diminished or disappear these functions have to be reproduced or enhanced elsewhere if our planetary life-support system is to continuing functioning in the manner on which we have come to rely. If eco-hydrological research tells us anything it is that that is clearly not happening, which makes what we do in upland protected areas even more important.

Secondly, we must never forget also that water is married to its diametric and symbolic opposite, fire. The story of fire is well told on the road to Radium. Fire doesn't just affect forests, it also affects how much water forests can hold and release over time. Water is one of the most important and least appreciated forest products.

We need to know much more about the relationship between insect pests, fire and water, especially in our mountain park headwaters. These are exactly the things we are studying in Kootenay. In this resides huge opportunity. If the national park model of integrated watershed management could be perfected and then expanded outward from our protected headwaters, and applied downstream, the West of the future would be a very different place. Not only would we be able to assure a more reliable water supply and temper the impacts of climate change, the national park integrated watershed management example could become a foundation for a truly sustainable Western Canadian society.

A second great public policy achievement in the West could be built upon the first. We have created the Canadian Rocky Mountain Parks World Heritage Site, now let's use it to demonstrate to the world how we can follow the water in our rivers and lakes back to the headwaters of our history.

From there we can identify that point in time where we made a wrong turn, in terms of taking the importance of our water resources for granted. From there we can correct that mistake and start again downstream from these mountains toward sustainability. Through persistent and thoughtful interpretation and communication there is no reason such a process could not begin on the road to Radium.

Matterhorn of the Rockies

Mount Assiniboine Provincial Park

ON A CLEAR DAY, FROM A HIGH PASS or ridge, one can see 3,618 metre Mount Assiniboine from a hundred kilometres away. It stands sharply and easily recognizable above all the peaks in the southern Rockies. Its remoteness, sheer size, and imposing steepness have made it a place to which hikers and climbers have made pilgrimages since Europeans first came to these mountains. Even today, a visitor to the Rockies is not considered serious within devout mountain circles unless he or she has visited this mountain.

It seems that a disproportionate number of "power places" can be found on the West Slope of the Mountain Parks. We have already described Lake O'Hara. Tucked beneath the Great Divide separating Alberta from British Columbia, Lake O'Hara is the centre of a grand landscape that radiates outward from its shores to create a mountain paradise defined by common rock types, still reflections of enormous peaks which en masse shape uniquely local weather patterns that are expressed in a remarkable local vegetation complex. All of these features are presided over by the known presence of grizzly bears, which provides an added dimension of the sublime to walking through the high meadows at the base of the mountain. The combination of these

MAP OF MOUNT ASSINIBOINE PROVINCIAL PARK
Courtesy of Ali Buckingham, Parks Canada.

features imbues this concentrated area with signature qualities. Lake O'Hara, quite literally, feels like and smells like no other place in the Rocky Mountains.

Sense of place is defined differently at Mount Assiniboine than in surrounding parks. Though the peaks around it are tall and spectacular, its alpine meadows and turquoise lakes are as perfect as in any in the Rockies, and the presence of the great bear ensures that visitors here are kept at the same heightened level of awareness as they are at Lake O'Hara. All of these elements are eclipsed by the overwhelming presence a single imposing wonder – the mountain itself. This great stone tower completely dominates the surrounding landscape. Even when unseen in darkness or in storm, this peak exerts a powerful, sometimes terrible presence that can overpower the perceptions of those who stand beneath its sheer walls. The staggering scale of this mountain makes it difficult to comprehend its full physical and aesthetic dimensions or to represent them in word or image.

Archaeological evidence indicates that the first people to visit and frequent the mountain were the Ktunaxa, who lived on the west side of the continental divide. Although there is no proof that Native peoples lived year round near this particular landmark, they would have seen it regularly as they made their way across passes connecting to trading partners on the Great Plains. Because it was a difficult mountain to miss, early explorers did not fail to note the wind-strafed pyramid even if they didn't visit it. Later, more experienced travellers remarked on the similarity between its imposing bulk and the dominating shape of the Matterhorn in the Alps.

The first man to record seeing the mountain was Father De Smet who crossed White Man's Pass in 1845. On his primitive map he marked a big pyramid that in all likelihood was seen from the summit of the pass. In 1884, George Dawson, the genius who headed the Geological Survey of Canada, was working in the eastern part of the Rockies. He recorded seeing the glistening wedge from the summit of Copper Mountain near Banff. In 1885, it was he who gave the mountain its present name. He named it for the Stoney people, a group of Plains Sioux who migrated

REFLECTING ON MOUNT ASSINIBOINE
Archaeological evidence indicates that the first people to visit the mountain were the Ktunaxa peoples who lived in the Columbia River Valley. Later visitors remarked on the similarity between its imposing bulk and the shape of the Matterhorn in the Alps in Europe.
Photograph by R.W. Sandford.

into the eastern Rockies once they became equestrian. It was a practice of this tribe to boil their food, including meat. This they did by dropping hot rocks into water-filled skin bags sunken into hollows in the earth. The people were originally called Stone-Boilers, but this name was shortened to Stoney. Their own name for the tribe, however, was Assiniboine.

Due to the size of the mountain, it is not surprising the European sense of place in the Mount Assiniboine area was first established by mountaineers. The first recorded formal expedition that actually went to the mountain was led by Tom Wilson, the famous Banff horse guide and outfitter credited with being the first European to see both Lake Louise and Emerald Lake. His client was one Robert L. Barrett, a Chicago paper manufacturer and business magnate with a mad desire to climb mountains for sport. In 1893 he and Wilson, with George Fear as cook, rode from the Sunshine area in what is now Banff National Park, with the hope that Barrett would have an opportunity to attempt the big peak from a camp below the face. The season was late, however, and Barrett never got his chance at the mountain.

The first attempt to actually climb Mount Assiniboine took place in the summer of 1899. The expedition was ostensibly led by American Walter Wilcox and included Henry Bryant and Louis Steele. The party left Banff on July 22 with a complete outfit but no climbing guide. They took a route proposed by Tom Wilson that followed Healy Creek to the Sunshine area and over Citadel Pass. Beleaguered by a snowstorm, they camped below Mount Assiniboine at a site Wilcox recognized from his first visit to the mountain in 1895. While Wilcox went back to retrieve a rucksack that had fallen from one of the horses, Bryant and Steele tried to scale the mountain. In 1899 the glacier that pours down the north side of the mountain was much longer than it is today, reaching almost all the way to Lake Magog. The two climbers used this ramp to gain access to the snowfield above. Though the snow conditions made progress slow, the two reached the 3,000 metre mark on the mountain before they were forced back by the advance of yet another storm. Despite a minor accident on the descent, the two made it safely back to the lake where they camped for four days waiting for conditions to improve. During this time Wilcox made many of his famous early photographs of the lake and surrounding panoramas – photographs that are still inspiring. No further progress, however, was made on climbing the mountain during that trip.

The following year another attempt was made on Assiniboine by two amateur climbers from Chicago. Turned back from the summit by the first vertical cliff bands, the brothers Willoughby and English Walling appear to have made something of a mess of the whole affair. Their defeat was made even more ignominious when they lost their way on the trip back from the mountain. If anything, their expedition is notable only for the fact that theirs was the first to use Swiss guides in an attempt on Mount Assiniboine.

A few failures on a large mountain, in the eyes of the mountaineering community at least, can add immeasurably to that mountain's reputation. Mount Assiniboine, it appeared, was a major challenge and the first to climb it would be worthy of laurels and high public praise. It was clear also that the mountain would not be impossible. Quite simply, it would be conquered by the first person to arrive at the mountain when it was in good condition with enough supplies to make a prolonged push for the summit. To this end, expeditions became increasingly secretive. In a very quiet way, a race was on for the peak.

In the busy 1901 season Wilcox and Bryant were back again, this time with professional Swiss guides. They made a very determined effort to climb the mountain from the southwest but the conditions were not right. It was late in the season and first rain then snow greeted them as they approached the peak. Though they reached the highest point yet attained on the mountain, the expedition was driven back by avalanches and bitter cold. Wilcox was greatly disappointed.

Word quickly got out about the latest failed attempt on the "Canadian Matterhorn." The failure of the Wilcox expedition was analyzed in detail among climbers camped in the Rockies that summer. It just so happened that 1901 was a big year for Canadian climbing. That summer the Canadian Pacific Railway brought to the Rockies none other than the "Prince of Mountaineers" himself, Sir Edward Whymper. Whymper had made the first ascent of the real Matterhorn in 1865. Surely – to be consistent with his great accomplishments in the Alps – the famous climber would be after the summit prize on Mount Assiniboine. As fate would have it, though, the sixty-two-year-old Whymper had no intention of risking his fame and his life on a mountain he was not sure he could climb.

James Outram heard about Wilcox's unsuccessful attempt while visiting Whymper in the Yoho Valley. Outram's interest in Assiniboine was doubtless fuelled by a promise made by his outfitter, Bill Peyto, who claimed he could get Outram's expedition to the foot of the mountain in only two days. They set out from Banff on August 31, 1901, and true to his word, Peyto had the Outram party at the base of the mountain on the evening of the second day. On September 2, Outram's party tried from the southwest and failed. The weather was clear the next day and, making use of a cache established in their previous attempt, they made for the peak from the south arête. Spending nearly two glorious hours on the summit, they descended by the north face, traversing the mountain as they returned to camp. They broke camp the next day and headed slowly back to Banff. Another storm struck the mountain as they did so, forcing them to plod through heavy snow. The day they had chosen to climb may have been the only window.

The first ascent by a woman took place in 1904, when Gertrude Benham, a famous English climber, made the ascent with two local

The mountain itself is so big
it influences local weather.
Weather fronts from the
Pacific coast and Great Plains
often collide around Mount
Assiniboine, making it one
of the stormiest areas of
the Rockies. Local weather
changes by the minute.
Visitors can often feel the
tensions between opposing
weather fronts.
Photograph by R.W. Sandford.

guides. Though many other expeditions would come to the mountains
seeking ever more challenging routes, the reputation of the Assiniboine
area in the 1920s was established, not by climbers per se, but by walking
tours offered by Arthur Wheeler. These great loop trips took enthusiasts
on long outings in the very best country in the Rockies. Assiniboine was
one of his most popular destinations. As it happened, one of Canada's
famous mountaineering accidents occurred on one of these walking
tours. It was an accident that explains a great deal about the nature and
character of Mount Assiniboine and why it is regarded as an almost
mythical feature in the mountain West.

THE AGONY OF MRS. STONE

IN 1921 CONRAD KAIN WAS invited to accompany Winthrop and
Margaret Stone on one of Arthur Wheeler's celebrated Walking Tours
to Mount Assiniboine. Kain's relationship with the Stones began at the
Alpine Club Camp's Mount Robson camp in 1913. By the time the Stones
had reached Mount Assiniboine in July of 1921, Winthrop considered
himself an expert climber who no longer needed a professional guide
to make his way successfully to the summits of his alpine ambition. The

Stones had already been to the Assiniboine area with the ACC in 1920 and were anxious to set out for their own adventure. They very much wanted to "crown a big one" in 1921. The big one they chose was Mount Eon, another giant over 3,000 metres located just south of Mount Assiniboine. Unfortunately, Conrad Kain could not be with them when they made their bold attempt.

Mount Eon appears to have been named by James Outram. Its name suggests a timelessness often associated particularly with the big mountains that compose the Great Divide of the Canadian Rockies. The deceiving scale of this monstrous 3,310 metre peak is masked by its close proximity to Mount Assiniboine. The first attempt on the mountain was made in the summer of 1920. Dr. A.W. Wakefield, H.G. Graves and L.H. Lindsay failed to get above 3,000 metres (9,842 feet) on the mountain due to worsening weather and insufficient scouting of the route. The trio reported plenty of rotten rock on the mountain. In 1921, Winthrop and Margaret Stone left Wheeler's camp on Friday, July 15 for a four-day excursion during which they hoped to make the first ascent of Mount Eon. Both climbers were in excellent physical condition and were well acquainted with the peak from a reconnaissance they did the previous year.

Having sent provisions and their gear ahead to Marvel Pass with a packer, the Stones made a leisurely crossing of Wonder Pass and walked past extraordinary Gloria, Terrapin and Marvel Lakes. They bivouacked a short distance south of the col that divides the east face of Mount Gloria. They spent Saturday, July 16 examining appropriate routes they could take to the summit. On the 17th of July, the couple rose early and, forsaking the northeast shoulder of Eon that foiled the 1920 attempt on the mountain, worked their way south and gained a ledge at about 7,800 feet (2,377 m) and passed around the southeast arête to the base of its wide south face where at its east end there was a yellow-capped outlying tower on the same level as the ledge by which they were certain they could access the summit. With the tower as point of departure, they climbed ledges and broken slopes for nearly 1,700 feet (518 m) before reaching the southeast arête. Another 800 feet (244 m) of climbing brought them to a band of snow up which they were able to kick secure steps in order to access a ledge above. They continued to follow broken ledges and short couloirs of unstable rock to a wide, steep and irregular chimney that opened with dangerously sloping topsides onto the summit. They reached the base of the summit chimney at about 6:00 p.m. It was here that Winthrop Stone, feeling the summit now

their friends on the peak. Mr. Raimon of Brooklyn, New York set out from Wheeler's camp with provisions in an attempt to find the missing climbers. He met two other Americans while en route and implored them to aid in the search. When the party still failed to materialize, the Americans sent packer Reno Fritten to the Trail Gang's camp, where they learned from Frank Gombert and Jack Betteridge the location of the Stones' bivouac, which the two horsemen had visited on Sunday, July 17. Gombert led the Americans to the camp and found it empty. Returning to Assiniboine Camp they were pleased to discover that a packer named Childs had already been dispatched to Banff for more qualified help.

On Friday, July 22, a week after the Stones had departed on their expedition, the Swiss guide Rudolf Aemmer arrived at Assiniboine Camp with Bill Peyto, having made the forty-five-mile (seventy-two-kilometre) journey from Banff to Mount Assiniboine in only one day. In consultation with the horsemen who had scouted the area surrounding the bivouac for clues of the route the Stones had taken, it was decided that the south side of Mount Eon was likely the best place to begin the search.

On the morning of Saturday, July 23, Aemmer set out with Bill Peyto, the packer Childs and a member of the North West Mounted Police who had been dispatched to the scene by the Superintendent of Rocky Mountain National Park, as Banff was known then. Ascending Marvel Pass they found the Stones' bivouac just as they had left it eight days before. After making their way up to a broad ledge of Mount Eon and onto the summit of a south spur, they were at last offered a good view of the lower reaches of the mountain's south face. In the failing afternoon light, after long and careful scanning of the mountain with binoculars they were just about ready to abandon the search. Then, when they had given up all hope, they heard it. It was someone calling from a distant point to the west. Startled, they looked again.

On a stone ledge a quarter of a mile away and three hundred feet beneath them (about 0.4 kilometre and 91.4 metres), they spotted Mrs. Stone. They fired a shot to announce to Mrs. Stone that her agony was nearly at an end. Working around the mountainside they were soon on a ledge above her. Rudolf Aemmer descended to the ledge and Mrs. Stone was raised toward the rescue team above. But the eight exposed days alone without food had taken their toll. She was too weak to walk. Aemmer carried her on his back around the base of Mount Eon, a distance of a mile (1.6 km) over the broken and unstable ledges, and down through the moraines to timberline where they bivouacked for the

ASSINIBOINE LODGE
The Marquis degli Albizzi and
a ski instructor from Lake
Placid, Erling Strom of New
York, opened a tourist lodge
below Mount Assiniboine in
1929. Strom ran the lodge until
1966, when he relinquished
management to his daughter,
Siri. Erling Strom continued
to visit the lodge in summers
until 1978, which marked his
fiftieth year in the Rockies.
At the time of this writing,
Assiniboine Lodge had been
operated for twenty years
by Sepp and Barb Renner
who maintain its rustic
charm and grant visitors the
same intimate experience of
place the first adventurers
experienced when they found
their way to this remote peak.
Photograph by R.W. Sandford.

night. She was too weak to be moved from this primitive camp. Fortunately Dr. Fred Bell of Winnipeg joined the party to care for Mrs. Stone.
For two days they waited for her to gradually gain enough strength to
permit her to be carried by stretcher to Trail Centre Camp. All hands
were needed to carry the stretcher the fourteen miles (22.5 km) to Trail
Centre where Miss Brown, the manager of the Camp, and Mrs. Fred Bell,
did everything they could to revive her tortured body and soul.

The effort applied to Mrs. Stone's evacuation so exhausted the rescuers that a fresh party was called forth to recover Winthrop Stone's body.
Arthur Wheeler, who at the time of the accident had been engrossed
in an official boundary survey further north, arrived in time to initiate
the search. Wheeler's party was comprised of Aemmer, Edward Feuz Jr.,
Conrad Kain, Lennox Lindsay and Mack and Elizabeth MacCarthy. The
packer Ralph Rink was responsible for supplying the party. On August
2, the recovery team arrived at Trail Centre, where they were grateful
to find Mrs. Stone in a much-improved state and in the company of her
youngest son Richard. Elizabeth MacCarthy, a close friend of Margaret
Stone's from their years together in the Purcell Range, chose to stay
with her friend while her husband and the others looked for Winthrop
Stone's body.

On August 5th, 1921, the recovery team successfully followed the Stones' route to near the base of the chimney just below the summit of Mount Eon. Upon reaching the 10,000 foot ledge (3,048 m) at the southeast arête, Feuz spotted Winthrop Stone's body. Above the snow band Kain recovered his ice axe. Noting how badly broken the summit formation was, the climbers avoided Stone's chimney route to the summit taking instead a badly broken line to the west to the peak, which they reached at 3:00 p.m. By examining Stone's route they were able to clearly establish that Stone had, indeed, made the first ascent of the mountain before he plunged to his death. The recovery team built a cairn in Stone's honour and planted his ice axe in the centre. After photographing the cairn, the climbers retrieved the ice axe for Stone's family.

Aemmer and four others received a special citation from the American Alpine Club for their role in the rescue of Margaret Stone. For Aemmer the rescue was nothing less than a matter of honour. He spoke sincerely and for all the professional guides in the Rockies when he said, "Real guides cannot be heroes. When somebody gets into trouble in the mountains, we go after him, take the necessary risks, and bring him down. Nothing else counts."[2]

Today, with helicopters and trained rescuers, Margaret Stone would not likely have been so long on Mount Eon. But despite improvements in mountain rescue techniques, the peaks in Mount Assiniboine Park are still wild. Today a dozen parties will climb Mount Assiniboine during a good window of weather. What we have saved in protecting these peaks is a baseline against which anyone with courage and enough strength can make themselves whole by overcoming fear and exhaustion to reach the peak. But you don't have to climb the mountain to bask in its great shadow. All you have to do is visit it.

THE CREATION OF MOUNT ASSINIBOINE PROVINCIAL PARK

UPON THE URGING OF THE Alpine Club of Canada, British Columbia set aside 5,120 hectares of the area on February 6, 1922 as Mount Assiniboine Provincial Park, the seventh in a fledgling park system. One large and five small shelters, known as the Naiset Cabins, were later constructed at Assiniboine as part of an arrangement whereby the Alpine Club of Canada granted Arthur Wheeler a lease to use the properties at two dollars per annum. In 1927, Wheeler sublet the buildings to a half-Russian, half-Italian nobleman who happened to be the Winter Sports

FALL GLORY

"If you are worn out and tired from the daily grind of routine existence. If you need revitalizing and a real rest. If you are nervous, neurotic or dyspeptic. Come and try it for a week or two. The cure is certain and for the remainder of your life the pages of your memory's scrapbook will be replete with scenes and experiences that will recur again and again with the thrill of joy."
From Arthur Wheeler's Walking and Riding Tours to Mount Assiniboine 1920 (a pamphlet in the possession of the author)
Photograph by R.W. Sandford.

Director at Lake Placid in New York. All accounts suggest that Marquis Nicholas degli Albizzi was a genuine character. Certainly, few can question his impact on the Assiniboine area.

In the spring of 1928, Albizzi and his friend Erling Strom, who taught skiing at Lake Placid, planned a winter visit to the Assiniboine area. Local outfitters and guides thought the expedition a little impractical and discouraged them from such madness. Undeterred, the duo made their difficult way through the downed timber of the burned-out valleys to the safety of the Naiset Cabins. The weather broke after they arrived and they enjoyed seventeen days of outstanding skiing. So enthusiastic was Albizzi about the potential of the great peak as a visitor attraction that he approached the CPR with a proposal to build a major lodge in the meadows below the mountain. It opened in 1929, but not without problems. The Marquis quickly grew disillusioned with the place and it fell into the hands of outfitter Bill Brewster, who ran it only in summer. Erling Strom, returning from a visit home to Norway, engaged the use of the lodge in the winter months then gradually assumed responsibility for the buildings all year round. Strom ran it until 1966, when he relinquished management to his daughter, Siri. Strom continued to visit his beloved Assiniboine until 1978, the year that marked his fiftieth year in the Rockies.

In 1973, the park area was increased sevenfold to its present size of 39,050 hectares. It is one of the best-loved places in the Rockies. It is the place in which Arthur Wheeler's mountain spirit appears to have come to reside. You can't seem to escape his presence.

Though some visitors still walk into Mount Assiniboine using Wheeler's favourite route from Sunshine, many people now helicopter to the fabled peak. Assiniboine Lodge has played a significant role in the history of this area of the Canadian Rockies. There is something in the simplicity of the architecture of the main lodge and the tiny line of cabins, which resonates with the character of the place. Visitors often express a feeling of experiencing an underlying current at Mount Assiniboine that somehow connects the landscape to the fundamental universal rhythms that unify form and meaning in art, poetry and music. There is some kind of indwelling quality of place and it touches a deep chord in those who visit what Wheeler called "this land of forests primeval, of lakes and exquisite blues and greens, of cascading torrents, flower-strewn uplands, wildly tumbling ice-falls, towering rock peaks and cloud-capped mountains massed with snow."[3] At Mount Assiniboine, you get to the heart of the mountain landscape immediately, where it doesn't take much time to confront the timeless.

Though Mount Assiniboine is a remarkable place in its own right, it derives much of its wildness from being contiguous with Kootenay to the west and Banff and Kananaskis to the east. What resulted from putting all of these pieces back together again is far greater than the sum of its individual parks. You don't have to climb Mount Assiniboine to appreciate sense of place in the Rockies. The extent of what we saved begets a powerful sense of naturalness rising from the bottom of the valleys right to heights of the peaks.

PART THREE

The West We Want: Creating a Culture Worthy of Place

18

Respecting and Honouring the Great Bear

The Grizzly as a Symbol of the West We Want

To ensure our identity as a people, what we want the West to be like in the future must include the presence of the great bear. The grizzly bear is the single most prominent symbol of what we saved in the mountain West. Without the grizzly the West would not be wild. Without the great bear we would soon become another anyplace in an increasingly homogenized world. Coming to terms with what we share with the grizzly, however, is a serious meditation, but essential for those who would define the current and future importance of the Canadian Rocky Mountain Parks World Heritage Site to our understanding of where and how we live. Because our views of the great bear and how we might share our existence with it have been shaped by them, that meditation might begin with consideration of what those who came before Euro-Canadians thought about the grizzly.

SPIRITUAL CONNECTIONS TO THE BEAR

In many North American Native cultures, specific responsibilities concerning relationship radiate outward from the individual to the immediate family, the extended family, the band, the clan and the tribal group. Relationships within most Native cultures, however, do not stop with the human realm. By necessity they extend beyond, into the environment. Native peoples developed special connections to the land, animals, plants, the sky and the elements.[1] Central among these were the relationships they had with the animals that provided their food and all their other material needs. Animals, however, were more than just sources of food. Animals aid Native peoples in their everyday lives and appear in their dreams and meditations. Because they were created before humans, animals are considered closer to the sources of all life and can, through their powers, act as allies, guides and familiars in the search for individual wholeness.

While this may appear, at first, to be a simple proposition to which we might aspire, it is not. Despite contemporary claims to the contrary, this is not an easy connection to develop and sustain. It requires generations of careful observation of the land and intimate knowledge of the behaviour of all the major animals with which you share your habitat. Then you have to gradually draw on that behaviour as a basis for examining and strengthening human traits and purifying human desires. Through fasts and vision quests, you have to derive your own spiritual nature from the power embodied in the animals around you. If you practice the above for thousands of years, you can create a religion based on your relationship to animals. Each animal teaches Native peoples a different lesson. In the West there are buffalo lessons and elk lessons. You can learn from the beaver and from the wolf. If you are very special, you can aspire to the power of the bear.

It is not only Native North Americans who have had this relationship with the bear. Anthropologists have discovered that when it comes to bears, there are a great number of similarities in the cultures of boreal peoples throughout the Northern Hemisphere. The bear appears in initiation and healing ceremonies, in shamanic rites, in the quest for spirit guardians and in various ritual dances.[2] There are also similarities between many cultures in the rites associated with the hunting of bears, and similar tales and myths have surfaced in widely separated geographical regions that associate the bear with various aspects of human thought and action.

As David Rockwell indicates in *Giving Voice To Bear,*[3] bears and First Nations people have been sharing habitat for a very long time. Both have walked the same trails, drank and fished out of the same streams, dug out and fed on the same roots and harvested the same berries, seeds and nuts for thousands of years. A great mutual respect developed between

Native peoples and bears. Nowhere is this more true than with the grizzly.

SIMILARITIES BETWEEN BEARS AND HUMANS

THE FIRST THING THAT WAS apparent to Aboriginal peoples was how similar bears are to people. The body of the bear is disturbingly similar to the body of a human. When skinned, grizzlies look rather like stalky, powerful, short-legged men. Bears can walk upright and, like humans, they have binocular vision. Their hind feet are very human-like and the prints they leave in soft mud or melting snow can appear surprisingly like ones that might be left by a man.[4] Bears are dexterous and can rotate their forepaws. There is even evidence that they may use tools.[5] Native observers also noticed that bears snore when they sleep, just like tired people.

Native peoples further observed that bears have a relatively long infancy. They also have a fierce maternal devotion that is not unlike what people show to their children. Bear cubs stay with their mothers twice as long as other large mammals of comparable size. This is likely because so much of what a bear knows is probably learned as opposed to being instinctual. There were also critical similarities in diet between people and bears. They often ate the same proportions of certain foods.

TRACKING THE GREAT BEAR

Colleen Campbell is a volunteer researcher who works under the direction of Dr. Mike Gibeau, a grizzly bear expert working with Parks Canada in Banff National Park. By knowing where the bears are travelling and what they are eating, park managers can minimize the threat of human contact. As we learn the seasonal habits and food preferences of resident grizzly populations, we can learn to live safely in their midst. *Photograph by R.W. Sandford.*

The diet of bears is often composed of 80 percent vegetable matter. The diets of Native groups using the same habitat were often composed of 70 percent vegetable matter. It has been suggested that people ate marginally more meat in these circumstances simply because they were better at obtaining it.[6] According to some First Nations groups, bears are just like people except that these furry relatives do not make fire.

THE BEAR AS HEALER

THOUGH EUROPEAN CULTURES seldom think this way, in many Native cultures the great bear is seen more as a healer than a threat. It was out of the bear's remarkable capacity for self-healing that the myth of the Medicine Bear emerged. It was clear to careful Native observers that the bear knew the secrets of plants. In many Native myths, the bear is portrayed as the plant gatherer, a mysterious herbalist gathering medicines straight from nature. Here is what the Lakota man Two Shields observed about the herbal knowledge possessed by the great bear:

> *The bear is quick-tempered and is fierce in many ways, and yet he pays attention to herbs which no other animal notices at all. The bear digs these for his own use. The*

bear is the only animal which eats roots from the earth and is also especially fond of acorns, Juneberries and cherries. These three are frequently compounded with other herbs in making medicine and if a person is fond of cherries we say he is like a bear. We consider the bear as chief of all the animals in regard to herb medicine, and therefore it is understood that if a man dreams of a bear he will be expert in the use of herbs for curing illness. The bear is regarded as an animal well acquainted with herbs because no other animal has such good claws for digging roots.[7]

Bears also represent a spiritual symbol for many First Nations people. Bears are ancient and possess an earlier and more vibrant proximity to the Great Spirit at the heart of the world's mystery. Many Native initiation rites seek to bestow upon a novice the wisdom the bear received through its ritual death. In such rites, the individual is removed from his or her family and village and goes alone to a special place. In their extended isolation, candidates for spiritual enlightenment often go without food or water. Such isolation and depravation serve as a ritual death during which the novice is visited by what may later become a guiding animal spirit. Assuming one survives this trial, he or she is born into a new life and new status within the tribe.

HUNTING THE BEAR

NATIVE PEOPLES ALSO HUNTED bears. Before the arrival of the horse and the gun this was a very dangerous proposition with highly significant ritual association. Every hunter knew the physical and spiritual power of the bear. There was a good chance a hunter would be mauled or killed in simply approaching such an aggressive animal. Still, there was nothing more heroic. Killing a bear was often celebrated as a more courageous act than killing a man or taking a scalp in battle. A hunter could possess no greater trophy than a bear-claw necklace. In killing a bear, you took the life of something more ancient and perhaps greater than yourself.

Among the Blackfoot Tribes, the grizzly has been called the Real Bear. The black bear was not held in anything close to the same esteem. The killing of the Real Bear was a sacred act and during the hunt, the name of the bear was never spoken. Instead he was called Old Grandfather, Old Man, Old Honey Paws, or simply Crooked Tail. This tradition of not naming the bear is common in tribal cultures throughout the circumpolar world. You did not speak the name of the bear, for the bear would hear you, for he heard and understood the languages of all the Native peoples. Today, there are yet clans and societies within tribes for whom it is taboo to name the Real Bear. Those who know the bear best do not speak of him, except euphemistically, and then only with the greatest of respect.

Though customs differ, the Native peoples of the coast also possess a great respect for the great bear. Traditionally, grizzlies are considered the closest animal relative to humans. On the rare occasion they were hunted, special rituals and songs were offered preceding the kill. A successful hunt was usually followed by a ceremonial feast.

BIRTH AND REBIRTH

AFTER OBSERVING THE BEAR over centuries, humans began to realize the bear was a symbol not just of the survival of winter. It was a symbol that hinted at a solution to the largest question of them all – the question of what lies beyond death.

The enigmatic bear, more than any other teacher, enacted the answer to this question. It passed into the earth each autumn and endured the death of winter and emerged again in the spring. When the bear emerged, it appeared that the winter had little effect on it and sometimes the miracle was double, for the bear often emerged with young. Birth and rebirth. Somehow the bear knew when to retire from the world and when to re-enter. It seemed to emerge before the snowmelt, as though its very heat initiated the spring. The first tendrils of spring vegetation seemed to rise from the ground for the bear's pleasure. The departing snow revealed the frozen carcasses of reindeer, moose, bighorn, and deer.

It was clear that the bear was a master of renewal whose life cycle was tied to the wheel of the seasons. It had knowledge of when to die and when to be reborn. In the winter den it did not eat, drink or excrete. Its entire life followed the solar cycle. Was the she-bear's meticulous motherhood a sign? Was the bear's behaviour a sign?[8]

If you lived in a pre-literature society of primitive hunters seeking to make sense of an often-hostile world, the behaviour of the bear could not fail to impress. This behaviour might also inspire the beginnings of what might later be defined as religious feelings. According to Shepard and Sanders, the powers of the bear and its relationship to humans become embedded in early morality stories in almost all early circumpolar cultures.

**A GRIZZLY WITH
TWO CUBS**

While most visitors consider
the grizzly bear to be a
uniquely mountain species, its
range in the Canadian West
was originally concentrated
on the Great Plains. The
Rockies are actually marginal
habitat for the Great Bear and
as such can be considered
its last stand in the interior
of North America. Due
to their low reproductive
rates, their diverse habitat
needs and their expansive
inter-jurisdictional range
requirements, bears are
good indicators of overall
ecosystem health. The
stability of bear populations
is now seen as a measure of
how well we are protecting
the integrity of our mountain
ecosystems.
*Photograph courtesy of Parks
Canada.*

THOUGH IT WOULD
HAVE BEEN sur-
prising if earlier
explorers had not
seen one, the first
European to record
seeing a grizzly was a
young Hudson's Bay
Company appren-
tice named Henry
Kelsey. Poor and
uneducated though
he was, Kelsey made some very important natural history observations
in Canada. Kelsey was the first European to see the marvel that is now
known as the Canadian prairies. On August 20, 1691, he was also the
first to see a bison in what is now the Canadian West. The same day, a
hundred and fourteen years before the first specimen was collected by
the Lewis and Clark Expedition on May 5, 1805, twenty-year-old Henry
Kelsey saw his first grizzly bear. Kelsey's journal is written in verse.
His entry for August 20, 1691 is the first description of the grizzly in the
English language:

> *To day we pichet to ye outtermost Edge of ye woods*
> *this plain affords Nothing but short Round*
> *sticky grass and Buffillo & a great sort of a Bear w*
> *is Bigger than any white Bear & is Neither White*
> *nor Black But silver hair'd like our English*
> *Rabbit ye Buffillo Likewise is not like those to ye*
> *Northward their horns growing like and English*
> *Ox but Black & short*[9]

Any resemblance the grizzly had with an English rabbit rather ended
with comparisons of size and the colour of its coat. Kelsey went back
and did a rhymed introduction to his journals of 1691. It is obvious that
it didn't take long for Kelsey to learn about the ferocious nature of the
great bear:

> *And then you have beast of severall kind*
> *The one is a black a Buffillo great*
> *Anotherr is an outgrown Bear w, is good meat*

His skin to gett I have used all ye, means I can
He is mans food & he makes food of man[10]

The grizzly instantly became a popular symbol of what had to be put right in the West if it was to be settled. The bear also became part of an emerging heroic mythology associated with developing European skill in coming to grips with the dangers of the Wild West. Guidebooks for missionaries and travellers, often written by people who had never seen a bear, became commonplace. In the literature of the day and in the popular press, the terrible image of the bear quickly began to shape what people expected to hear about travel in the North American West. Published exploration accounts were deemed incomplete if they didn't offer at least one story of a bear encounter. The more exotic the tale, the better. Though it would be easy to question the veracity of many of the early published stories, some stand out for their capacity to describe the remarkable behaviour of the great bear. The stories also lead, ultimately, in the direction of truth.

THE BEAR'S EMBRACE

AN INTERESTING EARLY BEAR story that is sometimes told in Jasper concerns an early fur trader named Ross Cox who, after working with John Jacob Aster's American Fur Company at Fort Astoria at the mouth of the Columbia, decided to join their Canadian rivals, the North West Company. Cox crossed Athabasca Pass from west to east with the fur brigade in 1817. It is not Jasper that is at the heart of the story but an encounter with a grizzly, which took place in the area of the Flathead River in the spring of 1816. This tale tells us two things. It explains the extent to which Native peoples conflicted with bears and it gives definition to the terrible embrace of the bear that later became known as the "bear's hug." The suggestion that Native peoples lived in some sort of primeval harmony with all the creatures with which they shared the mountain West is not supported by the Ross Cox account:

I have seen several of our hunters, as well as many Indians, who have been dreadfully lacerated in their encounters with bears: some have been deprived of their ears, other had their noses nearly torn off, and a few have been completely blinded. From the scarcity of food in the spring months they are then more savage than at any other season; and during that period it is a highly dangerous experiment to approach them.[11]

From this account we learn that bears are more aggressive in the spring. Cox surmises that this is probably due to the shortage of food. It has not yet occurred to anyone that this may also be due to the fierce female defence of the young. The rest of the story concerns ten Canadian fur traders and one of their number, "pauvre Louisson," who felt the bear's terrible embrace:

> The third evening after quitting the fort, while they were quietly sitting around a blazing fire eating a hearty dinner of deer, a large half-famished bear cautiously approached the group from behind an adjacent tree; and before they were aware of his presence, he sprang across the fire, seized one of the men (who had a well-furnished bone in his hand) round the waist, with the two fore paws, and ran about fifty yards with him on his hind legs before he stopped. His comrades were so thunder-struck at the unexpected appearance of such a visitor, and his sudden retreat with "pauvre Louisson," that they for some time lost all presence of mind, and, in a state of fear and confusion, were running to and fro, each expecting in his turn to be kidnapped in a similar manner; when at length Baptiste Le Blanc, a half-breed hunter, seized his gun, and was in the act of firing at the bear, but was stopped by some of the others, who told him he would inevitably kill their friend in the position in which he was then placed. During this parley Bruin relaxed his grip of the captive, whom he kept securely under him, and very leisurely began picking the bone which the latter had dropped. Once or twice Louisson attempted to escape, which only caused the bear to watch him more closely; but on his making another attempt, he again seized Louisson round the waist, and commenced giving him one of those infernal embraces which generally end in death. The poor fellow was now in great agony, and vented the most frightful screams; and observing Baptiste with his gun ready, anxiously watching a safe opportunity to fire, he cried out, "Tire! Tire! mon chere, si tur m'aimes. Tire, pour l'amour du bon Dieu! A la tete a la tete!" This was enough for Le Blanc, who instantly let fly, and hit the bear over the right temple. He fell, and at the same moment dropped Louisson; but he gave him a right ugly scratch with his claws across the face, which for some time afterwards spoiled his beauty. After the shot, Le Blanc darted to his comrade's assistance, and with his "couteau de chasse" quickly finished the sufferings of the man stealer, and rescued his friend from impending death; for with the exception of the above-mentioned scratch, he escaped uninjured. [12]

THE CANADIAN VERSUS THE AMERICAN BEAR

THE INTRODUCTION OF THE repeating rifle marked the beginning of the end for most grizzly populations in the United States. Surviving bears became more wary and their range retracted into the mountains. Everywhere they were, however, they were hunted. Soon the trappers and miners were replaced by homesteaders and ranchers who shot bears on sight. The livestock industry began to expand grazing into the last niches in which the grizzly still remained. By 1920, the bear was eliminated from most of its former American range.

Canadians are sometimes smug about the fact that we still have grizzly bears. Their smugness is unwarranted. In Canada, the attitude toward bears was not much different than it was in the United States. During the fur trade era, bear hides were legal tender in what is now Western Canada. Hudson's Bay Company records tell us much about the abundance of the grizzly on the plains and in the mountains prior to the coming of the railroad. Bears were sometimes taken in great numbers. During the winter of 1871–72, records indicate that some 750 grizzly bear hides were taken in the area of the Cypress Hills in what is now southwestern Saskatchewan.[13] The grizzly disappeared quickly from the Great Plains in Canada. The same myths and biases about the ferocious nature of the grizzly were just as much a part of folk culture here as they were further south.

The completion of the Canadian Pacific Railway in 1885 initiated a wave of prairie settlement. The bears of the Great Plains disappeared soon after. Fewer people and a slower rate of settlement, however, left space in the mountains for bears. The prevalent attitude toward the grizzly remained an openly hostile one. People looked for excuses to kill them.

When the great Himalayan explorer and mountaineer, Dr. Tom Longstaff, came to the Canadian Rockies in the summer of 1910, he brought with him the typical bias of the day concerning bears. They were relentless, bloodthirsty killers and that was all there was to it. Though he had to seek high and low just to find a grizzly, Longstaff still deemed it an act of self-defence to kill one. In fact, he likely only wanted the trophy and the bragging rights. Here's how Longstaff described killing three bears in one day in the Bugaboo Pass area of the Purcell Range southwest of Banff:

> *Suddenly I saw three grizzlies emerge from the timber, below and ahead of me, slowly making their way uphill. Running along the ridge till I got above them I sneaked down as near as I could get unseen. Grizzlies run with their dam for a full two years, and I now saw that the party consisted of an old dam with two three-quarter-grown cubs. I could never expect a more exciting introduction. I was not disappointed. Grizzlies are unattractive and dangerous brutes; moreover they were a serious menace to our horses. Not only will grizzlies attack them but also horses are easily stampeded by bears and we might lose them for days. I took the dam first and rolled her head over heels down the slope. Thinking her dead I took the biggest youngster, but only broke its foreleg. However, the old dam got up and came roaring up-hill towards me. They were now all giving tongue and the result was far more appalling than all the six*

*tigers I have met put together. Perhaps in consequence of the savage noise they made
it took me two more shots to finish the old one. Then another for the youngster. The
third unwounded one was now pretty close and roaring like a fiend. Its nose was full of
porcupine quills, which may have soured its temper. It required a second shot too, but
it never got up to me.*[14]

The hunting of bears was no longer a sacred rite, as it was in the days
when the bear was a respected symbol of a prior human relationship to
nature. Bears were hunted out of a practical need to protect livestock or
to preserve community security. Bears were also eagerly hunted simply
for sport.

Attitudes toward bears and toward wildlife as a whole would not
begin to change until both became greatly depleted in the West. Only
the creation of the world's first national parks, in Yellowstone in 1872
and Banff in 1885, offered the great bear respite from overwhelming
pressure on its range and threats to its very survival.

THE CREATION OF OUR NATIONAL PARKS

WHILE IT WAS CLEAR BY THE 1870s that settlement was changing the
West dramatically, the creation of national parks in North America was
not inspired by a movement to preserve western wildlife. At least not
at first. The object of the first national parks was, primarily, the preservation of scenery. The impetus toward this preservation was Niagara

Falls. As early as 1830, it was noted that the continent's greatest known natural treasure was being beaten to death by "sharpsters," "hucksters" and private developers who acquired the grandest views, then forced visitors to pay exorbitantly just to watch the water fall.[15] Things would be different in the West. The grand scenery would be protected for all time for everyone to see.

Despite the creation of these reserves, wildlife was vanishing from the West at an unprecedented rate. Part of the problem was that animals were not even safe in the newly created parks. Under the influence of the livestock industry, predator control programs were introduced in the mountain national parks to ensure that "vermin" in the form of wolves and coyotes would not spill out of these reserves into neighbouring ranch and farm country. The programs were very successful. It soon became apparent that it was not only the buffalo that had disappeared from the West. Almost every other wild species was also in decline. The popular image of the Wild West was under siege. This problem did not go away with the creation of national parks.

DO NOT FEED THE BEARS

THE PROBLEM OF BEAR FEEDING is as old as our national parks. The moment bears stopped being hunted in national parks, they became less wary of people. It soon became clear to the bears that they could feed on garbage provided they did not injure people in so doing.

The arrival of the automobile institutionalized the bear problem in our national parks. Black bears very quickly came to identify an automobile with food. They took to sitting cutely on the roadside waiting for passing cars. When the cars stopped, they would amble over and wait for handouts. Enthralled visitors couldn't help themselves. They began to compete with one another to get the best photographs of people feeding a begging bear. The food was rich and nutritious. The bears liked it. When the cars stopped coming, the bears started to hit campsites and to come into town to look for food. When Park Superintendent S.J. Clarke and Chief Game Guardian Howard Sibbald drove a party of Ottawa officials to observe the killing of a problem bear west of Banff in July 1915, it made big news in the local newspaper. The female black bear that was the source of the problem was killed and her two cubs deposited in the Banff Zoo.[16] Though the park service could hardly have seen it at the time, this was the beginning of a vicious circle that has yet to be broken in the mountain national parks. Unwitting or uninformed

BEAR FEEDING

Since the inception of Canada's national parks system in 1885, park managers have been fighting what sometimes seems like a losing war against the human habitation of wildlife. While photographs like this are now actively discouraged in the mountain parks, they were once the mainstay of the tourism souvenir trade.

Photograph from the Byron Harmon Collection courtesy of the Whyte Museum of the Canadian Rockies.

visitors feed bears, the bears become habituated to human food, they start taking it wherever they can find it and, in order to preserve the safety of those who started the feeding in the first place, the bear has to be killed.

In 1916, park wardens reported that the town of Banff was literally "overrun" with bears. The policy of shooting problem bears on sight was initiated in some parks. In February of 1918, Parks Commissioner J.B. Harkin granted blanket permission for wardens to kill all bears "encountered, roaming at large, within any townsite in your park."[17] Wardens were also given blanket permission to shoot any bear found raiding provisions or stores outside of townsites. Though wardens were instructed to go to great lengths to justify killings outside of townsites, growing human presence in the parks had defined parks policy. Bears were to be killed if they posed a problem to people – even though it was people offering food who first posed the problem to the bear.

By the mid 1920s, black bears had become the delight of visiting motorists. Stories abounded of their boldness. Visitors, for the most part, thought them cute. Park officials knew they had a problem on their hands. In 1928, superintendents from the mountain national parks gathered to discuss the problem and to make recommendations that would reduce the threat to public safety and minimize government liability without compromising the thrill visitors got from seeing bears. Their conclusions are interesting even today:

> ... bears should be killed only after they become a nuisance; the decision on that point to rest, as at present, with the Superintendent. It is understood that the Superintendent will at all times exercise the best judgment with a view to protecting the public and at the same time see that there will be enough of non-dangerous bears to provide the thrill that the tourists get from seeing live bears in the open.... It is deemed good policy to endeavor to educate the public through Parks literature and especially through the chauffeurs operating in the Parks as to the danger of bears and other wild animals. It is specially important that the number of bears frequenting outlying camp grounds should be kept down because the danger there is much more serious than in the larger camp grounds. It is not deemed worth while [sic] yet to develop a policy of killing bears in the fall or other suitable time in order that a revenue be derived from their skins. It is considered that warning posters should be erected, especially with a view to protecting the Department against claims for damages.[18]

FOOD AND GARBAGE

IT WAS IN THE MID 1930S that the American live trap concept of removing problem bears began to be employed in Canadian national parks. A large metal box on wheels, called the Black Maria, was built for the use of wardens and put into wide use. Bears were trapped and moved to remote areas. Not all park superintendents were completely sold on this new technique. Though devices of this kind are still in use, some of the more enlightened superintendents of the day argued that it might be just as effective to burn garbage so that bears would no longer be attracted to towns, campgrounds and dumps. This, too, would become parks policy, but not until much later when the problem of increasing visitation demanded wholesale rethinking of bear-management strategies.

The bear problem continued to grow after World War II when visitation increased and the car began to replace the train as the most popular and economical way to travel to the mountain national parks. Visitation to Banff National Park increased nearly ten-fold from 1900 to 1950.[19] In terms of bear-management issues the main problem was garbage. Visitors wanted to see bears and dumps became the place they went to see them. Some of the larger accommodations, like Jasper Park Lodge, had their own dumps and encouraged select guests to visit them if they hadn't already seen bears on the golf course or among the cabins on the property. Bears often congregated in these places in huge numbers. Jasper Park Wardens once reported seeing twenty-four bears at one time at the Jasper Park Lodge, and the situation was not much different in many other places in the mountain national parks.[20]

The popularity of bears in Jasper and the extent to which they were fed at Jasper Park Lodge during this period is well documented in *The Bears of Jasper*, a travel book written by a freelance journalist named Harper Cory and published by Thomas Nelson and Sons in 1946. Cory was a nature writer with some twenty books to his credit when he came to Jasper, likely at the expense of Canadian National Railway, to write entertaining little book on the "Jasper Comedians," the black bears at Jasper Park Lodge that frequented the park roadways in order to entertain visitors. Some of the pictures in this book, which show people feeding animals, would make the hair on the back of the neck stand up, for any contemporary student of bear problems in the national parks today. There are bears standing at the doors of cabins at Jasper Park Lodge begging for food from nattily dressed guests, staff feeding groups of bears, and small children face-to-face with begging cubs. While such antics would be unthinkable today, Cory's book typifies the attitude of the time toward bears in the mountain national parks. Here is how Cory introduces us to the black bears of Jasper National Park:

> The wild bear in his native habitat is a more accomplished entertainer than the animal in the circus or the zoo. The latter, educated to perform rote actions and responses; his inventiveness is killed in ratio to the speed with which his life is forced into a groove. The wild bear, especially in a district where he is treated with consideration, as in Jasper and other of the National Parks of Canada, is a walking mass of inventiveness, liable to spring all manner of surprises in his urgent desire to attract attention of the right sort – that is, attention accompanied by sweet edibles. He knows more amusing tricks than any man could teach him, and he rarely exhibits them needlessly. He is the world's most accomplished mendicant, but he will work – not too hard of course – for his reward. Therein, his behaviour most resembles that of human beings.[21]

What Harper Cory and other writers of popular works on wildlife of the day didn't understand was that the feeding of these animals was beginning to cause series problems in the mountain national parks in both Canada and the United States. Once bears were habituated to garbage in places like Jasper they became problems along roadsides, in campgrounds, outlying lodges and even in town. The problem was aggravated in the early fall when Jasper Park Lodge closed for the season. Bears got hungry and then got aggressive. Attempts to close the

**THE FUTURE OF THE
GREAT BEAR**

In preserving the Great
Bear, we preserve our own
unique heritage and sense
of place, and assure a
sustainable tourism future.
As undisturbed ecosystems
are now seen to be central to
moderating or even slowing
climate change effect, in
saving our natural places, it
may turn out that our natural
places will save us.
*Photograph courtesy of Parks
Canada.*

dumps were closed and bears began to disappear in numbers. In the end, however, the work conducted by the Craigheads would become the foundation for much of what is known about grizzlies in Yellowstone and elsewhere in North America today, including the Rocky Mountain parks in Canada.

BEAR ATTACKS: THEIR CAUSES AND AVOIDANCE

GRIZZLY BEAR RESEARCH in Canada's mountain parks came into its own with a book published by a Professor of Environmental Science and Biology at the University of Calgary in 1985. The moment it was released, Stephen Herrero's *Bear Attacks: Their Causes and Avoidance* began to reshape the way people thought about bears.[28] The approach that Herrero used in his famous book is very interesting. Herrero realized that people had a primal fear of bears. He also knew that the media was obsessed with bear maulings. (Even today, the forty thousand deaths a year caused by automobile accidents do not get media attention. A bear mauling, even though it is less likely to happen to you than being struck by lightning, is instant front-page news.) Though he must have occasionally winced, Herrero did not back away from the gruesome nature of his subject area.

By carefully classifying the kinds of encounters people had with black bears and grizzlies and by scientifically assessing the behaviour of both bears and humans in each of these circumstances, Herrero proved you could look at these situations and learn from them. Herrero's observations suggest that conscious and pre-meditated malice toward humans is probably outside the mental capacity of bears. Through his work, Herrero broke through outdated myths associated with bear aggression and allowed a generation of campers, hikers and backpackers to rethink the role they could play in allowing the bear to continue to contribute to their experience of wildness in the mountain West.

Though some of the accounts he shares in the book are horrific, they are no more so than you would find in any fatal automobile accident file. What we begin to see, however, when we look objectively at the evidence Herrero provides, is important. We begin to see that there are certain situations in which we place bears, where instinct can over-power learning and natural caution and the bear may charge and even attack. Herrero offers that the more we know about these situations the more we can avoid them. Herrero further offers that by knowing and understanding patterns of bear aggression we can anticipate the safest possible action in an encounter with a bear and increase our chances of avoiding injury or death.

Herrero's scientific examination of the causes of bear attacks and rec-ommendations on how to avoid them are not foolproof. Herrero himself is circumspect about his capacity to help others reduce the chances of injurious encounters with bears:

> *Regard me as a scientific handicapper. I study a bear's history – actually a lot of bears – and suggest where you should place your bets. I think I'm a good handicapper because I've been able to look at the track record of many grizzly bears throughout North America. And I am painfully aware that if I give the wrong advice, someone may suffer injury or death.*[29]

Although avoidance of injury from bear attacks cannot be reduced to a simple formula, Herrero did lead us to a new concept. By combining the principles of safe travel in bear country with a growing contempo-rary understanding of the feeding, mating and rearing behaviour of bears and their distribution and movement patterns, we may be able to change our relationship with the bear. If we know the kinds of habitat bears favour at different times of the year, in an area in which we want to travel we can begin to predict where bears might be and what they might be doing on a given day, in a given season, in a given habitat. This understanding combined with knowledge of what to do in the event of a confrontation provides a big step in minimizing conflicts that might be fatal to both people and bears. By applying what Herrero teaches us, about bears and about ourselves, we may be able to learn to share habitat more safely with bears and permit more peaceful coexistence between the two species.

The wonder of Herrero's book goes far beyond the suggestion of the vision of a culture capable of sharing habitat with predators like bears. The classic nature of this book resides in its overall prescience. Though the first edition was written two decades ago, it prefigured the manner in which people would look at bear safety in the future. It predisposed backcountry users to a higher awareness of bears and what could be done to avoid them. It predicted the widespread use of bear repellents like the universally popular bear spray that hikers carry with them in bear country today. It recommended bear-management strategies based on ecosystem integrity that are the norm in national parks today. In his cool, objective and highly scientific way, Herrero also dispelled the hysteria associated with the role the grizzly actually plays as an indicator of ecosystem health in the mountain West. In 1985, Herrero pointed out that there would be no ecosystem collapse if we killed all the bears in our national parks and surrounding areas. Herrero allotted the great bear, and its smaller cousin the black bear, their rightful place in the ecosystems of the West. Bears are important, not because our ecosystems would fail without them, but because they represent the fullest expression of the diversity and natural beauty that the West possessed when first Europeans first arrived on this continent.

Stephen Herrero's work went far beyond the publication of *Bear Attacks: Their Causes and Avoidance.* His research findings began to influence bear management inside and outside Canada's mountain national parks. Even today, hardly a grizzly project of note in Canada is undertaken without his input.

Because the findings of scientists like Stephen Herrero are so easy to understand, a great number of non-scientists involved with bears consider themselves expert. This, as Thomas McNamee points out, makes practicing bona fide science difficult for genuine experts. Sometimes it seems that there are as many self-acknowledged experts on bears as there are armchair experts on mountaineering. Real expertise on bears, however, does not come from reading about them. It comes from experience in observing them. From the domain of first-hand experience have come some surprisingly credible observers who have become an expert on their own terms. An important divide was crossed in North America when enlightened hunters and hunting guides began to see the great bear in a new light. There are still conflicts but we are beginning to think differently about what they might mean to our relationship to the bear and its future in our West.

EMBRACING THE BEAR

In *Bear Attacks*, Herrero described an encounter involving Patricia Van Tighem and her husband Trevor Janz, which took place on the Crypt Lake Trail in Waterton Lakes National Park on a cold Sunday morning in September of 1983:

> They were returning from camping overnight and it was snowing lightly, but not enough to obscure their vision. Patricia remembers the wind blowing into their faces before they were attacked by a grizzly bear. Trevor was 100 to 130 feet ahead of Patricia and was singing softly when he suddenly saw the head of a bear below the trail about fifty feet to his left. He had no way of knowing that eighty feet away there was a partly consumed bighorn sheep carcass on which the bear, a female grizzly, and her two yearling cubs had been feeding.[30]

The grizzly mauled both Trevor and Patricia terribly. When the horrifying encounter was over, Patricia had lost an eye and much of her face.[31] Seventeen years later, after scores of operations, untold pain and personal trial, Patricia Van Tighem wrote *The Bear's Embrace: A True Story of Surviving A Grizzly Bear Attack*, a book about her survival and painful but still incomplete recovery. It is not a book for the faint of heart, for it tells of mental anguish, suffering and unendurable physical pain. It is an important book, however, because it starts when the bear mauling ends. It tells what happens after you have been attacked by a bear. Throughout the painful descriptions of her injuries, the difficulties in getting the kind of care she needed, the failed surgeries and the months in hospitals and institutions, you feel Van Tighem gradually rising above her injuries and disfigurement to reach for a larger meaning for what has happened to her. Here the book becomes much more than just an engaging account. It goes places that even the author may not have fully foreseen. In the end, Van Tighem does something that we all must do if we are to grant the natural world the right to exist and the capacity to sustain us: we must accept that we are part of nature and allow ourselves to be embraced by it. In other words, we must accept the bear's embrace.

THE DIVIDE UNCROSSED: LEARNING TO LIVE WITH THE GREAT BEAR

DECIDING TO EMBRACE the bear is one thing, actually doing so is quite another. There arc a great number of attitudes and habits that we have to continue to work to change if we are going to successfully learn to safely share habitat with bears over the long term. Some of the things we have to change are deeply rooted in the collective human psyche. Others are just habits that have to be reconsidered if we want to realize our healthy ecosystems as highly desired and precious tourism resources in the future.

One divide we will likely never cross is the innate fear many people have of bears. The origins of this fear lie deep within the collective unconscious of our culture. It is to this primal fear that the media appeals with bold headlines about bear attacks. Sensational bear stories have always served to feed supposition at the expense of fact. Suppositions, as we have indicated elsewhere, often have a long life. As William Kittredge once noted, the public has a taste for second-hand dangers. Getting past the image of the bear as a terrifying and incomprehensible force of wild nature is one of our greatest long-term challenges.

SCIENCE, SCIENTIFIC AGREEMENT AND BIOPOLITICS

IF ONE CONSIDERS THE GOALS and method of science, one can see that differences of opinion between scientists over how bear populations should be managed are a given. If you accept the obvious importance of remaining bear habitat in the West to a growing and resource-hungry population, you can also see that it is impossible to keep bear research from being politicized. It must be stated, however, that is not the purpose or function of pure science to act upon its research findings. That is the job of politicians and decision-makers within the organizations charged with managing our Mountain Parks. The structure that exists today in North America is that research is conducted, findings validated, and results presented to those responsible for making collaborative decisions about land use. As much as we would like science to tell us everything we should do to manage landscapes wisely, it cannot. Good science, it seems, often ends up asking more questions than it answers.

One divide we have yet to cross is the one that reconciles humans as part of natural environmental processes. To what extent can we interfere with an ecosystem and still have it remain "natural"? How natural is natural? And where does the bear fit into this scheme? Circumstances do not always allow us to gather all the facts we need in time to make sound decisions. Sometimes we have to make educated guesses. It is at this juncture that we leave the world of science and enter the troubled dominion of biopolitics.

Like all worlds unto themselves, biopolitics is a diverse domain. It includes the public relations imagery that shapes our notions of what is a desirable way of life in the West. Within this domain are public relations strategies that make us think we still live in a wild and untrammelled West. Even though the original Canadian Pacific Railway ambition of settling Western Canada was fulfilled in the twentieth century, developers and community planners conspire to give us a sense that we are still living in the Wild West. We name subdivisions after the animals and plants they replaced and still give ourselves airs when in the company of visitors, pretending we still live on the edge of a frontier. We have not figured out that the West *would* be a paradise if humans spread themselves among the remaining wildlife species instead of completely replacing them.

The world of biopolitics also extends to the complex domain of land-use jurisdiction. When we examine what each of the jurisdictions in the Mountain Parks have in common, we realize a number of divides that can be crossed through co-operation. We have already realized that national parks, as generous as they often are in area, do not always preserve the quantities of the right kind of habitat to ensure the survival of key indicator species such as bears. Our research has also allowed us to realize that the ranges of bears often extend far beyond national and provincial parks into other jurisdictions where other forms of land use are encouraged. We know from Kananaskis Country and projects like the Foothills Model Forest that animals like bears can survive in multiple land use areas if they carefully managed.

There is still much to be hopeful about. More than at any other time in modern history, there is willingness to work together to find ways to preserve enough of the right kind of habitat and enough corridors to that habitat to assure the survival of the great bear over time. The cultivation of the common willingness to work together toward the future of the bear and its place in Western culture is what the Mountain Parks are all about. There is also evidence that what we are doing is working. In

the Canadian Rocky Mountain Parks World Heritage Site, healthy populations of wild grizzlies can be found within an hour's drive of a city of a
million people. In this the people who live in and around the Mountain
Parks should take great pride, for it suggests that if we can learn to share
habitat safely and successfully with the great bear, it is still possible to
create the West we want.

19

Seeing What Is Hidden in Plain Sight

Triumphing Over Diminishment and Loss

HOW LOCALS AND VISITORS ALIKE experience the Rockies has changed dramatically over the past fifty years. Along the entire spine of the Rockies, from Canada to the United States, communities are losing their unique character and becoming more and more alike and more urban in character. As a large proportion of the present local population has been in the region for only a short time, what they discover in themselves through the experience of the new and exotic landscape they now call home is very different than the relationship to place experienced by First Nations people or by earlier generations of non-Native residents. Because the landscapes of the Mountain Parks never fail to astound, inter-generational pride in place makes it possible to redress some of the injuries and losses related to place that have accrued through time, or to at least compensate for them. But more and more, locals are confronted with evidence that we face in this region potential losses that are almost beyond imagination.

There are three sets of statistics that put into relief the direction and flow that history has and continues to take, with respect to human influence on the ecological history of the mountain West as it pertains to the Mountain Parks. The first statistic is the change in the size of the population of the resort town of Banff. In 1900, the population of Banff was 271 people. Fifty years later, it was 2,357. Fifty years after that, in 2000, it was about 7,000. As we will see in the next chapter, caps on the population size of the town of Banff may have very positive ecological effects on the park. The next statistic is equally interesting. In 1900, there were about 5,000 visitors a year to the park. Fifty years later that number had multiplied nearly ten times to 413,000. In the fifty years since, the number of visitors has multiplied another ten times.[1] Now we have nearly 4.5 million visitors a year. The third statistic that deserves very careful analysis is the growth of the regional population.

In 1885, in all 100,000 square miles (258,999 square km) of the territory that is now Alberta, there were only 15 non-Native people. In the fall of 1885, when the Canadian Pacific Railway was completed, there may have been 3,000 people living in the entire Bow Valley. Now more than 1,500,000 people live in the river basin alone.

We are only now taking time to properly examine how these changes have impacted where and how we live, and how they will affect our future. Since World War II, tourism has been moving toward greater mass, toward increased visitation, toward globalization, toward improving standards of amenities and higher financial yields. It has worked. Tourism has become the economic engine of the mountain West and many livelihoods depend on it. But there is concern that this success may not be sustainable if we are unable to prevent large-scale ecological change.

It was not until a blue-ribbon scientific assessment called the Banff Bow Valley Study was completed in the fall of 1996 that we came into possession of a thorough assessment of the cumulative effects of human interaction with the landscape on the broader ecological history of the mountain West. The report acknowledged that ecosystems within the Bow Valley had co-evolved with a variety of natural disturbances that helped maintain a diversity of vegetation types and wildlife habitat. The report noted that natural fires, as well as fires set by Aboriginal people, were important to the evolving health of the montane and subalpine areas of the valley. Floods were also an important part of the natural succession of life in the valley. Flooding along the Bow River and its tributaries was essential for maintaining healthy riparian communities. Avalanches cleared areas of trees and shrubs, opening them up for new growth that was essential for the perpetuation of many wildlife species. It was also observed that insect infestations and disease also played a natural role in the long-term renewal of valley ecosystems.

The report then noted that, since the arrival of European settlers in the valley, the nature of the disturbances has changed. The park was becoming "islandized" by urban development and other forms of human use. Towns, lodges, highways, railways, trails and other facilities have eliminated or altered many natural valley communities. Increasing numbers of residents and park visitors contributed to air pollution, sewage discharges, solid waste, and demands on potable water. It was also noted that sensitive wildlife avoided areas of high human activity, further compounding the problem of diminishing natural habitat. Transportation corridors through the park were understood to fragment the landscape and block natural movement of wildlife through the region. It was also noted that transportation corridors were avenues by which exotic plants were being introduced into the park and into the rest of the World Heritage Site. Nearly eighty years of fire suppression had led to the gradual aging of forests and a loss of important wildlife habitat. The report recognized that, though the hunting pressure that had so diminished wildlife early in the twentieth century had subsided, wildlife mortality pressures continued along the highway and the railway.

Consistent with what Ian Syme witnessed, the Bow Valley Study also noted that predator-prey relationships had been altered in Banff National Park over the past century. Most species of large carnivores were exterminated from the park and surrounding areas twice, between 1910 and 1950, as part of a provincial initiative to control rabies. Elk numbers were controlled through culls and translocations as late as 1960. Though not well documented, it appears that ungulates, upland game birds and some large carnivores were hunted as sources of food by wardens and other park users until the 1950s.

These were not the only ecological impacts that human presence had on the valley. Aquatic resources have been compromised by a range of impacts from water level control and impoundment, loss and degradation of aquatic habitat through development of transportation corridors, the increased urbanization of Banff and Lake Louise townsites resulting in releases of nutrients and other chemicals, pollution deriving from garbage landfills, and past mining activity. Aquatic ecosystems have been further impacted by gravel extraction and atmospheric pollution. The aquatic ecosystems themselves have also been severely affected by over-fishing and by the introduction of non-native fish and other species.

The direction and flow of ecological history indicate that since European contact, mountain ecosystems in many parts of Canada are moving in the direction of greater disturbance and disruption of natural processes, resulting in diminishing native biodiversity. The diminishment and loss that have been a central ecological theme in North America since the beginning of the Pleistocene continues unabated.

Through initiatives like the Bow Valley Study, we have come to possess a far greater understanding of the natural systems that surround and support human societies. Much of that research has been focused on thresholds, interdependence, and interactivity of complex systems of environmental resources such as climate, oceans, forests, mountains and agricultural lands. As Thomas Homer-Dixon has indicated, over the last decades the public has generally held the view that the earth's environmental systems are resilient and stable in the face of human impacts.[2] Over the past two decades, however, the perception of science has shifted: these systems may respond slowly and incrementally over time before suddenly changing their character. In other words, natural systems exhibit "threshold effects."

In 2007, the Fourth Assessment Report of the Intergovernmental Panel on Climate Change (IPCC) assessed the then-current scientific knowledge of the natural and human drivers of climate change, observed changes in climate, estimates of projected future climate change, and the ability of science to attribute changes to different causes. Its key findings include the fact that global atmospheric concentrations of carbon dioxide, methane and nitrous oxide have increased markedly as a result of human activities since 1750 and now far exceed pre-industrial values. The report pointed out that global increases in carbon dioxide concentration are due primarily to fossil fuel use and land-use change, while increases in concentrations of methane and nitrous oxide are primarily due to agriculture.

The IPCC has concluded that the global mean surface temperature will continue to rise and that we might expect projected increases of somewhere between 1.1 °C and 6.4 °C by the year 2100. As of 2007 at least, IPCC models predicted that if something is done to mitigate greenhouse gas emissions, mean global surface temperature could still rise by somewhere between 1.1 °C and 2.9 °C. Or it may rise as much as 2.4 °C and 6.4 °C within this century if we carry on as we are now. The huge range in these predictions reflects uncertainty related to how humanity will respond to the need to reduce greenhouse gas production. Put bluntly, our planet's mean surface temperature could rise by 1.1 °C if we do something about human population growth, energy

KOOTENAY RIVER VISTA
Kootenay National Park is
more than just a highway.
It protects the headwaters
of the Kootenay River. The
780-kilometre-long Kootenay
is a major tributary of the
Columbia which is confusing
to some in that it flows out of
Kootenay National Park and
flows within a kilometre of
Columbia Lake, which is the
headwaters of the Columbia
River. The Kootenay then
flows out of Canada into
Montana and Idaho before
flowing back into Canada and
joining the Columbia near
Castlegar, British Columbia.
Photograph by R.W. Sandford.

consumption and energy conservation; or it could rise two and half times that if we don't.[3]

The consequences of climate change would be manifold. We can expect weather disturbances, heat waves, droughts, forest fires, violent storms and floods. Polar icecaps will shrink and weaken. We have already seen evidence of this. In 2000, an icebreaker made its way through the thin and melting ice to a two-kilometre-wide pool of open ocean at the North Pole. By 2007, the entire Northwest Passage was free of ice in summer. Sea levels will rise just a few centimetres or nearly a metre. If the latter, coastlines worldwide will shrink and lowlands will disappear. Huge numbers of people will have to be resettled.

As thermoclines of global climate advance poleward, plant communities and animal species have to struggle to keep up. Plant communities, in particular, are slow to respond to changing climate. At the close of the last ice age, two species of cold-adapted spruce advanced northward with the retreating ice. They now form the great northern forests of Canada and Alaska. They advanced northward at only three to fifteen kilometres a century. The velocity of the northern movement of climatic zones in the next century, however, may be much more rapid than what happened at the end of the last ice age. The future of slower-paced native floras and faunas is uncertain. Many native animal species and plant communities are trapped in isolated reserves, islandized by agriculture and urban sprawl. Plants and animals in these situations have no place to go.[4] Many parks and reserves will no longer remain within the biogeographical regions they were created to represent.

As E.O. Wilson has suggested, it may well be possible to transplant some threatened plant and animal species northward or inland. But it is impossible to physically move entire ecosystems. Among the most vulnerable ecosystems are the alpine and arctic tundra. In the event of even a modest amount of global warming, they will be pushed upward and pole-ward into oblivion. Thousands of mountain species from lichens to mosses, some of our most cherished wildflowers, and mammals such as pikas, marmots and bears, all the way to polar species such as penguins and polar bears, could disappear.

There are other ramifications that could present themselves through such climate change. The problem with rapid upward change in the surface temperature of the earth is that it makes our weather more unpredictable, altering patterns of rainfall and hence impacting agriculture and food supply. It would melt glaciers and icecaps, and reduce snowpack and snow cover, altering the flow and reliability of our rivers and the levels of our oceans.

Projections have been made on how climate change might affect national parks that have been created in the mountainous regions of Canada.[5] Climate change projections for the southern mountain national parks indicate that winter and spring precipitation is expected to increase, while summer precipitation is expected to decrease. Warmer spring and fall temperatures will extend the melting seasons of glaciers by at least one month, in the southern Rocky Mountains. Lower-elevation glaciers are projected to retreat rapidly as a result of projected climate warming. Accelerated glacial retreat would increase summer runoff until the glaciers have been largely depleted. However, once these glaciers have melted, input to streams could decrease substantially within only a few years.[6] Scientists have observed high concentrations of persistent organochlorine compounds in glacial ice and snow in the mountain ranges of western Canada. These pollutants have accumulated over decades via long-range air transport. A rapid glacial melt may release these trapped pollutants in sufficient quantities to be of concern for downstream aquatic ecosystems.

There will also be changes in the make-up of mountain ecosystems. Banff National Park, for example, contains montane, subalpine and alpine vegetation zones. Forty-one species in the park are at the limits of their ranges, and are therefore particularly sensitive to climate change. Both latitudinal and elevational boundary shifts should be expected. A temperature increase of between 1°C and 6°C will cause vegetation zones to shift upwards by approximately 500 to 600 metres or a range of about 1,600 to approximately 2,000 feet, the equivalent of one vegetative zone in mountainous regions. This may result in the loss of some alpine species that will be unable to compete with subalpine or montane species that expand upward. One scientific study modeled the loss of mammals in montane habitats from climate change and predicted that an increase of 3°C would result in species losses of 9 to 62 percent from mountaintops.[7]

The migration of animals and birds through the region will also be significantly affected by climate change. The current wintering zone for the park's ungulate herds is in the montane regions of the lower river valleys in most of the parks that compose the World Heritage Site. The montane zone provides a shallower snow pack, allowing these animals to move with relative ease. Though winters are expected to be shorter and spring run-off earlier, a projected increase in winter precipitation may impair the movement of these species. In response to these changes, ungulates may migrate down valley to find food throughout the winter.

The fire regime in the mountain national and provincial park region will be affected by climate change. Forest fires are projected to become more frequent. The intensity of fires may also increase as a result of drier summer conditions. Higher summer temperatures and less severe winter cold spells are expected to increase forest disease and insect attack, such as those by species of bark beetle on lodgepole pine communities and high elevation spruce and fir forests. Fires are likely to become more intense when they occur in forest stands affected by these insect species. Higher temperature fires will have impacts on water storage in vegetation and soils and influence run-off patterns in ways that we cannot presently fully predict.

The impact of climate change on popular recreational activities like downhill skiing in western Canada has not been adequately studied. An increase in winter snowfall may result in better ski conditions, however warmer temperatures in late fall and early spring may result

AVALANCHE HAZARD

Avalanches are a serious and much under-estimated winter hazard in the mountain West. In a big avalanche, millions of tonnes of snow can move several kilometres in just a few seconds. Despite enormous efforts committed to public education, the number of avalanche deaths remains unnecessarily high.

Photograph by Frances Klatzel.

in a shortened season. In addition, increased temperatures may push quality ski conditions to higher elevations, potentially increasing the pressure to expand ski facilities upward. The potential increase in avalanche activity due to increases in snow pack and higher winter temperatures may increase the disruption of ski operations and highway and railway corridors in the park.

On the positive side, warmer temperatures are expected to increase the length of the summer season for activities such as hiking, camping, golfing and rafting. Deeper snow pack may continue to restrict the accessibility of some high-elevation trails. However, trails in lower areas would experience an increase in season length. Higher stream water levels may impede backcountry trail users and, at times, pose an extra risk to visitors. Rafting may benefit from high late-summer water levels resulting from increased glacial melting, as long as there is a large enough volume of ice to still be melted. Higher spring peak flows, however, may threaten park infrastructure like bridges, culverts and trails. Decreased summer precipitation and higher evapotranspiration rates may increase irrigation requirements for golf courses.

Recent studies have indicated that the climate in the Canadian West is warming at a rate that exceeds the global average. In Alberta, for example, mean annual temperature has increased in the range of 1 to 2.5 degrees Celsius over the last century. We are already experiencing higher winter and nighttime temperatures. Snow and ice are declining as warmer, shorter winters convert snow to rain. Mean annual stream flows on the Canadian prairies have been decreasing since 1947. Over time, changes in precipitation are expected to have substantial impacts on total water supply.

While the southern Great Plains move in the direction of desertification, the climate in the western mountains has also begun to change. For the last century, the strategy for protecting global biodiversity has been to protect representative parcels of each important eco-region. The foundation of this entire global program, of which our mountain national and provincial parks are an important part, is

PRACTICING PROBING FOR BURIED AVALANCHE VICTIMS
Because there are more inexperienced people skiing in the backcountry and because skiers at established resorts do not always take out-of-bounds warnings seriously, the avalanche hazard remains the prominent winter public safety threat in the Canadian Rocky Mountain Parks World Heritage Site. Although ski patrols at established ski areas are well-trained in search and rescue techniques, avalanche victims seldom survive long if they are buried. *Photograph by R.W. Sandford.*

that these representative areas will remain biogeographically stable. But the Alberta climate change vulnerability assessment argues that global climate change impacts are already invalidating this assumption. The maintenance of global biodiversity will require us to aim to protect what will effectively become "a moving target of ecological representativeness."[8]

Protecting existing landscapes will require that disturbances be managed, new stresses will need to be controlled and habitat modifications will likely be necessary in order to reconfigure protected areas so that they can survive emerging climate conditions. Whole ecological systems are already advancing northward. Current ecological communities are disassembling and re-integrating into new assemblages. These changes could bring about a huge dislocation of human settlement. That relocation will likely be inland and uphill toward cooler temperatures and reliable water supplies. The Canadian West will be a different place by 2050.

The implications of these changes could dramatically change our culture. As climate change impacts accelerate, as they almost certainly will do, governments will have to do a great deal more to ensure the

A MOST UNDESIRABLE END

For all their glory, the Rocky Mountains parks can be a very dangerous place. The actor in this photograph has been positioned in exactly the posture in which many avalanche victims have been found after being buried in the near cement-like conditions of a big slide. Such accidents generally can be avoided by knowing the avalanche conditions and by never skiing out-of-bounds at an established ski area.
Photograph by R.W. Sandford.

reliable and predictable availability of the basic environmental resources and of goods and services that make our large cities and prosperous urban way of life possible. A whole new global economy will emerge to provide the environmental needs that nature at one time provided free on our behalf. The sheer scale and urgency of the project will require this to be so. More and more of our resources will have to be spent on managing natural, agricultural, forest and urban ecosystems so as to ensure the vitality of the basic processes that form the foundation of the environmental stability upon which our continued prosperity depends.

Though we are presently looking at a complicated future, we have to see that there is a huge window of opportunity in this. Never before have we had a greater reason to create a vision of the West we want and to act on it. Never before has there been a greater urgency to get past the frontier free-for-all that once again defines our age, to create a vision of what we want our West to be like at its future and ultimate best. By protecting the core of the central Rocky Mountain ecosystem, we have laid down the foundation for the next iteration of scientifically informed public policy in the mountain West. So what might we do next?

It took about fifty-five years to lay down the foundation for the protected area system that presently defines the ecological and cultural milieu of the mountain West. Due to the urgency created by population growth, landscape change and accelerating climate impacts it is not likely we will have that much time to affect change. We might have ten to twenty years at most – and the next five are the most critical. There are at least seven things we might consider doing. To transform the West around our founding landscape values, we won't have time to do one step before we advance to the next. We will have to move simultaneously on all fronts. Fortunately, some of these steps are already being undertaken. What we seem to lack, however, is urgency, and that is something we can either have now, while we still have choices, or later when we don't.

The first thing we should do is acknowledge the true nature of our accomplishment in the mountain West. We have to think in larger terms about what we have, appreciate what we have done, acknowledge what we have learned by doing it, and be unabashed in creating a vision for the future based on the foundation of past success. Though we may not have consciously intended to do it – or even known we were doing it – the creation of the Mountain Parks and surrounding buffers is one of this country's greatest cultural achievements. It is a triumph of persistent, forward-thinking public policy. This accomplishment, in my estimation at least, should trump the history of development and fragmentation we presently celebrate as being so central to our identity in the West. We need to keep in mind that the real history, the one that will matter most to the future, is not what we built, but what we saved.

Breakthroughs in understanding the dynamics inherent to self-willed, self-generating ecosystem function will be as important to the future as the discovery of electricity was in the past. Those discoveries can only be made where such systems still exist. Our greatest future wealth may reside in the fact that we still have such places.

It is not enough, however, to tell people what we have. Due to the galloping impacts of population growth, landscape change and climate warming, what we have now could well be history before we can explain its loss. What we need is a desirable vision of this world transposed over the next. No one is going to create this vision for us. Governments might ultimately bless and perhaps even fund what we do regionally, but they are not going to do the work. The vision has to come from somewhere. Whatever the future holds for this region, it is going to be created on the ground by selfless people working together toward a common vision and linked to one another through the Internet. Ideally, whatever we do next should be informed by science and should be founded on ecosystem values. This isn't going to be easy. We are going to have to get out of our intellectual, institutional and jurisdictional silos to achieve and create a larger vision, but once again the Central Rockies Ecosystem provides a means to do so. The compelling natural character of the Rockies drove the first iteration of the mountain West. It can drive the next.

The second thing we might consider is that we have to stop making things unnecessarily worse. Instead of trying to avert climate change, we are dismantling natural systems that serve as protection against climate extremes. At the same time we are going full speed ahead in making landscape changes that will not diminish but amplify climate impacts. Sooner or later, we are going to have to stop inappropriate development in the mountain West if only because, in terms of energy and climate impacts, it is not sustainable.

Third, there is an urgent need to link scientific research outputs to public policy inputs. We have to build a bridge between science and public understanding so that we can establish a common vision of the value of what we have in the context of global and climate change. Presently, we don't act fast enough on what science tells us. It has been estimated that it would cost $30 trillion a year to provide the planetary ecological services that nature presently provides to us free. It might only cost one one-hundredth of that to protect and expand much of the world's existing ecological function. Viewed this way, E.O. Wilson argues, conserving biodiversity can be seen to be the best deal that nature has offered humanity since agriculture. We need to realize and then act on this fact.

Fourth, we need to build a strong local culture around ecosystem productivity. The most effective way to incorporate ecosystem-based sensibilities into the fabric of our culture is through land-use policy. Only by tying all human activity directly to a landscape ethic can all the energies of our unique Western mountain culture be harnessed in support of sustainability. Only then will we be able to use art, literature and popular culture, grounded in solid science, to inspire in the public imagination a new sense of pride in what we possess, in terms of ecological wealth in the mountain West and why it is important to our future. We need to articulate a simple but sensible ecosystem ethic and communicate it outward, in a way that will constantly reinforce local understanding of the value of what we possess in the mountain West that is unique to where and how we live.

We need high-profile public champions for the expanded bioregion. Every time we turn on a television or radio, we need to hear the message. We have to get past worn-out environmental clichés about the importance of ecosystems, which put people into nostalgic sleep. We need some edge. We need to teach Westerners the value of what ecosystems do and provide – for us and for the world. And we need to do it now.

To survive economically – which is to say ecologically – we need to create a culture commensurate with the remarkable nature of the landscape we occupy. We can't do that without the sincere support of the tourism industry. The tourism industry, however, has made this commitment without expecting every gesture in support of ecosystem understanding to be rewarded with further development approvals.

If we want to keep what we have, we will have to find ways to participate in the creation of an economic foundation compatible with an ecologically sound future. If we don't, then the future could take away from us all that we have worked to protect. This suggests that, whether we like it or not, we have to do a far better job of articulating the economic value of the ecological wealth we possess, so that our whole society can redefine itself in the context of what that wealth might ultimately mean to them.

Finally, we need to embody our society's need to be positive and persistent while being flexible and adaptive. Those locals and visitors who have come to know and love the western mountain landscape all have community and family lives. Our knowledge of mountain geography and ecosystems allows us to be highly influential witnesses to climate impacts in our time and to extend that influence beyond the mountain community to everyone around us.

We have to dispel the myth that we can't do anything about what is happening, that we have to essentially sit back and watch as our world and everything that matters in it declines, that we have to accept the diminishment and loss that began in the Pleistocene to persist into our epoch to become the central theme of our historical era.

Now is not a time to be timid. We can't retreat because there is no place to retreat to. We should go up not down. We should expand our ecosystem ideal and see if, in making our ecological wealth apparent to ourselves and to others, we can't shape a different kind of future than the one obviously before us. We've done it before. We can do it again. We can create the West we want.

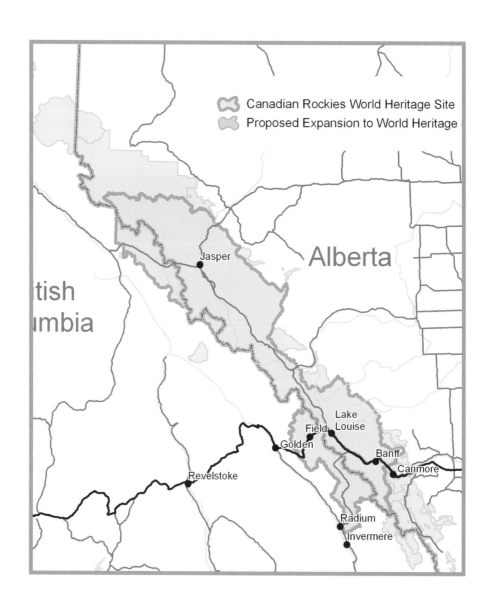

20

Expanding the World Heritage Site Designation

Managing for Future Integrity Instead of Loss

THE REALIZATION THAT WE HAVE done some very significant and positive things in terms of the management of land use that we haven't yet fully appreciated is a source of great hope for the future in the mountain West that is increasingly rare in our time. That hope was put into obvious relief in a global context for perhaps the first time through the United Nations International Year of Mountains in 2002.

The International Year of Mountains evolved out of the Rio de Janiero Earth Summit in 1992, where it was realized that the health of the planet's mountain ecosystems was just as serious an environmental concern for humanity as tropical deforestation, desertification and climate change. It was concluded in Rio that many of the mountain ranges in the world were under real threat. Our extreme landscapes were literally being eaten alive. The International Year of Mountains was declared so that we could focus on these threats and what we might do to counter them.

The reaction in the Mountain Parks to the proposed UN Year was very interesting. Many felt that the celebration wouldn't be of much value because mountain ranges in Canada were not under the same kinds of threats as the mountain regions in places like the Andes or Himalayas.

POND NEAR KINBASKET LAKE

Parts of British Columbia that were part of Hamber Provincial Park when it was originally formed remain ecologically intact, despite large-scale reservoir construction and extensive forestry activity. These areas would be excellent candidates for inclusion in an expanded World Heritage Site re-designation. *Photograph by R.W. Sandford.*

Our country was too big, too sparsely populated and too wealthy to have the kinds of problems other countries had in their mountains. As we had been wise enough to protect large national and provincial park blocks and adjoining multiple-use forest areas in our mountain regions, the International Year of Mountains would simply be a celebration of our success in protecting mountain ecosystems. This, however, did not turn out to be the case. The biggest challenge faced by organizers during the International Year of Mountains in Canada was to get people to see what was happening right in front of their very eyes.

In examining the state of our mountain ecosystems against the backdrop of the pressures facing mountain regions all over the world, it became apparent that mountain ecosystems in Canada are no less threatened than elsewhere on the planet. We have resource development, settlement and human-use issues, tourism pressures, and problems with habitat fragmentation and loss. We have ecosystem health issues and problems with introduced species.

Just as elsewhere in the world, the people who live in our mountain areas are often obliged by the harsh nature of economic reality to suffer exploitation by lowlanders who apply political and economic pressures in ways that compromise local connection to place and respect for the fragility of ecosystems. All this, we discovered, happens in and around our mountain national parks, which are the extreme landscapes to which we have afforded our highest level of protection and most intense management commitment.

In mountain areas outside national parks, our culture's appetites are eating up more than just the view. At a forum held in Jasper in 2000, representatives from every national park in western and northern Canada gathered to talk about the relationship between heritage, tourism and ecological health. It became apparent that the problems we face inside our parks are nothing compared to what is happening on and beyond their boundaries. There were few national parks, even in the remotest parts of the Arctic, that were not experiencing extensive oil and gas exploration or mining development on or near their boundaries. In some of the more remote parks, the number of people travelling for the purpose of resource exploitation is many times greater than those who visit for reasons of personal transformation or adventure.

Just as elsewhere in the world, the flow of history in Canada is leading toward a direction of reduced biodiversity and increasing cumulative human impact in all of this country's mountain ranges. We often save extreme landscapes only when tourism and adventure are deemed the most profitable human use, and then only after resource interests have eaten away at them first.

As has occurred elsewhere, the hysterical but largely unfulfilled prophesies of the extreme environmental movement has spawned a counter-movement within the industrial tourism sector. American-style public relations strategies are being employed widely by the tourism industry, especially in the mountain national parks. If you don't like the fact that a landscape has been slated for any kind of protection, or if you feel in any way limited in the activities you may want to undertake in a given area, you can create your own advocacy group to fight for and expand your rights.

The self-centred public relations of special interests have proven to be very dangerous to our hope of long-term sustainability. What kind of cultural landscape do we live in when all meaning and value is reduced to economic terms? You get a world in which wishes are often disguised as facts. You get a world of logical and rhetorical fallacy in which weasel words and special pleading define the future of our most cherished places. Combine this with a form of political correctness in which disagreement is confused with disrespect and you can justify almost

for others, plus the approval of management plans with an emphasis on protection of the natural environment. As a result, the World Heritage Committee, at its 2006 meeting, passed a resolution encouraging an expansion of the Canadian Rocky Mountain Parks World Heritage Site.

The expansion of the designation will demonstrate the global ecological value of what we already possess, so its economic value can be appropriately recognized. The broader designation also offers the opportunity to reposition ourselves in the global tourism marketplace. We may wish to use the expanded designation as a foundation for articulating and aggressively marketing interpretations of the important role the careful local management of ecologically stable national and provincial parks and protected places plays in moderating regional climate impacts, as a way of distinguishing the Canadian Rockies region in the world tourism marketplace. We may also wish to seek broader designation in the name of watershed protection, for the benefits in doing so will greatly reduce the cost of dealing with water quality in towns and cities downstream.

Re-designation could be accompanied by scientific research activities related to evolving ecosystem dynamics. Such research could be linked directly to public education that underscores a vision of the West we want. Increased public understanding of the economic value of properly functioning ecosystems would inform evolving public policy, and create a foundation for this country's second great landscape-based national public policy achievement. It may sound impossible but it isn't. History tells us a great deal about the power of mountain place to define identity

Vast areas of the eastern slopes in the foothills eco-region adjacent to the entire length of the current World Heritage Site are still in pristine ecological condition. Presently these domains act as buffers protecting the core of the World Heritage Site. Many of these areas, including the White Goat, Siffleur and Wilmore Wildernesses, are worthy of higher designation in and of themselves. Such designation need not mean an end to current human activities, including hunting and guiding.
Photograph by R.W. Sandford.

for the Canadian West. At the risk of repeating one of the central themes of this book too often, we have done it once. We can do it again.

There are other benefits to extending the designation. Without altering a single land-use regulation, the enlarged World Heritage Site will encompass a broader range of ecosystems and habitats, including the montane grasslands of the Front Ranges and Foothills on the east side, and wet-belt forests on the west slope of the Great Divide. The broader array of habitats and ecosystems will provide more resilience in the event that climate change causes latitudinal and elevational shifts of current ecosystem complexes. This would mean a greater likelihood of maintaining this region in the closest possible semblance of its original state.

With the exception of bison, which may yet be reintroduced, all the large mammal species that historically occupied habitats in the World Heritage Site are still present. All naturally occurring fish species are still present, as headwater streams provide remnant habitat for once-abundant species such as bull trout and west-slope cutthroat trout.

The extended designation will also speak very positively to the World Heritage Committee's criteria for preservation of integrity. Integrity is a measure of the wholeness and intactness of the natural and/or cultural heritage and its attributes. Examining the conditions of integrity requires assessing the extent to which the property includes all elements necessary to express its outstanding universal value.

For all properties nominated under criteria of integrity, biophysical processes and landform features should be relatively intact. However, it is recognized that no area is totally pristine and that all natural areas are in a dynamic state and to some extent involve contact with people. Human activities, including those of traditional societies and local communities, often occur in natural areas. These activities may be consistent with the outstanding universal value of the area where they are ecologically sustainable. In addition, properties nominated under integrity criteria should have sufficient size and contain the elements necessary to demonstrate the key aspects of processes that are essential for the long-term conservation of the ecosystems and the biological diversity they contain.

The benefits of such designation, however, do not stop with ecosystems. Beyond the region's geological, biological and ecological significance is an entire domain of cultural significance that has yet to be brought into consideration, even within contemporary management frameworks that define current use of this far-flung group of protected places. These mountains are the headwaters of western Canadian literature and poetry. They are the inspiration for art, music and dance, and dozens of recreations that utterly define Western identity. These mountain landscapes are the source of our cultural inspiration and the image of what Canada is, in the world's imagination. They are the backdrop to everything we are and do in the mountain West.

Our final decision on what areas we would like include within this globally significant re-designation is pending. The high level of protection we afford these landscapes will ensure that the Western culture we created in response to the grandeur of the landscapes in which we live, continues to thrive and that we plan to establish our uniqueness through that culture. In telling the world that these places matter, we are announcing that where and how we live is central to our identity as Canadians. By deciding in favour of these broader designations, we will be announcing to ourselves and to the rest of Canada that we are on the threshold of creating a culture commensurate with place. In so doing we will be telling the world that we have made a clear decision on the kind of West we want. That world will then come to Canada on our terms, to see that West and to see how we created it.

21

Creating a Culture Commensurate with Place

WHAT WE HAVE CREATED BY WAY of the Canadian Rocky Mountain Parks World Heritage Site is unique in the world, and invites us to think in different terms about how we might live in association with this remarkable landscape in the future. By re-affirming local values derived from our strong historic connection to place, we can make our history work for us in the service of a bright future. This, I believe, can be accomplished through the re-telling of our history in the expanded context of our greatest cultural achievement: the creation of our National and Provincial Parks and their collective designation as a World Heritage Site. This re-telling should begin with what we have done well and what we can do well in the future. One thing we have done well relates to our growing understanding of the role fire plays in the succession of mountain ecosystems. Because this leads us back to a greater understanding of why protected areas exist, this is a story Parks Canada doesn't mind sharing.

TORCHING SMOKEY THE BEAR

AS FIRE ECOLOGISTS LEARNED more about the natural history of Rocky Mountain valleys, it became clear that for thousands of years Native

MAKING SURE WHAT NEEDS TO BE BURNED CATCHES FIRE
We can set small, frequent, low-temperature fires with careful prescribed burns. This emulates a natural fire regime and keeps fuel loads to a minimum. Conversely, suppressing fires and allowing fuel to build up can produce 1,100°C fires that burn forests and destroy even microbes in the soil, such that it takes three hundred years for to recovery, with lasting impacts on wildlife, ecological stability, erosion and stream flow.
Photograph by R.W. Sandford.

large chrome coffee carafe. A large metal cover screws into the top. When this is removed one finds a metal wand that can be screwed back onto the outside of the tank, to create a device that can literally change the world.

By opening the right valves and lighting the end of the wand, one can create liquid fire by simply pouring the fuel in the same way you pour water from a watering can. I watched Studd as he advanced along the base of the ridge and made his way up the steep slope to meet a fire line created by Ian Pengelly and Tom Davidson. He looked like a Pied Piper from hell. As he moved nonchalantly up the hill and through the forest, flames popped out of the ground and followed him. A great roaring followed the fire into the forest above.

As the smoke cleared, the afternoon winds stopped blowing from the west. Cool, denser air began pouring slowly down the mountainsides into the valley. Night would soon put the fire to sleep. Pengelly explained that Parks Canada had to be very careful to keep its fire program operative within constraints acceptable to the local residents upon which it relied for support. He was very conscious that the smoke from prescribed burns in the park could create discomfort among people with respiratory problems who lived downwind. For this reason Pengelly and his colleagues kept the area of each burn to less than 200 hectares and carefully monitored conditions. A firebreak had also been created between the park and the neighbouring communities of Harvey Heights and Canmore. Pengelly hoped that the people who lived downwind in the Bow Valley would appreciate that the Fairholme fires would ultimately contribute to the natural biodiversity of the park and the region, making it a safer, more interesting and ultimately a more worthwhile place to live in the future.

RE-WILDING THE WEST

OUR IMPROVED UNDERSTANDING of fire and our growing ability to manage it to the benefit of both ecosystems and people in the Mountain

Parks has opened the door to other opportunities to restore ecosystems that have been adversely impacted by human actions in the past. One way to reverse the trend of diminishment and loss of ecological integrity and diversity that began in the Pleistocene, and we have carried on in our time, is to consider re-introduction of lost species. The restoration of previous ecological conditions, however, is fraught with complications. Only a very committed society can even contemplate turning back the ecological clock, for once a species is gone, a whole new ecology forms around its absence.

In association with Parks Canada's International Year of Mountains fire orientation program, I was also invited by Parks Canada to contribute observations on the viability of re-introducing the bison to the upper reaches of the Red Deer River in Banff National Park. This species had been present in the area of the Mountain Parks up to and slightly after European contact and had had a huge influence on the ecology of the mountain forests until it was hunted nearly out of existence in the nineteenth century. The bison was the largest terrestrial mammal to have survived the Pleistocene extinctions in North America. The idea was that re-introduction of this species would reverse the trend of diminishment and loss of species and ecological integrity within the World Heritage Site. But as I soon learned, the introduction or re-introduction of even a single species through the process of re-wilding can have profound ecological consequences.

Parks Canada invited a number of people to see where the proposed bison re-introduction might take place. We gathered at the Warden Office in Banff early on an overcast June morning, with the aim of flying into the Red Deer Valley. The group included local naturalist and ecosystem expert Peter Duck, respected outfitter Ron Warner and me. Our host, at least for the flight from Banff to Scotch Camp Warden Cabin, was Chief Park Warden Ian Syme. Accompanying him was Ian Pengelly, the Parks Canada's fire specialist who had earlier allowed me to try my hand at starting a prescribed burn in the Fairholme Range.

Pengelly had confided that the idea of re-introducing bison into its historic range was the brainchild of a number of senior Park Wardens like himself who wanted to do something really bold before they retired. They had chosen the upper Red Deer watershed because it was known historic bison habitat. There were two other important advantages to the area. In this area the national park abutted on its boundary with the Ya-Ha-Tinda Ranch, a 565-hectare Parks Canada holding in some of the best grassland habitat in the front ranges of the Rockies. Just as importantly, it was a long way from the Bow Valley where conflicts between human use and wildlife protection always seemed to make national headlines. In this remote place it might be possible to perform the ultimate experiment in reversing biodiversity diminishment and loss while contributing to the restoration of the park's original ecological integrity. The object, Pengelly said with pride, was to re-introduce the alpha herbivore in the North American West. It wasn't going to be easy, however, as the bison is one of the most difficult and dangerous of all species to manage and confine.

To understand how wonderfully remote the upper Red Deer River Valley really is, it is valuable to see the park from the air. Pilot Ken Gray flew us from Banff up the Cascade River Valley, where we dropped supplies at Stoney Creek Warden Cabin before following the Panther River

BISON

Historically, bison were part of the mountain ecosystem on the east side of the Great Divide. Efforts to restore the species as part of a "Pleistocene re-wilding" effort have met with little success. Bison are hard to contain and control. Their reintroduction would be expensive and complicated, especially given the increasingly islandized nature of the mountain parks and threats to existing species such as the mountain caribou, which will take considerable resources to address. *Photograph by R.W. Sandford.*

to the park's eastern boundary and out into the Province of Alberta. We then flew over the Ya-Ha-Tinda, then back into Banff National Park, following the Red Deer River to Scotch Camp. The reasons for holding our discussion at this remote Warden Service outpost soon become apparent. We were joined at Scotch Camp by park ecologist Tom Hurd, ecosystem specialist Cliff White, and University of Calgary bison restoration specialist Cormack Gates. Hurd, White and Gates were very excited about the grass on which Ken Gray had so smoothly landed the helicopter.

The big meadow at Scotch Camp had been purposely set alight in April, less than two months earlier. White explained to our amazement that green shoots had started to push themselves through the burned sod barely two hours after the fire scorched the mountain prairie. In barely two months, the fescue had completely restored itself and the meadow, creating almost unbelievably rich habitat for ungulates like deer and elk. Conditions so lush, White and Pengelly pointed out, could surely support bison.

Their point was clear. The stunning grassland ecosystem recovery rate in this valley is evidence of how valuable fire would have been historically as a range improvement tool. By burning carefully and regularly at low temperatures, Aboriginal peoples ensured that bison could continue to be supported even this far into the mountains. If it was done in the past, it could be done again.

These Park Wardens wanted to try but they knew they would never be given an opportunity to undertake such an expensive and controversial project without a great deal of public support. Peter Duck, Ron Warner and I were invited to offer our observations on the idea behind the restoration and to be candid about whether or not the kind of public support necessary to make it happen might be forthcoming. No one was shy about identifying the obstacles. The first challenge was the nature of the bison as a species. They are so big and powerful, they are almost impossible to contain.

Jasper National Park contains some of the best natural bison habitat in the Mountain Parks. In 1973, a small herd of some twenty-eight animals was airlifted into a remote northern region of the park. It wasn't long, however, before they migrated out of the park and into the surrounding foothills. In order to prevent havoc on private lands, twenty-two of the animals were recaptured. The others lingered in the area but did not survive. It may be that they needed more habitat to survive than they could find solely within the protection of the park.

The idea was to bring in pregnant bison cows, have them calve in a purpose-built paddock and then gradually introduce them into the valley so that they would imprint on the upper Red Deer as home range. Bison bulls that grew up in the valley would eventually be able to roam within a core area that would include the Panther and Cascade Valleys to the south, the Pipestone River and Baker Creek drainages to the west, and the Siffleur and upper Clearwater regions to the north and west. Should bison wander outside of these core areas and containment zones, they would be culled by First Nation ecosystem specialists in the employ of Parks Canada. In this way, First Nations participation in the culling would be formalized in a manner that was both practical and symbolic. It was proposed that the first run of management experimentation be thirty years.

The political challenges associated with the re-introduction of the bison are not insignificant. Though there are presently some 220,000 plains bison on commercial buffalo ranches in Canada, Canadian ecological specialists recently proposed this bison be listed as endangered in the wild. Commercial producers went ballistic due to the threat such a listing would pose in international markets.

Cormack Gates pointed out that area-specific species restorations were occurring with other troubled prairie mammals such as the black-tailed prairie dog and the black-footed ferret. He also cited the fact that media mogul Ted Turner was trying to restore a complete Great Plains ecosystem on his huge Montana ranch. This suggested to Gates that there was a "sweet spot" between economic, ecological and cultural interests that might permit restoration of Great Plains habitat and species. The challenge was to find that spot and do everything one could to enlarge it. Gates also cited the Charles M. Russell initiative, which aimed to restore prairie habitat in the American West, and another initiative in which the World Wildlife Fund helped add 25,000 acres to a restoration project on the Montana-Saskatchewan border. Gates pointed out that bison ranchers were also working on solutions such as the creation of common ranges as large as 600,000 acres. Whether all these initiatives will actually work, however, remains to be seen.

Cliff White wanted to talk about ecological considerations. "Is what we have here now, right?" he asked. "Or is it simply a product of what we have done, perhaps incorrectly, over the last century?" Bison, he pointed out, move differently on the landscape than other ungulates or even cattle. Bison do not congregate in the riparian areas like cattle do. They exert different grazing pressures. Bison wallow and tend to trample small pines and spruce trees, which encourages new patterns of grass and forb growth. They also tend to establish their own trails. Cliff's point was that the landscape you end up with over time is very different with bison than what results when the major ungulates are deer, elk and moose. Part of the significance of this restoration proposal was that it offered more options with respect to the era to which we want to return, in terms of replicating ecological integrity.

White was asking an important question. Which ecological integrity do we want to reproduce? The one with deer, elk and moose, or the one that existed before we established the current wildlife assemblage, which included and in fact was dominated by the bison? Ian Pengelly also weighed in on this argument. In his opinion it is crucial to determine clearly the point to which you want to return in the ecological history of the World Heritage Site as a function of Parks Canada's management objectives. Pengelly pointed out that the protected area's current ecosystem dynamics included a strong link between elk, caribou, predators and fire. He noted that there were – at last count – less than half a dozen mountain caribou in Banff National Park and only two hundred or so remaining in Jasper. He wondered if caribou were disappearing because humans were reintroducing fire and allowing wolf populations to re-establish themselves instead of eliminating them as vermin. He wondered if caribou would have even been present in these mountains had humans not decimated wolf numbers historically.

INDIAN PAINTBRUSH
Indian Paintbrush *(Castilleja coccinea)* presents a range of flower colours, from pink through bright red to nearly black. It may be the wildflower that is most emblematic of the Canadian Rocky Mountain Parks World Heritage Site. *Photograph by R.W. Sandford.*

He also wondered if the ecological combination of bison, predators and fire wasn't a more representative and stable one. He wondered if that composition might better fit our idea of the West we really want. If it did, he said, we should start managing toward it.

THE WEST WE WANT

CELEBRATIONS CAN BE important, especially if they make us examine the roots of our success and the direction that success might be taking us. The International Year of Mountains offered Canadians at all levels of experience an opportunity to reaffirm their connection to place, and to expand their knowledge of Canada's mountain heritage. By analyzing how locals came to have a "sense of place," and by examining what people search for when they travel to see our mountains, Canadians began to see just how remarkable our protected mountain places really are in a larger global context.

In re-examining what makes what we have so meaningful to ourselves and others, we learned that the people who live in mountain communities in western Canada have a lot more in common than we ever imagined. Most of those who live in Canada's mountain places today were not born where they now live. They came from elsewhere and experienced transformation in the mountains. They fell in love with the local landscape and culture and stayed to become "locals by choice."

We discovered that residents in what were locally considered to be very different and often rival mountain communities often felt very similar about what was important to them concerning where and how they lived in the mountain West. This, in combination with a number of other circumstances, led to the birth of the Heritage Tourism Strategy in the Mountain Parks. Though this idea has lost some of its initial momentum it still possesses great promise as a vehicle for helping to further develop and sustain a culture that is unique to place in the Rockies.

In a simple world, Parks Canada, or a select group of community-minded residents, might be asked to identify those tourism activities that were most appropriate to the wilderness image and long-term health of the park. Activities deemed inappropriate would somehow magically cease to exist and the image of the park as pristine wilderness would be immediately restored. Unfortunately, the real world is far too complicated to accommodate such simple solutions. Even if you could agree on what was appropriate in the context of changing environmental realities, issues of rights stemming from long years of residency and heavy investment in existing infrastructure cannot be ignored. No one in business in Banff was going to leave the park voluntarily just because their operation is held by some to be inappropriate to their version of park values.

The first objective of the Heritage Tourism Strategy is to make sure that all visitors to the Mountain Parks are aware they are in a park and World Heritage Site and to ensure they know what that means in terms of responsibilities, a unique aesthetic, and the recreational opportunities available to them here.

While this strategy may appear self-evident, the challenge of making people aware of the special circumstances that make Mountain Parks unique is more complicated than it might at first appear. The problem of grounding visitors in the values that are at the heart of our national park heritage begins with how we advertise our parks as attractions. In an examination of the brochures available to Banff visitors, for example, it was noted that less than one-quarter of these indicated that their attraction was in a national park or World Heritage Site and that this unique designation required any form of special consideration on the part of the visitor. Without specific direction, visitors cannot be expected to act differently in a national park, provincial park or World Heritage Site than they would in any other tourism situation. To ensure our long-term success as a tourism destination, we have to preserve the unique nature of the park. We can succeed at this if we do everything we can to ensure that all visitors understand they are in a special place and a World Heritage Site, and why this is different and special.

The second objective of the Heritage Tourism Strategy is to encourage and develop opportunities, products and services consistent with heritage values. The point this objective makes is that we cannot continue to attract visitors to Mountain Parks to participate in activities that have little or nothing to do with the heritage of the park without expecting that heritage to be compromised. The more distractions there are from the true heritage of the park, the more visitors will come for these distractions. People coming for the distractions will replace those coming for the heritage. Instead of enjoying the World Heritage Site for the heritage for which it was preserved, visitors will come in increasing numbers to enjoy experiences unrelated to the true purpose of the reserve. As this continues to happen, tension over appropriate use will grow and the tourism sector in our parks will increasingly come under criticism as being in opposition to the fundamental purpose of protected areas.

With growing regional populations and a city growing up on the eastern boundary of the Canadian Rocky Mountain Parks World Heritage Site, Banff, for example, will face increasing difficulty in sustaining its international reputation as a wilderness park. The net future impact may ultimately be a decline in the image of Banff as an international destination, which could result in a very much altered tourism climate. In order to help preserve the wilderness character of the park and, at the same time, sustain its vital tourism reputation, the tourism community in Banff may wish to reassess what it offers. It has become clear that one way to assure a bright tourism future is to develop new products and services that mirror the heritage values locals hold dear to them, as a Mountain Park and World Heritage Site community.

New realizations about the complex nature of the parks' ecosystems are also prompting changes in the way we think about the areas that compose this World Heritage Site. The third objective of the Heritage Tourism Strategy addresses ecological concerns by encouraging environmental stewardship initiatives upon which sustainable heritage tourism depends.

AT MOUNT SHARK
Bob Sandford and some of his family at Shark Mountain. The Kananaskis is as worthy of World Heritage Site designation as the adjacent national parks.
Photograph by M. P. Rogeau.

The Heritage Tourism Strategy recognizes the enormous importance of evolving environmental sensitivity, especially within our national and provincial park and World Heritage Site context. The strategy makes it clear that heritage tourism cannot stand on its own without appropriate environmental practices that ensure the integrity of the natural systems upon which this form of tourism depends for its authenticity and sustainability.

In the past two decades, a great deal of progress has been made in the implementation of recycling programs and in the development of greater efficiencies in waste, water and energy management. Some tourism businesses have become leaders in the development of these systems and in the sharing of these advancements within their industries. But environmental considerations in the Mountain Parks cannot stop at recycling and waste management. As better and more complete science allows more accurate monitoring of the health of park ecosystems, it will become increasingly important for the tourism community and national and provincial park administrations to work effectively together to address common environmental problems. The historically adversarial relationship between these agencies and the tourism sector must be replaced with a greater mutual acceptance of the fact that healthy ecosystems are just as important to the tourism industry as they are to the park.

The strategy also recognizes that ecosystems involve complex relationships and that it will not always be possible to make clearcut decisions relating to ecosystem management based on available information. For this reason, it is particularly important that everyone who lives and works in the World Heritage Site have a solid, current and consistent understanding of the heritage values and environmental

HELEN CREEK

A trail that begins across from the Crowfoot Glacier, on the Icefields Parkway, switchbacks upward toward vast alpine meadows that surround Helen Lake. Because of their similarity in appearance, the peak and valley are named for the Dolomite Mountains in northeast Italy. Grizzly bears are often seen in the area of Helen Lake's outlet creek. *Photograph by R.W. Sandford.*

considerations that drive management plans for this area.

The fourth objective of the Heritage Tourism Strategy is to strengthen employee orientation, training and accreditation programming as it relates to sharing heritage understanding with visitors. The people who live and work in this World Heritage Site establish, to a very great extent, the attitudes and habits of visitors who rely on them for example and direction, with respect to how they can maximize their national park experience. The Heritage Tourism Strategy seeks to harness local experience and appreciation of place as a basis for focusing visitor appreciation on the unique nature, history and culture of our World Heritage destination. This strategy demands that locals come to a common understanding and acceptance of what our heritage is and how we want it presented to visitors.

In the West, and in Alberta in particular, where individualism is highly cherished, coming to a common appreciation of our heritage may be difficult, perhaps even impossible. The Heritage Tourism Strategy does not presume, however, to want to make everyone think the same way about our mountain heritage. It does, however, propose that we all may want to start with the same information as a basis for reassessing what is important about our heritage and that the information be, as much as is possible, accurate and relevant.

The Heritage Tourism concept still makes a great deal of sense, but to be successful it may need to be revived at the regional level represented by the World Heritage Site. Its revitalization must not be made to rely solely on the good will and enlightened self-interest of the tourism industry. A strategy of such wide reach will only be made to work if it is adopted as a regional development strategy and embraced as a tool for land-use planning in and around the World Heritage Site. Adopted in this way, however, the strategy embodies the kinds of values that help us decide on a regional basis how we will deal with global change and the impacts associated with global warming. An integrated approach to how we want to manage the World Heritage Site crystal around which we have developed our current circumstances will also help us determine what kind of mountain West we want to have in the future.

WHAT IS OUR HERITAGE?

HISTORICALLY IT HAS ALWAYS been understanding and appreciation of nature that has been at the heart of true Rocky Mountain localness. This tradition has been encouraged by a local culture that is interested in wild landscape and the fulfilling experiences you can have in it. In the Rockies, landscape has always been seen as a powerful transformational force in human life. For generations, visitors and locals in the Rockies have observed that in realizing the country they could realize themselves. The history that has always been most important to us as locals is the history of our developing relationship to that nature. True localness has been traditionally tied to weather, land and landscape, and the ways people meet their patterns and demands. For these reasons, our heritage can be defined as a tradition of people coming to live and work here who develop an interest in understanding and celebrating the unique qualities of local nature, history and culture. It is in this way we become locals by choice.

There is little doubt that over time we have gradually been moving away from our historic local grounding in place. There are a number of obvious reasons for this. Though increasingly strong communities compose its heart, the population remains frantically transient. Many of the people who live and work here know the history and geography of where they grew up but not of the place they currently live. And even those who have made the choice to stay are not immune to the acceleration of lifestyle that seems an inescapable part of contemporary culture. Busy people have less and less time to ground themselves in the nature that surrounds them.

Like communities everywhere, we also suffer the effects of the global homogenization of culture based on media and standardized business and communications processes. Even in Canada's western mountain national parks, politics and economics are gradually beginning to impact people as much as or more than they do the landscape. In the midst of this, place is changing, too. Even those who have only lived in the Rockies a short while observe that their surroundings are changing. Our understanding of the nature of natural places is also being radically reformed by new knowledge of the dynamics of ecosystems and new awareness about what is required to sustain their integrity. It is hard to keep up with all that is happening.

But we have done one thing right that makes this region the envy the world. We have not spent all of our natural capital. The fact that we have saved important functioning elements of our natural and cultural history allows us latitude others do not possess in choosing the future we want. What we have saved keeps the door open to the most important of all cultural options: the opportunity to create a new and inspired vision of what kind of West we would like to create for ourselves and for our children.

Only now are we beginning to understand the importance of what we have preserved in terms of the watershed of the West. Only now are we beginning to imagine what this bold act says and could say about our identity and our true prosperity. Re-casting our history against the backdrop of such an extraordinary inter-generational public policy achievement allows our culture room to move in a time when natural systems everywhere are under great stress and are changing rapidly.

By caring about our mountains we have learned how to create a culture commensurate with place. But the frontier era is over and the West awaits its next historic age. We should not be satisfied to simply get what we get. It is up to us to create the West we want.

Notes

CHAPTER 1

1   Papers Relative to the Exploration by Captain Palliser of the Portion of North America which lies between The Northern Branch of the River Saskatchewan and the Frontier of the United States; and Between the Red River and Rocky Mountains; Presented to both Houses of Parliament by Command of Her Majesty, June 1859. (George Eyre and William Spotiswoode, London, 1859 and 1860), 3.

2   Ibid., 4.

3   Stephen M. Meyer, *The End of the Wild* (MIT Press, 2006), 42.

CHAPTER 2

1   "Endless Summits: Mountains of Canada," *Canadian Geographic* (September–October, 2001).

2   Personal communication, Desmond Collins. This quote echoes Stephen Jay Gould's book, *Wonderful Life* (W.W. Norton and Co., 1990).

3   Michael J. Benton, *When Life Nearly Died: The Greatest Mass Extinction of All Time* (Thames & Hudson, 2003).

4   Peter Ward, *The End of Evolution: On Mass Extinctions and the Preservation of Biodiversity* (New York: Bantam Books, 1994).

CHAPTER 3

1   Paul Martin, *Twilight of the Mammoths: Ice Age Extinctions and the Rewilding of North America* (University of California Press, 2005).

2   See John A. Byers, *American Pronghorn: Social Adaptations and the Ghosts of Predators Past* (University of Chicago Press, 1998).

CHAPTER 4

1   Wallace Stegner, *Beyond the Hundredth Meridian* (University of Nebraska Press, 1982), 256.

2   Ernest Thompson Seton, *Lives of Game Animals: An Account of those Land Animals in North America, North of the Mexican Border, which are considered "Game," Either because they have Held the Attention of Sportsmen, or Received the Protection of Law (8 Volumes)*, Charles T. Branford Company, Boston, 1953. See also Dan Flores, *The Natural West: Environmental History in the Great Plains and Rocky Mountains* (University of Oklahoma Press), 187.

3   David Thompson's Narrative of His Explorations in Western America, 1784–1812, Edited by J.B. Tyrrell (Toronto: The Champlain Society, 1916), 441.

4   Paul Kane, *Paul Kane's Frontier*, including *Wanderings of an Artist among the Indians of North America* (University of Texas Press, 1971), 87.

5   William T. Hornaday, *Our Vanishing Wildlife* (Charles Scribner's Sons, 1913), ix.

CHAPTER 5

1   Alfred W. Crosby, *Ecological Imperialism: The Biological Expansion of Europe, 900–1900* (Cambridge: Cambridge University Press, 1986), 182–186.

2   See Elizabeth A. Fenn, *Pox Americana: The Great Smallpox Epidemic of 1775–82* (Hill and Wang, 2001).

CHAPTER 6

1   R.W. Sandford, *The Canadian Alps* (Altitude Publishing, 1990), 8–28.

2   If you have visited the Middle East you may have noticed that most of the mountains described in the Bible fall within the category of hills by Canadian standards. Though we will never know the exact nature of the plant and animal communities that may have existed upon these hills two thousand years ago, it seems unlikely that they would have differed in a wholesale way from what existed on the lower slopes or on the valley floor.

3   Dolores LaChapelle, *Earth Wisdom* (Los Angeles: The Guild of Tutors Press, 1978), 10.

4   Edwin Bernbaum, *Sacred Mountains of the World* (San Francisco: Sierra Club Books, 1990), 116.

5   Francis Keelyside, *Peaks and Pioneers: The Story of Mountaineering* (London: Elek, 1975), 10.

6   Ibid., 40.

7   Ibid., 47.

8   There are two good books on the Otzi Iceman: See Brenda Fowler, *Iceman: Uncovering the Life and Times of a Prehistoric Man Found in an Alpine Glacier* (New York: Random House, 2000), and Konrad Spindler, *The Man In The Ice: The Discovery of a 5000 Year-Old Body Reveals the Secrets of the Stone Age* (Toronto: Doubleday Books, 1994).

9   See Dirk Meissner, "Frozen Aboriginal Hunter Providing Wealth of Information," *The Calgary Herald*, June 14, 2001. See also John Gray, "Anthropology re: Kwaday Dan Sinchi," *The Globe and Mail*, August 4, 2001.

10 Chris Jones, *Climbing In North America* (University of California Press, 1976), 4.

11 *Journal Kept by David Douglas During His Travels in North America, 1823–1827* (New York: Antiquarian Press Limited, 1959), 258–59.

12 Johnson's Chart of Comparative Heights of Mountains (London, 1864).

13 Donald Creighton, *John A. Macdonald, The Old Chieftain* (Toronto: Macmillan, 1965), 120.

14 E.J. Hart, *The Selling of Canada, The CPR and the Beginnings of Canadian Tourism* (Altitude Publishing, 1983), 59.

15 Ibid., 60.

16 Wm. Spotswood Green, "Climbing in the Selkirks and Adjacent Rocky Mountains," *The Alpine Journal*, No. 127 (February 1895):290.

17 Walter D. Wilcox, "Early Days in The Canadian Rockies," *American Alpine Journal*, IV (1941):177.

18 Charles E. Fay, The Casualty On Mount Lefroy, Addresses at a Memorial Meeting of the Appalachian Mountain Club, October 21, 1896, page 13.

19 R.W. Sandford, "The Columbia Icefield, A Centennial Celebration," Parks Canada, 1998, page 6.

20 Ibid., 9.

21 Letter dated September 1896, from J.H. Stallard, The Bungalow, Menlo Park, San Mateo Co., California, Canadian Pacific Archives.

22 Letter dated September 25, 1896, from D. McNicoll to T.G. Shaughnessy, Vice President, Canadian Pacific Railway, Montreal, Canadian Pacific Archives.

23 Edward Cavell, *Legacy in Ice: The Vaux Family and the Canadian Alps* (Banff: The Whyte Foundation, 1983), 7.

24 E.J. Hart, *The Place One Takes Bows From: Exploring The Heritage of the Banff-Bow Valley* (EJH Literary Enterprises, 1999), 102.

25 James Monroe Thorington, "Edward Feuz Sr.," *Canadian Alpine Journal*, xxix, no. 1 (1944–45):128.

26 R.W. Sandford, *High Ideals: Canadian Pacific's Swiss Guides, 1899–1999* (The Alpine Club of Canada and Canadian Pacific Hotels, 1999), 15.

27 Ibid., 17.

28   A.O. Wheeler, *The Selkirk Range*, Vol. 1 (Ottawa: Government Printing Bureau, 1905), 326.

29   Christian Klucker, *Adventures of an Alpine Guide* (London: John Murray, 1932), 173.

30   E.J. Hart, *Diamond Hitch* (Summerthought, 1979), 51.

31   James Outram, *In the Heart of the Canadian Rockies* (Macmillan, 1905), 65.

32   Ibid., 59.

33   The Alpine Club of Canada has remained this country's foremost national mountaineering organization. In the International Year of Mountains it boasted more than 6,000 members from all over Canada and the United States.

34   Hart, *Selling of Canada*, 65.

35   Andrew J. Kauffman and William L. Putnam, *The Guiding Spirit* (Footprint Publishing, 1986), 61.

36   Ibid., 248.

37   Howard Palmer, *Edward W.D. Holway, A Pioneer of the Canadian Alps* (The University of Minnesota Press, 1931), 3.

38   Sandford, *High Ideals*, 28.

39   Whyte and Harmon, *Lake Louise, A Diamond In The Wilderness* (Altitude Publishing, 1982), 36.

40   Basil Gardom, Canadian Pacific Railway Co., Alpine Hut of Field Stone Construction in Abbots Pass at Lake Louise, Alberta, blueprints in the Canadian Pacific Archives.

41   Whyte and Harmon, *Lake Louise*, 36.

42   Kauffman and Putnam, *Guiding Spirit*, 74.

43   Keith Haberl, *Alpine Huts: A guide to the facilities of the Alpine Club of Canada* (The Alpine Club of Canada, 1995), 61.

44   Jim Scott, *Backcountry Huts & Lodges of the Rockies & Columbias* (Johnson Gorman Publishers with the Alpine Club of Canada, 2002), 7–8.

45   Ibid., 12.

46   R.W. Sandford, *At The Top, 100 years of guiding in Canada* (The Alpine Club of Canada, 1996), 23.

47   Ibid., 23.

48   Ibid.

49   This information provided by Linda Heywood of the Association of Canadian Mountain Guides, and is correct as of September 8, 2007.

CHAPTER 7

1   See Lorne E. Render, *Mountains and the Sky* (Glenbow Alberta Institute in association with McClelland & Stewart West, 1974).

2   See Roger Hall, Gordon Dodds and Stanley Triggs, *The World of William Notman: The Nineteenth Century through a Master Lens* (McClelland and Stewart, 1993).

3   See *Great Days in the Rockies, the Photographs of Byron Harmon, 1906–1934*, Ed. Carole Harmon (Oxford: Oxford University Press, 1978).

4   Walter J. Phillips and Frederick Niven, *Colour in the Canadian Rockies* (Thomas Nelson and Sons Ltd., 1947).

CHAPTER 8

1   *David Thompson's Narrative of His Explorations in Western North America, 1784–1812*, Ed. J.B. Tyrrell (Toronto: The Champlain Society, 1916), 445.

2   Quote is from *The Columbia River: Or scenes and adventures during a residence of six years on the western side of the Rocky Mountains among various tribes of Indians hitherto unknown; together with "A Journey across the American Continent"* by Ross Cox (University of Oklahoma Press, 1957), 283. See also *Journal of a Voyage on the North West Coast of North America during the Years 1811, 1812, 1813 and 1814* by Gabriel Franchere, Transcribed and translated by Wessie Tipping Lamb, edited with an introduction by W. Kaye Lamb, The Champlain Society, 1969.

3   Pamphlet in the possession of the author, titled *The Canadian Pacific: The New Highway to the East: Across the Mountains, Prairies and Rivers of Canada*, published by the Canadian Pacific Railway, Montreal, 1888.

4   Walter Dwight Wilcox, *The Rockies of Canada* (New York and London: G.P. Putnam's Sons / The Knickerbocker Press, 1900).

5   Walter Dwight Wilcox, *Camping in the Canadian Rockies* (G.P. Putnam and Sons, 1897), 16.

6 James Outram, *In the Heart of the Canadian Rockies* (London: Macmillan Company, 1905).

7 H.E.M. Stutfield and J. Norman Collie, *Climbs and Exploration in the Canadian Rockies* (Longmans, Green and Company, 1903).

8 A.P. Coleman, *The Canadian Rockies: New and Old Trails* (Henry Frowde, Toronto, 1912).

9 Originally published in 1911, Mary T.S. Schäffer's book *Old Indian Trails of the Canadian Rockies* was republished by Rocky Mountain Books in 2007.

10 James Monroe Thorington, *The Glittering Mountains of Canada: A Record of Exploration and Pioneer Ascents in the Canadian Rockies 1914-1924* (Philadelphia: John W. Lea, 1925).

11 Kain, Conrad, edited with additional chapters by J. Monroe Thorington, *Where the Clouds Can Go* (New York: American Alpine Club, 1935).

12 Ralph Connor (pseudonym of Rev. Charles William Gordon), *The Sky Pilot: A Tale of the Foothills* (Fleming H. Revell Company / Grosset & Dunlap, ca. 1899); *The Black Rock: A Tale of the Selkirks* (Street & Smith, 1900); *The Man from Glengarry* (Grosset and Dunlap, 1901); *The Patrol of the Sundance Trail* (New York: Hodder & Stroughton, and George Doran, 1914).

13 Howard O'Hagan, *Tay John: A Novel* (New York: Clarkson N. Potter, Inc., 1960).

14 Sid Marty, *Headwaters* (Toronto: McClelland & Stewart, 1973).

15 Jon Whyte, *The Fells of Brightness: Some Fittes and Starts* (Longspoon Press, 1983); *The Fells of Brightness: Wenkchemna* (Longspoon Press, 1985); *Indians in the Rockies* (Altitude Publishing, 1984); *Tommy and Lawrence: The Ways and Truths of Lake O'Hara* (Banff: The Lake O'Hara Trails Club, 1983).

16 Thomas Wharton, *Icefield: A Novel* (Edmonton, NeWest Publishers, 1995).

17 Sid Marty, *Men for the Mountains* (McClelland & Stewart, 1978); *Leaning on the Wind: Under the Spell of the Great Chinook* (Harper Collins, 1995); *Switchbacks* (McClelland & Stewart, 1999).

18 Sid Marty, *The Black Grizzly Bears of Whiskey Creek* (McClelland & Stewart, 2008).

19 Ben Gadd, *Handbook of the Canadian Rockies*, Second Edition (Corax Press, 1995).

20 Brian Patton and Bart Robinson, *The Canadian Rockies Trail Guide*, Seventh Edition (Summerthought, 2000).

21 See Don Gayton, *The Wheatgrass Mechanism: Science and Imagination in the Western Canadian Landscape* (Fifth House Publishers, 1990), and *Landscapes of the Interior* (New Society Publishers, 1996).

22 See Kevin Van Tighem, *Coming West: A Natural History of Home* and *Home Range: Writings on Conservation and Restoration* (Altitude Publishing, 1995).

CHAPTER 9

1 Rick Bass, "On Willow Creek," in *Heart of the Land: Essays on Last Great Places,* Joseph Barbato and Lisa Weinerman, Eds. (Vintage, for the Nature Conservancy, 1994), 9.

2 Wes Jackson, *Becoming Native to this Place* (Washington, DC: Counterpoint, 1994).

3 Alfred W. Crosby, *Ecological Imperialism: The Biological Expansion of Europe, 900–1900* (Cambridge University Press, 1984), 194.

CHAPTER 10

1 Ronald Rees, *New and Naked Land: Making the Prairies Home* (Western Producer Prairie Books, 1988).

2 T.E. Lawrence, *Seven Pillars of Wisdom* (1926; Penguin Modern Classics, 1975).

3 See R.W. Sandford, *The Weekender Effect: Hyperdevelopment in Mountain Towns* (Rocky Mountain Books, 2008).

4 Terry Tempest Williams, "Winter Solstice at the Moab Slough," in *Heart of the Land: Essays on Last Great Places,* Joseph Barbato and Lisa Weinerman, Eds. (Vintage, for the Nature Conservancy, 1994), 4-5.

5 Ibid.

CHAPTER 11

1   R.W. Sandford, *The Book of Banff: The Insider's Guide to What You Need to Know to Be a Local in Banff* (Friends of Banff National Park, 1994), 204.

2   Ibid.

3   Sandford, *Book of Banff*, 205-206.

4   Ibid.

5   Ibid., 46.

6   There is a fine book about the history of early outfitters and guides in the mountain national parks: Hart, *Diamond Hitch* (Summerthought, 1979). It not only tells the stories of many of the most interesting guides and outfitters, but also tells us about the clients they had and where they went during the golden age of the horse in the Rockies.

CHAPTER 12

1   Christine Mill, *Norman Collie, A life in two worlds, mountain explorer and scientist, 1854–1942* (Aberdeen University Press, 1987).

2   H.E.M. Stutfield and J. Norman Collie, *Climbs and Exploration in the Canadian Rockies* (Longmans, Green and Company, 1903), 107 -108.

3   James Outram, *In the Heart of the Canadian Rockies* (Macmillan Company, London, 1905), 385.

4   James Monroe Thorington, *The Glittering Mountains of Canada: Old Trails of the Rockies* (John W. Lea, Philadelphia, 1925), 79.

5   Ibid., 81.

6   Don Harmon (photographs) and Bart Robinson (text), *Columbia Icefield, A Solitude of Ice* (Altitude Publishing, 1981), 80.

7   See Dalton Muir and Derek Ford, *Castleguard* (National Parks Centennial, published under the authority of the Minister of the Environment, 1985).

8   Jon Rollins, *Caves of the Canadian Rockies and Columbia Mountains* (Rocky Mountain Books, 2004).

CHAPTER 13

1   George Kinney and Donald "Curly" Phillips, "To the Top of Mount Robson," in *The Canadian Alpine Journal*, Vol. 2., No. 2 (The Alpine Club of Canada, 1910): 40.

2   Ibid.

3   Conrad Kain (translated by A.W. Wallace), "The First Ascent of Mount Robson From the Southwest," in *The Canadian Alpine Journal*, Vol. VI (The Alpine Club of Canada, 1914): 22.

4   A.D. Barnosky, *Heatstroke: Nature in an Age of Global Warming* (Island Press/Shearwater Books, 2009).

CHAPTER 14

1   Any examination of Coleman's technical work will put to rest the notion that the science of geology was not well advanced by the time Coleman took his degrees in Canada and Europe. For those without a good grounding in geology, Coleman's technical work can look as if it were written in a foreign language. A melaphyre is a porphyritic igneous rock with dark-coloured aphantic groundmass and varied phenocrysts.

2   E.W.D. Holway "New Light on Mounts Brown and Hooker," published in *The Canadian Alpine Journal*, Vol. IX (The Alpine Club of Canada, 1918): 45. In his article, Holway explains that the quotations of Douglas to which the alpine literature refers are from "A brief memoir of the life of Mr. David Douglas, with extracts from his letters," in *Companion to the Botanical Magazine 2*, 1836, pages 79–182.

3   A.P. Coleman, *The Canadian Rockies: New and Old Trails* (Toronto: Henry Frowde, 1912), 121.

4   Ibid., 187.

5   As Coleman's description of this ascent is vague, there is some confusion as to which mountain he climbed to get his bearings in the Fortress Lake area. Since they could look east toward Fortress Mountain and Mount Quincy and still see the White Pyramid to the south, it is likely they ascended the ridge to the east of Chisel Creek that overlooks Fortress Lake to the north and Mount Quincy to the east.

6 Coleman, *Canadian Rockies,* 157.

7 Ibid., 169.

8 The assertion that Coleman made the first ascent of Sunwapta Peak has been made before by other historians. Coleman's description in the text of his book, however, casts some doubt. The problem is that he describes the mountain as being at the headwaters of the Sunwapta. The actual head-waters of the Sunwapta River is the Athabasca Glacier below Mount Athabasca. The peak directly east of this glacier is Nigel Peak, which is generally held to have first been climbed by surveyors in the employ of the Boundary Commission in 1918. It is almost certain, given the time that it took and his description of the mountain, that the Coleman party did climb Sunwapta Peak, which lies slightly south and east of where the party camped on the confluence of Jonas Creek and the Sunwapta River. See Robert Kruszyna and William L. Putnam, *The Rocky Mountains of Canada North,* Seventh Edition (1985). The first ascent is not credited to Coleman but to J. Simpson in 1906.

9 Coleman, *Canadian Rockies,* 187.

10 In terms of maps, it is also interesting to note that, in the back cover of the book, we find a Canadian Pacific Railway map of its transcontinental route, complete with the names of every community along the main line. In exchange for assistance in making his eight trips through the Rockies, Coleman was not reluctant to quietly promote the railway in his widely read and highly popular account of exploration and science in the mountains of the West.

11 H.E.M. Stutfield and J. Norman Collie, *Climbs and Exploration in the Canadian Rockies* (Longmans, Green and Company, 1903), 153. The publication of Douglas's actual journal notes from the upper reaches of Athabasca Pass three years after the first printing of *The Canadian Rockies: New & Old Trails,* exposed the extent to which Douglas's text had been transformed before his notes were first published in the *Botanical Magazine* in England:

After breakfast at one o'clock, being as I conceive on the highest part of the route, I became desirous of ascending one of the peaks, and accordingly I set out alone on snowshoes to that on the left hand or west side, being to all appearances the highest. The labour of ascending the lower part, which is covered with pines, is great beyond description, sinking on many occasions to the middle. Half-way up vegetation ceases entirely, not so much as a vestige of moss or lichen on the stones. Here I found it less laborious as I walked on the hard crust. One-third from the summit it becomes a mountain of pure ice, sealed far over by Nature's hand as a momentous work of Nature's God. The height from its base may be about 5500 feet: timber, 2750 feet; a few mosses and lichen 500 more; 1000 feet of perpetual snow; the remainder, towards the top 1250, as I have said, glacier with a thin covering of snow on it. The ascent took me five hours; descending only one and a quarter. Places where the descent was gradual, I tied my shoes together, making them carry me in turn as a sledge. Sometimes I came down one spell 500 to 700 feet in the space of one minute and a half. I remained twenty minutes, my thermometer standing at 18°; night closing fast in on me, and no means of fire, I was reluctantly forced to descend. The sensation I felt is beyond any description, striking the mind with horror blended with a sense of the wondrous works of the Almighty.

This original journal account makes no mention of the heights of either Mounts Hooker and Brown which were obviously added later. A botanist with any amount of experience in the Rockies would be able to figure out instantly from this description that Douglas must have known, at least approximately, the true altitude of Mount Brown. Treeline in this part of the Rockies is, depending upon slope and exposure, at between 6,800 and 7,200 feet (2,072–2,194.5 metres). Douglas puts treeline at about 2,700 feet (823 metres) above the pass, suggesting that the pass would be at about 4,100–4,500 feet (1,250–1,371.6 metres) in altitude, not all that far off from its actual 5,736 feet (1,748.3 metres). It seems impossible that Douglas wouldn't have known that treeline could not deviate to a very great extent at this northern latitude. Why a reputable botanist like Douglas would choose to exaggerate the heights of these mountains remains a mystery.

CHAPTER 15

1 Irene M. Spry, ed., *The Palliser Papers, 1857–60* (Toronto: The Champlain Society, 1968), 309.

2   Thomas E. Wilson, *Trail Blazer of the Canadian Rockies* (Calgary: Historical Paper Number 3, Glenbow Alberta Institute, 1972).

3   Ibid., 16–17.

4   Ibid., 30.

5   Ibid., 35.

6   Ibid., 36.

7   Ibid., 37.

8   Ibid., 52.

9   R.W. Sandford, *Yoho: A History and Celebration of Yoho National Park* (Altitude Publishing, and the Friends of Yoho National Park, 1993), 53.

10   For a more complete account see R.W. Sandford, *Yoho: A History and Celebration of Yoho National Park* (Altitude Publishing, and Friends of Yoho National Park, 1993), 59–61.

11   Stephen Jay Gould, *Wonderful Life: The Burgess Shale and the Nature of History* (New York & London: W.W. Norton, 1989), 53.

12   Ibid., 52.

13   See Stephen Jay Gould, *The Hedgehog, the Fox and the Magister's Pox: Mending the Gap Between Science and the Humanities* (Harmony Books, 2003), 202.

CHAPTER 16

1   The historical information about the history of the automobile in the mountain West is abridged from R.W. Sandford, *Roads to the Future: The History of the Alberta Motor Association* (Alberta Motor Association, 2001).

2   Sandford, *Roads to the Future*, 6.

3   See Bob Hahn, *Kootenay National Park* (Rocky Mountain Books, 2000). Bob Hahn is a Park Warden with a lifetime of experience in Kootenay. This book should be cherished for its loving insights into a national park that does not receive the attention it deserves because of the highway focus visitors and locals bring to their appreciation of it.

CHAPTER 17

1   Conrad Kain, *Where the Clouds Can Go: The Autobiography of Conrad Kain*, Edited, with additional chapters by J. Monroe Thorington, Third Edition (New York: The American Alpine Club [1938, 1954] 1979), 381.

2   Rudolf Aemmer spoke these words upon being awarded a special citation by the American Alpine Club in 1909.

3   This quote is from the same 1920 brochure produced by Arthur Wheeler, in the possession of the author.

CHAPTER 18

1   See Joseph Epes Brown, *Animals of the Soul: Sacred Animals of the Oglala Sioux* (Element Books, 1997), xiii.

2   David Rockwell, *Giving Voice to Bear: North American Indian Myths, Rituals, and Images of the Bear* (Key Porter Books, 1991), xii.

3   Ibid.

4   Some researchers believe that the uncanny similarity of the bear's hind foot is at the root of many Sasquatch and Yeti stories.

5   Doug Peacock, *Grizzly Years* (Owl Books, 1990), 186–7. Peacock described a grizzly grasping a six foot log between its paws and moving it back and forth to scratch his neck.

6   Rockwell, *Giving Voice to Bear*, 5.

7   Brown, *Animals of the Soul*, 22.

8   Paul Shepard and Barry Sanders, *The Sacred Paw: Bears in Nature, Myth, and Literature* (New York: Viking Penguin, 1985), 56–57.

9   Henry Kelsey, *The Kelsey Papers*, with an introduction by Arthur G. Doughty and Chester Martin, The Public Archives of Canada and the Public Record Office of Northern Ireland, Ottawa, 1929. See entry for August 20, 1691.

10   Ibid., see introduction to the year 1690, page 3, following the French version of the introduction by the editors.

11   Ross Cox, *The Columbia River* (University of Oklahoma Press, 1957), 241.

12 Ibid., 242–43.

13 Robert H. Busch, *The Grizzly Almanac* (The Lyons Press, 2000), 105.

14 Tom Longstaff, *This My Voyage* (London: John Murray, 1950), 230.

15 Alfred Runte, *National Parks, The American Experience* (Lincoln, NB: University of Nebraska Press, 1987), 6.

16 Burns and Schintz, *Guardians of the Wild*, 19.

17 Ibid., 21.

18 Ibid., 73.

19 R.W. Sandford, *The Book of Banff* (The Friends of Banff National Park, 1994), 74.

20 Burns and Schintz, *Guardians of the Wild*, 209.

21 Harper Cory, *The Bears of Jasper* (New York & Toronto: Thomas Nelson and Sons, 1946), 2. To see this book visit the bear exhibit at the Jasper-Yellowhead Museum.

22 Burns and Schintz, *Guardians of the Wild*, 209; Paul Schullery, *The Bears of Yellowstone* (Roberts Rinehart, Inc., Publishers, in cooperation with the National Park Foundation, 1986), 83.

23 Burns and Schintz, *Guardians of the Wild*, 76.

24 Schullery, *The Bears of Yellowstone*, 11.

25 Thomas McNamee, *The Grizzly Bear* (New York: The Lyons Press, 1997), 98.

26 Ibid., 99.

27 Ibid.

28 Stephen Herrero, *Bear Attacks: Their Causes and Avoidance* (New York: Nick Lyons Books, 1985).

29 Ibid., 75.

30 Ibid., 31.

31 Herrero and other bear researchers have noted that attacking grizzlies will often direct their attacks toward the head and faces of other bears during aggressive encounters. The likely reason for this is that the bear is trying to break the jaw of an animal that presents a threat to it and thus disable its primary weapon. The bear uses its jaws to break the jaws of it's adversary. Bears will try to do this to other animals, including humans, in defense of food and young. This may account for the fact that many people mauled by bears suffer head injuries that include the tearing of the scalp, facial lacerations, damage to or loss of eyes and the breaking or tearing off of the lower jaw. For this reason most recommended strategies for playing dead in the presence of an attacking bear stress protection of the face.

CHAPTER 19

1 See R.W. Sandford, *The Book of Banff* (The Friends of Banff, 1994), 72–74.

2 Thomas Homer-Dixon, *Environment, Scarcity and Violence* (Princeton, NJ: Princeton University Press, 1999), 37.

3 See *Climate Change 2007: The Physical Science Basis*, Working Group 1 Contribution to the Fourth Assessment Report of the Intergovernmental Panel on Climate Change (Cambridge: Cambridge University Press, 2007), 13. It is also available at http://www.ipcc.ch/publications_and_data/publications_ipcc_fourth_assessment_report_wg1_report_the_physical_science_basis.htm

4 Edward O. Wilson, *The Future of Life* (New York: Alfred A. Knopf, 2001), 67–69.

5 All of these reports are abridged from Climate Change and Canada's National Park System, edited by Daniel Scott of the Adaptation and Impacts Group, Environment Canada, and Roger Suffling of the School of Planning at the University of Waterloo, published by Parks Canada in May of 2000.

6 One of the concerns here is that the depletion of glaciers may result in a diminished later summer flow in the Bow and other rivers that rely on glacial melt to sustain year-round volumes. Depending on the extent and nature of local changes, some rivers like the Bow could potentially stop flowing late in dry summer seasons.

7 See *Climate Change and Canada's National Park System: A Screening Level Assessment*, Daniel Scott and Roger Suffling, Eds. (Adaptation and Impacts Research Group, Environment Canada, 2000), 80.

8 David Sauchyn et al., Assessment of Biophysical Vulnerability, Report to the Government of Alberta, Prairie Adaptation Research Collaborative (University of Regina, 2006).

Index